SHOUT, SISTER, SHOUT!

The Untold Story of Rock-and-Roll
Trailblazer Sister Rosetta Tharpe

GAYLE F. WALD

Beacon Press
Boston

Beacon Press
25 Beacon Street
Boston, Massachusetts 02108–2892
www.beacon.org

Beacon Press books
are published under the auspices of
the Unitarian Universalist Association of Congregations.

09 08 07 8 7 6 5 4 3 2 1

This book is printed on acid-free paper that meets the uncoated paper
ANSI/NISO specifications for permanence as revised in 1992.

Composition by Wilsted & Taylor Publishing Services

Library of Congress Cataloging-in-Publication Data

Wald, Gayle
   Shout, sister, shout! : the untold story of rock-and-roll
trailblazer Sister Rosetta Tharpe / Gayle F. Wald. — 1st ed.
      p. cm.
   Includes bibliographical references (p.   ), discography (p.   ), and index.
   ISBN-13: 978-0-8070-0984-0 (hardcover : alk. paper)
   ISBN-10: 0-8070-0984-9 (hardcover : alk. paper) 1. Tharpe, Rosetta,
d. 1973. 2. Gospel musicians—United States—Biography. 3. Blues musicians—
United States—Biography. I. Title.

   ML420.T395W35 2007
   782.25'4092—dc22
      [B]   ·   2006016622

No, no, I'm not ashamed of my blues.
It's all the same talent,
a beat is a beat whatever it is.
Thomas A. Dorsey

CONTENTS

PREFACE: THE LONESOME ROAD

When you talked about Rosetta Tharpe you talked about a ball of energy. This woman would come out on the stage she'd have people laughing, she'd talk to them in a way that it was almost like she was related to them. And when she finished her act, they were standing. You know, they would love this woman. And she was a lovable person. I mean she was an approachable person. Even though she was a diva too, you know, because she did play the diva role.
Ira Tucker

The time: the early 1960s. The place: a television studio. The occasion: the taping of *TV Gospel Time*, a national program, before a live audience. A modestly dressed middle-aged woman takes the stage, launching into an improvised rendition of "Up Above My Head," a church standard, accompanying herself on electric guitar. Behind her the white-robed members of a full gospel choir clap their hands in time to the music.

> *Up above my head, I hear music in the air*
> *Up above my head, there is music in the air*
> *Up above my head, music in the air*
> *And I really do believe, really do believe joy's somewhere.*

It's a commanding enough performance, the woman singing and playing with jaunty confidence, despite the canned context. Then, two-thirds of the way in, during a guitar solo that serves as the bridge, something astonishing happens. The church faithful might see it as the Holy Spirit descending; for others, it's that magical moment when a really fine musician becomes lost in her music and yet remains utterly in control of its effects on her audience. The woman begins moving in tandem with the guitar, alternately swaying with it, leaning into it, and rocking it gently on her hip. At one point, she executes a little jump, high heels and long dress notwithstanding; at another, she makes a dramatic circular gesture with her right arm, allowing her hand to stray promiscuously from the strings for a teasing fraction of a second. Rapidly finger-picked notes press up against full-on power chords that linger languidly in the air. She squeezes notes from the high end of the pitch, relishing the gentle fuzz of distortion, then cajoles the instrument, commanding, "Let's do that again!" And so the guitar soars briefly once more, eventually making a perfect, gentle landing into the final verse of the song.

The woman in question is Rosetta Tharpe, a vocalist and guitarist of the Sanctified Church and one of the most remarkable—yet largely forgotten—musicians of the twentieth century. Beginning in the 1930s, she commenced a colorful career as gospel's original crossover artist, its first nationally known star, and the most thrilling and celebrated guitarist of its Golden Age—so called because it saw the emergence of the genre's defining artists, including Mahalia Jackson, whose fame would eclipse Rosetta's by the 1950s.

Yet unlike Jackson, whose celebrity developed around her reputation as a defender of gospel tradition, Rosetta earned notoriety for her instinct for creative insubordination and her practiced talent for show-biz flamboyance. From spiritual singing that could bust out in blues cadences—and, in private, touch on "blue" subjects—to a guitar virtuosity that set her apart from any other performer of her era, Rosetta's particular genius defied categorization. Her music incorporated elements of gospel, blues, jazz, popular ballads, country, rhythm and blues, and rock and roll. When she was at the top of her game, no one could touch her charisma or jaw-dropping talent.

Rosetta's exuberant self-expression clashed with the prevailing rhythms of her time, making her the kindred spirit of secular artists such as blues singer Bessie Smith. And like the persona of Smith's celebrated "Young Woman's Blues," who also sang about the "long lonesome road," Rosetta was often too busy living to settle down. In an age when church folk looked askance at divorce and shunned blues as the devil's music, she fled an unhappy first marriage to a Pentecostal preacher to become a star in pre–World War II New York. Her ebullient spirit propelled her out of storefront churches and tent meetings and into venues such as the Cotton Club, Harlem's legendary Apollo Theater, the left-leaning nightspot Café Society, and Carnegie Hall. Rosetta played all of these places, as well as the Grand Ole Opry and arenas, stadiums, high-school auditoriums, and churches around the country. Her dazzling guitar playing, which featured a finger-picking style unusual at the time, indelibly influenced Elvis Presley, Johnny Cash, Jerry Lee Lewis, Red Foley, Etta James, Little Richard, Bonnie Raitt, Ruth Brown, Isaac Hayes, and many others.

Before the Clara Ward Singers made gospel singing glamorous, Rosetta did gospel programs in sequined gowns and a series of dye jobs or wigs of different colors—sometimes she was a blonde, sometimes a redhead—riding grandly into town on her own tour bus. In the socially conservative 1950s, she staged her nuptials to her third husband in a baseball stadium in Washington, D.C., entertaining a crowd of tens of thousands by playing guitar in her wedding dress. She resisted the moral severity of the Pentecostal Church, while embracing its musical values of emotional expressiveness. Her 1945 crossover hit "Strange Things Happening Every Day," a humorous jab at religious hypocrisy that became a favorite of Memphis radio announcer Dewey Phillips (and subsequently of Phillips protégé Elvis Presley), may well be the first rock-and-roll song. And while Mahalia made her Newport Jazz Festival debut conditional on her singing on Sunday morning, with no secular music following her performance, Rosetta took the stage at the Newport Folk Festival in the summer of 1967 "garbed," as Anthony Heilbut puts it in *The Gospel Sound*, "in unfolksy [and unseasonal] mink."

She was a woman of many guises: she could play the sincere penitent, the deep spiritualist, the saintly believer, or she could play the humorous exhibitionist, the uninhibited flirt, the needy child. Just as she crossed and recrossed the line between secular and sacred sound, so Rosetta, according to jazz critic Richard Hadlock, could at times cross "into that territory normally reserved for comico-coquettish entertainers like Mae West and Pearl Bailey." No one could accuse her of disliking the grand gesture, whether histrionic tears or magnanimous, magnificent expressions of loving-kindness.

Rosetta's courage to follow her artistic convictions and pursue her ambitions set her apart from popular musicians on both sides of the sacred/secular divide. In the racially segregated rural and small-town communities where most black people lived before World War II, churches were defining institutions, and ambitious young musicians confronted the parting of paths between the church and the world as crucial career turning points. Those who pursued the secular path, from Muddy Waters and T-Bone Walker to Dinah Washington and Sam Cooke, inevitably paid a price for their choices in the reproach of the very communities that had nurtured and applauded their talents. In many cases, becoming a popular entertainer meant severing ties to these communities—if not permanently, then until success paved a golden path back into the good graces of the congregation.

Most African American musicians raised in the church had little option but to choose, as soul singer Al Green once put it, between lifting up their voices for God or taking a bow for their third encores. Rosetta, in contrast, attempted to inhabit an in-between place where the worlds of religious and popular music intersected and overlapped. She performed church hymns on secular stages. She breached standards of holiness and respectability by singing blues and jazz songs about worldly desires. Even when limiting herself to a church repertoire, she stuck out as a *loud* woman: loud in her playing, loud in her personality. In concert, she combined the spontaneous fervor of religious revivals with the practiced production values of Broadway variety shows. She could sing about the evils of worldliness with irreverent pleasure. And like the best preachers, she was capable of presenting herself as both larger than life (the furs, wigs, and jewelry) and as her audience's equal in human frailty and suffering (no one could say she hadn't sinned and paid for it).

Some—especially in the Pentecostal Church—preferred a musician with a little less swing in her spirituals and schmaltz in her style. Even secular fans sometimes objected to her theatrics. And yet even Rosetta's critics could not but marvel at the extraordinary guitar playing that became her hallmark as a performer. In that day it was still unusual to see a woman guitarist, in gospel or in any musical field. Not merely to play, but to wield the instrument with authority and ease, was to subvert convention and expectation.

Rosetta exploited her novelty as a "girl guitarist" to its fullest. Building on skills she had honed since childhood, she played for maximum visual as well as aural impact, simultaneously dancing the digits of her right and left hands in a see-if-you-can-do-this display of dexterity. Most self-accompanying players of the 1930s and '40s strummed along to their singing, subordinating the guitar to the vocals, but Rosetta gave the instrument its own distinct voice. And to be sure she got an audience's full attention, she pushed amplifiers to their ear-splitting limits, challenging anyone to outdo her in volume if not in flair.

Paradoxically, Rosetta developed her stage persona through a deep-seated religious faith acquired in childhood. Believing her talents to be divinely inspired, she saw herself doing God's work as a popular musician. It never mattered much to her whether her listeners were "saved," only that they got something from her music. Such generosity of spirit endeared her to an unusually broad audience, including working-class white and black Southerners, urban jazz aficionados, and European venerators of the ragtime and blues traditions. Although he counts Mahalia her artistic superior, "Sister did more than anyone else in introducing the music of the Negro church to the world," says gospel scholar Horace Clarence Boyer.

In hindsight, nearly everything Rosetta accomplished as a musician seems ahead of its time—sometimes not by years, but by decades. Felled by a stroke in 1973, when she was fifty-eight, she didn't have the opportunity to witness the flowering of soul, although it was a music she helped innovate through her own experiments in bridging worlds of sound. Indeed, it's hard to conceive of as seminal a figure as Elvis, whose genius similarly lay in his ability to confound the usual categories, without first imagining Rosetta.

But of course Elvis emerged in a world that venerated the achievements of white men above all others, while Rosetta was neither white nor male. Following the trail she blazed, other black women, including early rock and rollers Ruth Brown and Etta James, would envision the possibility of one day getting up in front of audiences to sing anything they liked. So fresh has her guitar work remained, moreover, that, watching one of her rare recorded performances, one has the impression of witnessing something both temporally distant and utterly contemporary.

Rosetta's life would bear out all of the contradictions and tensions of her song "The Lonesome Road," a blues she sang in a Sanctified style, portraying a desire for companionship that attaches itself to objects both sacred and secular. Her story defies the usual divisions: tragic or triumphant, self-aggrandizing or self-sacrificing, clay-footed or transcendent. In the course of a thirty-five-year professional career, much of it spent on the road, she withstood failed marriages, personal disillusionment, volatile economic circumstances, racial discrimination, and rejection by her church. Like so many others, she confronted the vicissitudes of fame and fortune in a gospel world as rife with backstabbing, competition, and hustling as any other musical sphere. The woman who once owned two homes and a Cadillac and required a large shed to house all of her gowns is today buried in an unmarked grave in Philadelphia. She combined independence and vulnerability, savvy and gullibility, sometimes in equal measure. Although she sang about the wages of sinful living, she pursued romantic relationships—primarily with men, but occasionally with women—wore pants before they were the norm for women, and swore like a sailor. She also maintained a lifelong affiliation with a church that regarded all of these behaviors as anathema.

Jim Dickinson, the legendary record producer, recalls what it was like to discover Rosetta when he was a teenager growing up in Memphis: "A female gospel singer playing electric guitar in a spangled evening dress was pretty unique in 1955." It's safe to say it is still pretty unique more than a half-century later.

1

COTTON PLANT (1915–1920)

This train is a clean train, this train,
This train is a clean train, this train,
This train is a clean train, ev'rybody's riding in Jesus' name,
This train is a clean train, this train.
Rosetta Tharpe

No doctor was in attendance when a black girl-child was born to Katie Harper on a farm just outside of Cotton Plant, Arkansas, in 1915. There were several white physicians in Cotton Plant, a relatively prosperous Mississippi Delta town about sixty-five miles west of Memphis, but no black woman would have bothered to call on them. The closest hospital was in Little Rock, more than seventy miles to the southwest, but even with the railroad, that was out of the question too. So Rosa, or Rosie Etta, or Rosabell—for she had many names before she became internationally known as Sister Rosetta Tharpe—was born on the grounds of the Tilman Cooperwood farm, where Katie Harper lived and worked. A midwife from the community was likely there to comfort and guide Katie when she gave birth to her first and only child at the relatively advanced age of thirty-two. The date of the birth was March 20, although no official certificate was issued; in those days, the only records country women like Katie kept were notes jotted down in family Bibles.

The girl Katie gave birth to was precocious from the start. It was said she began walking and talking before her first birthday. She had a gift of music in her, a God-given gift that she shared with her parents. Both Katie and her husband, Willis (or Willie) B. Atkins, a farm laborer, could sing—not in the manner of the trained vocalists who appeared at Cotton Plant's Francis Opera House, a room in a building on Main Street—but in the manner of black working people who sang for their pleasure, or at church, or as a distraction in the fields or the kitchens where they spent most of their waking hours. Like his wife, Willis Atkins had a clear, booming voice, the kind that "when he sang you could hear him across a field," remembers his grandson, Roy T. Scott.

Willis died soon after the second Great War, but Katie maintained that strong voice until 1968. Back when she gave birth, nothing would have been further from Katie's imagination than recording an album with Dizzy Gillespie when she was seventy-seven. And no wonder: neither Dizzy, nor modern bebop, nor LPs existed in 1915. Nor could Willis or Katie have predicted that their little girl, born into humble circumstances in the segregated South, would become gospel music's first national star and a pioneer of modern rock-and-roll guitar. Thirty years later, Rosetta would return to the area around Cotton Plant a bona fide celebrity in a fancy black roadster, thrilling the people there with her fine clothes, fistfuls of United States currency, and glamorous persona.

In 1915, however, these were fairy tales of a future beyond imagination. Back then, Willis and Katie raised Rosetta in the manner of all loving and well-intentioned parents of every station and background. They taught her to obey her elders, not to sass, and to remember the lessons she learned in church. As the cliché goes, children were to be seen and not heard—and such rules of conduct were particularly crucial for black children, for whom a careless word could spell mortal trouble. Unlike the state capital, Cotton Plant was never touched by the racial violence that rocked Arkansas in the early twentieth century, when fifty-four black people were lynched between 1910 and 1929.[1] Yet that didn't mean that the black citizens of Cotton Plant could speak freely. As ninety-three-year-old Sam Scott, Cotton Plant's oldest living resident, recalls, "a young man come in, a white man, you had to say Mister to him." Rosie would have been taught much the same racial etiquette, as a matter of survival.

At the same time, Rosie grew up with music in the air. Both Katie and Willis taught her to use her voice to sing, and both set her the example of playing an instrument, Katie the piano and mandolin, Willis the guitar and the mouth harp (harmonica). The area around Cotton Plant had other young people who imbibed these values: Louis Jordan, the bandleader and jump-swing innovator, born just ten miles down the road in Brinkley, blues musician Peetie Wheatstraw, and gospel singer Ernestine Washington.

Rosetta didn't know her father for very long. By her sixth year, she and Katie had departed Cotton Plant without him to settle in Chicago, and by the time Rosetta reconnected with the Atkins clan living in Camden, Arkansas, in the early '50s, Willis had already passed away. According to Donell Atkins, Willis's son by his third wife, Effie, Rosetta "didn't 'preciate being kept away from her daddy, because when she came she tried to pick up all the literature that she could about her daddy." Although Willis's ten living children by Effie—five boys and five girls, in addition to the five infants who died early—possessed among them only a few photographs of their father, they gave them to Rosetta, out of sympathy and respect for her fame as a musician. She promised to give them back, but never did. Thus, Willis Atkins lives on only in the memories of his surviving children.

That makes it difficult to know much about Willis's heritage, Donell Atkins says. Willis's mother may have had the surname Newton, but Donell isn't certain whether "Atkins is a slave name" or a name Willis's father took from another source. Family legend has it that Donell's grandparents on his father's side ran away from slavery.

Willis's own personal history is clearer. Roy Scott, son of Willis's daughter Elteaser, says he grew up hearing that his grandfather had had three separate families, including his mother's and "Auntie" Rosetta's. Born in 1876, just before the end of the relatively progressive and hopeful era of Reconstruction, Willis Atkins was married first at age twenty-four, to a woman by whom he had two children; then to Katie Harper; and finally, after he and Katie separated, to Effie, a woman twenty-six years his junior. By 1930, Effie and Willis were living on a rented farm in Ouachita County, in southern Arkansas, where Donell and Elteaser were born. Census records indicate that Willis could read and write, and that his oldest child by Effie, a daughter named Leona, attended school. In addition to farming, Willis worked for the Pacific Railroad, both as a switch man and as a tie-cutter, and later helped build highways, doing construction from Arkansas to Missouri. Donell remembers his father as robust and compact, a John Henry figure who, even in his older years, would march off without ceremony into the fields to cut wood. "I seen him pick up crossties and throw them over his shoulder and take them somewhere and stack them."

To know what Willis Atkins looked like, you have only to look at Donell. "Everybody said I feature my daddy," he attests. "I feature him a lot." Elteaser, now ailing and on dialysis, agrees. "He was Donell height, about Donell tall," she says of Willis Atkins. "My dad was kind of low. Dark brown skin. Dimples in his jaw. Gray hair." (He was fifty when she was born.) He was also a devout Christian. "I never heard him sing the blues and I never seen him drink," says Donell. "He was a beautiful man," adds Elteaser. "He was real religious. He never whipped none of us. When things happened to us he took us on his lap and prayed for us and that was about it. . . . He did the best he could. He didn't have too much to give us but he gave us love."

Katie Harper's heritage might be lost were it not for a document that she herself acquired from the U.S. Census Bureau in November 1959, when she was seventy-six years old, possibly so she could obtain a passport to accompany her world-famous daughter on an overseas tour. Bearing the stamp of the Commerce Department, the document, glued to a piece of cardboard, identifies the Katie Bell Nubin, then of 5046 Aspen Street in Philadelphia, as the Katie Harper born in 1883 and living in 1900 in Princeton, Arkansas, in Dallas County, about 120 miles to the southeast of Cotton Plant. Katie's parents, Levi and Agness J. Harper, almost undoubtedly had been slaves; Levi was born in 1845 in Louisiana, to parents from Louisiana, Agness around 1842, to parents from Arkansas and Louisiana.

Like most black Southerners, they made their living working the land. The 1900 census taker noted Levi Harper as an "owner." If this is so, then Katie may have grown up in relatively prosperous circumstances, since the vast majority of black people in the South in the late nineteenth and early twentieth centuries were either tenant farmers, meaning that they rented the land but owned the crops they produced on it, or sharecroppers, in which case they owned neither the land nor the fruits of their labor. Levi is entered in the 1880 census as a "renter," so it's possible that, in the twenty intervening years, he and Agness and their children managed to acquire their own farm.

Katie Harper grew up in a world that had precious little time for anything but work. Levi and Agness raised a large family, in part because, once they could perform even the most rudimentary chores, children were valuable additions to the family workforce. In all, they had five girls, Sallie, Dillie (or Dilly), Katie, Hanna, and Emma, as well as two boys, Rufuss and William—the latter probably named for an earlier William who died young. Like her parents and siblings, Katie received little if any schooling. The census enumerator of 1900 notes that at age sixteen Katie, like her father, Levi Harper, could neither read nor write. By that time, moreover, Agness had died, perhaps from the physical strain of giving birth to William, who was then one year old. Katie and her older sister Dillie (Sallie had moved out and likely married) thus greeted the new century as household and farm workers as well as caretakers of their younger siblings.[2]

How Katie Harper came to reside in Cotton Plant and how she met Willis Atkins are mysteries. Did she move there as a young woman, with other members of her family? Did she follow a husband, perhaps someone she married before Willis Atkins? Perhaps she migrated because she heard that good work could be found in a town that prided itself as "The Great Cotton Metropolis of Eastern Arkansas."

Cotton Plant once belonged to lands inhabited by Cherokee and other American Indians, who were forcibly removed after the formation of Arkansas Territory in 1819. As local lore has it, its name came from the plant that sprang up from the ground after William Lynch, a white man, "accidentally" dropped cotton seeds onto its fertile soil. A prosperous town grew up where Lynch's seed took root, but Cotton Plant declined in the late twentieth century. After the civil rights battle for school desegregation that raged in Little Rock in the 1950s, many of the young black people in Cotton Plant left to pursue their educations elsewhere, says Sam Scott. Like many other small towns across the country, Cotton Plant in the twenty-first century is in danger of extinction.

When Katie gave birth, Cotton Plant boasted a population of perhaps a thousand, with cotton farms, cotton gins, and a rapidly developing veneer industry that employed white and black men alike. Among the virtues of Cotton Plant noted by a 1905 version of *The Hustler*, a local newspaper, were its several Masonic lodges, its opera house, two banks, three hotels, a jewelry store, a shoemaker, a dentist, three lawyers, two white churches, and three "colored" churches. There was also a regular school system for white children and, for "Negro" children, the Cotton Plant Industrial Academy, originally a freedmen's school founded in the 1880s by the Presbyterian Church. "In a country like ours where two races mingle in business relations so freely, it is very necessary for both to be educated. This education must be both literary and industrial. Skilled labor is always in demand. A thoroughly cultivated literary mind is always the pioneer of industrialism," wrote *The Hustler,* in terms notably progressive for a racially mixed (approximately half-black, half-white) Delta town at the turn of the last century. "The school has given to the community around a different type of colored people, and it continues to rise higher and higher."[3]

For the newspaper's white editors, as well as for many black residents of Cotton Plant, a "different type" meant businessmen like Nat Darby, the town's most prosperous black citizen; highly cultivated individuals such as Florence Price, a Boston conservatory-trained composer who gave music lessons in town; and members of a black middle class that drew from Cotton Plant's small but significant service economy. According to Gwendolyn Stinson Gray, granddaughter of Nat Darby and daughter of one of the principals of Cotton Plant Academy, many black people owned farms and businesses in Cotton Plant in the early twentieth century. For example, although their property lay outside of Cotton Plant, the family of Pickens Black had thousands of acres and three airplanes: one to dust the farm, one to lift cargo, and a third for the family's private use. Scott Barnes, a black citizen in nearby Forrest City, owned a rock quarry. Nat Darby was a farmer and builder who variously owned cotton gins, orchards and potato fields, a lumber yard, a planing mill, a commissary store, and a silent movie theater. Tilman Cooperwood, owner of the farm where Katie worked, was a black man.

Their wealth didn't exempt these black families from segregation, of course; many lived in an area just south of town called Dark Corner. Nat Darby attended an African American church, belonged to a black Masonic lodge, and sent his children to Cotton Plant Academy. Participating in such vital black institutions, the Darbys and their social peers viewed themselves as models for and patrons to their less fortunate brethren. Like the Tilman Cooperwoods, remembers Gwendolyn Stinson Gray, they were "good livers," prosperous people "who knew how to survive on what they had and who shared things." Tilman himself was a particularly well established and resourceful man who owned a "pretty estimable piece of land." His interest "was not in standing in command over people," she says; rather, there was "interest in uplift." "The conditions were not the norms that you hear about. . . . When you were a sharecropper there you were part of the family."[4] Sam Scott recalls much the same of the Cooperwoods: "They were the type that wanted you to look up and want the best things in life."

Most black farmers—the majority in Cotton Plant—didn't share the advantages of its landowning middle class. When Rosetta was growing up, the children of these families helped their parents tend to crops and animals and keep house; at best, they attended school seven months of the year: two at the height of the summer and five in the winter. So active were the many farms in and around Cotton Plant that Sam Scott remembers white cotton lint floating down Main Street at harvesting time. *The Hustler,* in the racially romanticizing terms of the day, waxed poetic about black laboring people: "For miles out from [Cotton Plant] in every direction stretches vast fields which in the fall of the year present the appearance of an immense blanket of snow. So white, so grand, so beautiful that but for the moving black people here and there who are eagerly grabbing the white, fluffy stuff from the bowls [*sic*] and placing it in sacks, one would think it a grand painting, the result of the brush of some master artist."[5]

Sam Scott readily bursts the bubble of this fantasy of the happily laboring farm "Negro." Although the son of an educated woman, Scott spent most of his working life farming, and he vividly recalls what this entailed in the era before mechanization. "I can remember when people used to have but one mule . . . they got one mule and eight or ten acres of cotton." The owner of the farm "furnished the mule, he furnished the feed, then you give him half of what you made." Each farm had a "riding boss"—"somebody to tell you what to do and everything, almost like [here he laughs] an improved slave."

On the other hand, he has nostalgia for rural life in the nineteen-teens: fond memories of eating fresh meat and potatoes roasted in hot sand, of enjoying family time ("We were educated but we just, we believed in good living, you know"), and of Sunday evening entertainments after church. "Old folks would take the bed down," he recalls, "and young people would gather in a room" where they would dance to the music made by someone playing piano or perhaps guitar. They did square dancing and a dance popular in the nineteen-teens called slow dragging, in which "couples would hang onto each other and just grind back and forth in one spot all night."[6] "All night" in Cotton Plant meant until ten o'clock, early enough to give people a bit of sleep before Monday morning's rooster's crow.

Social divisions within Cotton Plant's diverse black population played themselves out not merely according to work and wealth, but according to religious affiliation. In general, wealthier black people belonged to congregations such as Westminster Presbyterian Church, which was affiliated with Cotton Plant Academy. Many working-class Southerners, on the other hand, were drawn to the new Pentecostal denominations that grew out of the Holiness movement of the mid-nineteenth century. Pentecostalism emphasized rigid standards of "clean" living—no alcohol, tobacco, gambling, social dancing, or other behaviors that might be construed as worldly—which meant that it exalted precisely the opposite of the conduct associated with the shameful stereotype of the lascivious, lazy, slovenly black slave. Yet in distinction to most Holiness denominations, Pentecostalism stressed the need for an experiential, lived faith, in which worshipers affirmed their baptism in the Holy Ghost through the "gift of tongues."

Katie and Willis were early adherents of the Church of God in Christ, or COGIC, the most important of these emerging Pentecostal denominations. For their parents' generation, few things had been more important and satisfying, in the years following Emancipation, than establishing their own places of worship, outside of white oversight. Yet while the majority of these churches, such as the African Methodist Episcopal (AME) Church, took forms of white Protestantism as a model, COGIC was almost single-handedly generated by the efforts of a black man, Charles Harrison Mason. Born in 1866, Mason was an Arkansas native and an ordained Missionary Baptist minister who had earlier split with mainstream Baptists because of his embrace of Holiness beliefs. Then, in 1907, Mason's life was transformed when he spent five weeks at a Holiness revival originally initiated by five black washerwomen in Los Angeles. The Azusa Street Revival, as it became known, began in early 1906 but gained quickly in strength and notoriety, particularly because its multiracial attendees had begun speaking a "Weird Babel of Tongues."[7]

Elder Mason himself underwent a tongue-speaking epiphany. "When I opened my mouth to say Glory," he would later report, "a flame touched my tongue which ran down to me. My language changed and no word could I speak in my own tongue. Oh! I was filled with the Glory of the Lord. My soul was then satisfied."[8] It was as though Mason were living out the words of Acts 2:4, in which, on the day of the Pentecost (the seventh Sunday after Easter), the people "were filled with the Holy Spirit and began to speak in other tongues as the Spirit enabled them."[9] Convinced that such outpouring of the Holy Ghost was essential to salvation, Mason—later, Bishop Mason—took his experiences back east with him, quickly attracting adherents to COGIC in Mississippi, Arkansas, Oklahoma, and Tennessee, particularly Memphis, which later became the international church headquarters.

In COGIC, Willis and Katie discovered more than an institution in which they could reaffirm, from week to week, a sense of black community and humanity. It also allowed them to express themselves in a way that connected them to the faith of their earliest enslaved ancestors, who gathered in "hush arbors" to perform African-based rituals like the ring shout. In a sense, Mason cultivated a style of worship in which modern black people, while reaffirming their essential dignity through Holiness living, might do so without abandoning the sustaining religious practices of the past. COGIC services were exciting and dramatic, with preachers who painted terrifying pictures of hell and soul-stirring images of heaven. Their music was lively and joyful, underscoring the pleasures of communal singing and dance as expressions of faith. At the same time, women were held to rigidly enforced standards of modesty, as an extension of Holiness living in the secular world. They were taught to dress without ornament and to shun makeup, jewelry, or any of the popular hair-straightening or skin-lightening products of the day. Such sanctions regulated and perhaps repressed their sexuality, but they also shielded them from degrading stereotypes of black women as Jezebels and temptresses.[10]

As in most Pentecostal and Holiness denominations, women in COGIC were banned from official ordination and lay preaching alike, but they enjoyed status in the church as evangelists, Sunday school instructors, and music teachers.[11] Like men, who enjoyed dignified titles such as "elder" or "pastor," regardless of their formal religious training, women in COGIC were anointed with honorifics such as "sister" and "mother." Not by coincidence is African American gospel the only indigenous U.S. music in which women performers, especially soloists, predominate. Rock and roll, a form Rosetta Tharpe would help to invent, has long been associated with masculine prowess and male musicians. But rock's gospel roots betray its feminine heritage—a heritage largely located in the Pentecostal Church.

Especially important for Katie and young Rosie—who had her first institutional exposure to religious song through COGIC services—Mason and his followers took a particularly liberal stand on the definition of "sacred" music. Instead of forbidding in church the everyday instruments associated with secular leisure, COGIC interpreted Scripture to dictate that congregants "shout" their faith with everything from tambourines and drums to trumpets and guitars. Indeed, whereas mainline Protestant denominations set strict limits on rhythmic music, or anything that might stir the body to movement, COGIC admitted into its musical repertory elements of blues, work songs, and ragtime, cross-fertilizing these in a glorious hybrid with slave spirituals and traditional hymns. Like speaking in tongues, exuberant singing and "holy dancing" affirmed the body, in its instinctive response to rhythm, as an instrument of God. Bodies, moreover, constituted unique percussive instruments. A great noise could be raised for the Lord through the collective clapping of hands and stamping of feet.

Katie's affiliation with COGIC indelibly shaped the life of her baby girl. The church provided Rosetta's earliest musical template, the sound palette on which she would draw throughout her career. COGIC established mother's and daughter's essential outlook on life as a striving for holiness, and imparted to them a profound and spirit-sustaining faith in God's protection. No matter how far she might stray from COGIC principles of holy living, or how far she might fall from the favor of the denomination's strictest and most unforgiving members, Rosetta's musical sensibility still bore the distinctive mark of Pentecostalism. In later years, when she raised her hands above her head in performance, she recalled COGIC doctrine urging the use of the outstretched arms in prayer; when she put a little swing in her spirituals, she echoed COGIC's liberal approach to blues. To use a gospel metaphor, when Rosetta "looked down the line" near the end of her life, all roads would lead back to the Pente-

costal Church—the source of her first audiences and of her own determined belief in herself, no matter the discouragements and setbacks the
world would throw at her.

Ironically, it was COGIC's historical links to slave religion that rendered
it an affront and an embarrassment to many middle-class blacks, who
considered its practices a "heathenish" throwback to "pagan" Africa, and
its charismatic leaders a dangerous influence on the people most in need
of racial uplift in the rapidly industrializing United States. For some
black Southerners who wanted to distance themselves from the trauma
of a degrading and dehumanizing slave past, Pentecostalism's roots in
slavery were a source not merely of embarrassment but of pain. To para-
phrase novelist Toni Morrison, for many, slavery was not a story "to pass
on." "Naturally enough when the Negro found himself free, he literally
put his past behind him," wrote John Wesley Work in 1915. "It was his determination that as far as within him lay, not one single reminder of that
black past should mar his future. So away went all those reminders into
the abyss of oblivion."[12]

The willful repression of the black past seemed to hold out the
promise of a more peaceful and prosperous black future, but it was not
to be. During Katie's and Willis's young adulthood, Reconstruction gave
way to the nightmare of a rising national tide of racism and racial violence. During the Red Summer of 1919, black soldiers returning from
service abroad—including veterans in uniform—were harassed, abused,
lynched, and even burned alive.[13] The historical overlap of these two
trends—the emergence of new Pentecostal-Holiness churches and the
increased repression of black people of all backgrounds and classes,
whether through violence or "ordinary" segregation—gave many even
more reason to fear the perpetuation of religious practices outside the
Protestant norm.

The progressive black intelligentsia of the early twentieth century
also found much to disapprove of in the demonstrative worship of the
"unlettered" classes. To the degree that Africans had historically been
portrayed as incapable of reason and suited only for labor, COGIC and
other Pentecostal denominations raised the fear of playing into the hands
of the white majority. What might seem like a sheltering cocoon of religious commitment to people like Katie Harper and Willis Atkins could

be construed, in the minds of others, as religious extremism. As one delegate to the 1900 National Negro Business League meeting put it, "I am one of those who believe the Negro must do something besides praying all the time. [Applause.] We started out directly after the surrender praying, 'Lord, give me Jesus and you can have all the world.' The white man in the South took us at our word and we got all the Jesus and he got all the world. [Laughter and applause.]"[14]

When Pentecostalism emerged, many non-Pentecostal black people took to calling believers like Katie Bell and her daughter "Holy Rollers," disparaging their shouts and ecstatic movements. The term particularly reflected the defensiveness of middle-class blacks, who saw Holiness and Pentecostal religion as a threat to the accomplishments and progress of "the race." Horace Clarence Boyer, a member of the Boyer Brothers gospel duo and a preeminent scholar of gospel, who was brought up in Faith Holy Temple Church of God in Christ, in Winter Park, Florida, notes that "Holy Roller" was virtually always used derisively. "You never heard that in polite society. It was just not to be done," he says. "We were born in the Pentecostal church, and we were very sensitive."[15]

Scorn from some segments of the black population didn't prevent Katie and little Rosie from attending COGIC services in Cotton Plant every Sunday, according to Sam Scott. Their church was rudimentary. In fact, it was not unlike the Baptist Missionary church the Scotts attended: a small wooden structure with slats where windows might have gone. Working-class people typically walked to church, which meant that they arrived for services dirty; in the days before Cotton Plant had indoor plumbing, when people arrived at church, "they would go to the pump and wash their legs and dry 'em off and put the talcum on." The big difference, as Sam remembers, is that at Shady Grove they had a piano and sang hymns like "Amazing Grace" "like it was wrote." But at the COGIC church Katie Harper and Rosie attended, they had "a different version, they put a little spirit in it, you know.... They would add to it, you know. That's what the difference. And they had the guitar for the back up, you know....After a while, they quit singing straight by the note, you know... [and] sometime they'll swing it." Sam Scott is mildly disapproving of this "looser" approach to liturgical music. " 'Amazing Grace' is *telling* you something, you know. So every song has got a message to it.... But I think if you want more out of it you have to sing it like it was wrote and what is meant."

Still, as children, Sam and his younger brother Cheatam enjoyed passing by the COGIC church on a Sunday afternoon to listen in on worship practices so different from their own. "We never had been used to that kind of, uh, I mean *service*, you know, and they would dance and shout in church, and we thought it was fun, I guess." He laughs. "So we would walk down there, when they first started. They'd have the guitar and the piano and all that stuff. . . . It was just amusing to us."

Sam Scott remembers Katie Harper as a "spiritual woman," but where Willis Atkins is concerned he draws a blank; in Sam's mind there is only an image of "the woman with the little girl who'd sing." Donell Atkins credits his father with teaching Rosetta songs when she was a child, but when the subject of Katie and Rosetta's departure from Cotton Plant comes up, he can only speculate from what he inferred from Willis Atkins. "Sister Rosetta's mother, she became a preacher, and at that time a preacher couldn't be married staying in a house with a man, so she left my daddy while he was at work and he never did hear from her no more. That's how it come out like that. I guess Sister Rosetta Tharpe's mother never did let her forget about her daddy. Who he were. But they never did try to contact him." Elteaser echoes her brother. "Her mother wanted to preach, you know, so she said she couldn't preach and be married, too. Rosetta was going out in the world, playing the guitar and everything, and she [Katie] said she wanted to preach and Rosetta would play her guitar."

Charles Mason's establishment of a COGIC Women's Department in 1911 could only have encouraged Katie to consider full-time evangelist work, particularly if she saw a better future for herself and her gifted daughter away from Cotton Plant. Perhaps Katie, a shrewd if untaught woman, understood that as the twentieth century progressed, the Emancipation Era pledge of forty acres and a mule—that is, the promise of black landownership—had drifted away, as the cotton lint wafted through the humid Cotton Plant air. If nothing else, becoming a missionary would have given Katie the opportunity to free herself and her child from the burdens of Southern life.[16] It's conceivable that Bishop Mason himself sent Katie out to evangelize.

Marie Knight, Rosetta's closest friend and her singing partner beginning in the late 1940s, tells a very different story from that of the Atkins clan. As Marie heard from Katie, she was forced to leave Cotton Plant because "the church world didn't accept her with a child out of wedlock."

"She said she never had the pleasure of actually being married to him," Marie recalls of Katie Harper. The disreputable pregnancy "carried down on her mind," Marie says. "She told me she used to go off and hide the larger she got with the baby...and the neighbors had to come to find her." Yet "the thing that settled Katie Bell down was Rosetta," she adds. Once she realized "she could make a living" through her child's rapidly developing musical gift, it became a natural next step to consider moving to a more metropolitan area, where the opportunities for missionary work were greater and the sinners more plentiful.

Whatever the case, Sam Scott remembers clearly that Katie Harper left Cotton Plant with only her child at her side. They were en route to Parkin, Arkansas, a town fifty miles or so northeast of Cotton Plant that was on the east-west rail line heading straight to Memphis, and from Memphis to St. Louis, St. Louis to Chicago. The route taken by most black migrants from Cotton Plant was also to be Katie and Rosetta's route.

2

GOT ON MY TRAVELIN' SHOES (1920–1937)

She belonged more to the world, I guess. I don't mean the worldly world,
but the people. . . . her voice was for people to hear and to know.
Camille Roberts

When gospel singers sing the familiar lines about putting on their "travelin' shoes," they're referring not to a day's trek, but to the ultimate journey, from this world to the next. Gospel songs focus almost entirely on the other world and its promises of everlasting life, unburdened by sorrow or suffering. That doesn't mean that gospel or Holiness religion are escapist, however; even as they celebrate the prospect of "going to see the King," they also give people strength to engage with the world, to stand the storms of everyday life. "Blues are songs of despair, but gospel songs are the songs of hope," observed Mahalia Jackson, widely considered the First Lady of the music's mid-twentieth-century Golden Age. "When you sing them you are delivered of your burden. You have a feeling that here is a cure for what's wrong."[1]

But the dozens of black sacred songs that celebrate "travelin'" also narrate the secular journey undertaken in the first decades of the twentieth century by millions of black Southerners as they migrated to the "Promised Land" of industrial cities such as Chicago, looking for economic opportunity and freedom from segregation and repressive violence.[2] Some, like Katie Atkins and her daughter Rosie, may well have landed in Chicago in search of opportunities to practice their religion in larger fellowships, thereby combining sacred and secular journeys. In any case, the pace of black migration to Chicago—considered part of "the North" by the migrants—was staggering: whereas in 1920 the black population of Chicago totaled 127,033, by 1930, according to statistics cited by migrant Richard Wright, it had swelled to almost 234,000.[3]

For Katie Atkins, Chicago represented economic opportunity as well as a place to save souls seduced by urban vices. As it did for many displaced black women, Katie's distinction as a Pentecostal enabled her to claim respectability, although she arrived there with a daughter and no husband.[4] Nevertheless, tensions were common between established black Chicagoans and their seemingly backward country brethren. For even as assimilated black urbanites devoted themselves energetically to the task of uplifting and educating the migrants, so they also sought to distance themselves from people who had the aura of outsiders—in their speech, the clothes they wore, the types of leisure they pursued, and, not least, their forms of religious expression.

Like a lot of migrants, Katie and her daughter were what Chicagoan Alva Roberts, a childhood friend of Rosetta's, calls "steady movers." At some point they lived on the West Side, in the neighborhood around the 1000 block of Thirteenth Street, recalls Musette Hubbard, who attended John M. Smith Elementary School with "Rosabell," as some Chicagoans remember her. (The name probably derived from Katie's short-lived marriage to a man named Bell, about whom little is known.) The girl Musette remembers was shy, while her mother distinguished herself, even by Pentecostal standards, for her puritanical attire. In her full-length, long-sleeved black dresses, "Mother" or "Ma" Bell looked old-fashioned, like someone out of the nineteenth century. Camille Roberts, Alva Roberts's in-law, remembers that Katie was "tall and sturdy" and dressed "like a missionary. Some might have thought she was a grandmother from her style of dress." They no longer had Cotton Plant lint on their clothes, but when Katie and Rosie walked down any main thoroughfare in black Chicago, their cosmopolitan neighbors saw the Sanctified Church writ large on their bodies and in their bearing.

Mother and daughter's first stop in the city may well have been its largest Church of God in Christ, located on Fortieth and State Streets on the South Side, just east of where most of black Chicago's storefront churches were located. Its pioneering members universally referred to it simply as "Fortieth Street." Such was the convention of the day, says Alva Roberts. She remembers how black children would identify themselves by their church membership: "I'm from 1319 West Thirteenth Street, and Elder P. R. Favors is my pastor!" they would stand up straight and announce.

When the children of Fortieth Street identified themselves to their peers, it was as members of the flock of Elder W. M. Roberts, a light-skinned man whose mother was the daughter of a slave woman and her Irish master. An early disciple of COGIC founder Charles Mason, Elder Roberts had his mentor's energy and resourcefulness. "I would say that the pastor was a man filled with a spirited urge," recollects Camille Roberts, who made the trip to Chicago from Atlanta with her mother and siblings around the same time as Katie and Rosetta. As custom had it, Camille's mother arrived with a letter of introduction addressed to Reverend Roberts from her pastor in Georgia, stamping her as a woman who would enrich the church and its reputation.

For Fortieth Street had a grand mission, despite its commonplace name. In the early 1920s, when Rosetta and Katie became members, it may well have been the largest COGIC congregation in the United States, larger even than the mother church of Bishop Mason in Memphis. By 1928, when the number of Holiness churches in Chicago had grown to fifty-six (from twenty in 1919), it was certainly the most respected COGIC church in the city.[5] "Papa Roberts," as he was fondly known, preached a practical, Booker T. Washington–style gospel of black self-reliance, even as he taught his flock to trust in God for all things. In the 1930s, he began broadcasting on WGCI, so that others could benefit from God's word.

Fortieth Street was a strivers' church, serious in its commitment to self-development. Veteran members of Roberts Temple Church of God in Christ, as it is now known, relate proudly that theirs was the first "black-built" church in all Chicago, not excluding the more well known mainline congregations. "We built that [church] from the ground," recalls Camille Roberts, who arrived in May 1922, a month after construction had begun. "We built just one floor at one time. I have a picture that says 1927"—the year church members had their first convocation upstairs. "See, [after that] we moved to a second floor. Then we expanded to property on the side. Then *it* expanded. Then we put a balcony. So that's how we grew."

Building their own church instilled self-respect in the members of Fortieth Street and further confirmed their faith in God's blessings. "The bigger churches, the people of other color would move out, and then other people would buy their churches," Camille explains, referring to the ways growing black congregations purchased synagogues and white churches when their membership relocated. "Pilgrim being one of the big churches. Ebenezer. They were white.... But ours was the largest at the time because we built it from the ground." Indeed, before the church acquired it in 1922, Pilgrim Baptist, at 3301 South Indiana Avenue, had served a Jewish South Side congregation as Kehilath Anshe Ma'ariv synagogue. Perhaps the single most significant church in the history of gospel music, because of its association with Thomas Dorsey, Mahalia Jackson, and others, Pilgrim Baptist made international headlines when it suffered a devastating fire in January 2006.

Becoming members of Fortieth Street in the early 1920s was definitive in the lives of Katie and her daughter. "I'm from 4021 South State Street and Pastor Roberts is my preacher!" Rosabell might have exclaimed to her school friends. In addition to giving them an identity, the church offered them a ready social network, a home base for Katie Bell's missionary work, and—through special collections for new arrivals and others in need—aid in establishing themselves amid unfamiliar surroundings. "I knew people that would take [Rosetta] and buy shoes, you know, for her, to see that she was dressed neatly," Camille Roberts recalls. "I don't mean fancy clothes.... People that could sew that could make things for her."

Most important where Rosetta's musical development was concerned, Reverend Roberts followed COGIC founder Charles Mason's liberal approach to sound. "They had a phrase: 'Rock Church Rock,'" says Camille, explaining her church's philosophy. "Music comes from God; it's the words that counts." Such were the teachings of Papa Roberts, who also embraced the COGIC mandate, derived from Psalm 150, to praise God with all manner of instruments, including the washboards and handmade guitars of poor rural folk. Whatever form it took, the music of prayer glorified God. As a church elder had once said, "The devil should not be allowed to keep all this good rhythm."[6]

Sunday morning services at Fortieth Street in the mid-1920s featured loud voices singing to the raucous accompaniment of tambourines, drums, triangles, a piano, guitars, and even brass, if a trumpet or trombone was available. (Not until 1928 did the church buy an organ.) Although there might be a featured soloist on a given Sunday, from week to week the "saints"—as Pentecostals called themselves—made their own music. Singing and playing were integral parts of the service, to the point where music and prayer merged. A shouting session could last the better part of an hour, its duration limited only by the energy of the congregation; often a member fainted or, if touched by the Holy Spirit, commenced ecstatic tongue-speaking and holy dancing. As Pastor Roberts preached, beginning with Scripture but then launching into an improvisational riff, the congregation buoyed him with their own shouted responses: "Yes, Sir." "Say it." "Praise the Lord." "Amen to that." Even in the Windy City, the un-air-conditioned building could be oppressively hot, and at the height of summer members fanned themselves to relieve the sweat and humidity. The dress code was somber, reflecting the seriousness of the Holiness enterprise, as well as the pride of people bent on achieving uprightness on their own terms, not through money or cultivation, but through sanctification.

In 1958, Rosetta would give her only two recorded accounts of her early performance history in Chicago. "I remember that my mother set me on her knees when she played the harmonium at church," she told the French interviewer François Postif. "I would tap 'Nearer My God to Thee' with a single finger and my mother accompanied me with her left hand. When we moved to Chicago, I was six years old, and I already played the guitar pretty well. One of our neighbors, Miss Foley, took an interest in me and hired my mother as a domestic to have me close to her. But one day, my mother had had enough of working for her, and the two of us set out to travel the church circuit."[7]

On her Mercury LP *The Gospel Truth*, recorded live before a COGIC audience six months after the interview with Postif, she told a similar story. "I started to playing music at the age of three years old," she testified. "[My mother] set me on her knee, and I would play an organ 'This Far by Faith' or 'Nearer My God to Thee.' I heard angels singing!" The congregation can be heard on the recording, responding with a shouted "Yes, Lord!" of encouragement.[8]

Rosetta's 1958 stories, although the products of a gospel celebrity fully practiced in the art of self-mythologizing, contain important emotional and factual truths. She confirms that her first musical experiences took place within the church, and that she played notes on the piano even before she plucked the strings of a guitar. She reveals that Katie worked as a domestic to supplement her income, and suggests that her frustration with her job fueled her determination to seek a living as a full-time traveling evangelist. Most important, she explains that she was considered a "special child" from early on, and how this indelibly shaped her own and others' images of her. Over the ensuing years, especially after she broke out as a national recording star, Rosetta changed her story about her age, her origins, and her personal life—omitting a marriage here, there neglecting the finer points of her capacity for immoderation. But she talked consistently of her giftedness until the day she died.

To Pentecostals, a gift was something to be used and used *well,* which meant the way the Lord intended. They had a saying in the church: "Your gift makes room for you." Growing up, says Geraldine Gay Hambric, a member of the Chicago-based Gay Sisters gospel trio, she learned from her mother that Rosetta was blessed with a gift of music and that Mother Bell was "a born healer, a real preacher." When their mother was pregnant with Geraldine, says Geraldine's brother Elder Gregory Donald Gay, she pleaded with Katie, who sometimes stayed with the Gays, to pray for her baby. The prayers apparently worked. When Geraldine was born, Elder Gay says, "she began playing piano with no lessons."

Katie, Geraldine recalls, occasionally wore a turban to set herself apart as a prophet. Rosetta, however, needed no special accoutrements to make her powers known. "I called [Rosetta's playing] 'fly,' " Geraldine says, noting that in those interwar years when gospel was developing in Chicago, "if you showed any kind of flyness with your music," you received special attention. "And she was so advanced, the music that I've heard from her."

"It was just her singing and her picking that guitar that just drew. You just got attached to it. She could really hit that, now," remembers Musette Hubbard. "You can sing, and it's a beautiful voice and everything, but if you sing with an *understanding* and the feeling of what you're singing it's altogether different. And that is what she did, more like to me. Even though she was young. It was a gift. Yes."

According to a story Rosetta was especially fond of repeating, at her Fortieth Street debut she was still so small that Papa Roberts had to lift her atop the church piano so the congregation could catch a glimpse of the pint-sized "singing and guitar-playing miracle." From that moment on, the members of the church couldn't get enough of the little girl with the too-big-for-her guitar and even bigger voice. Most youngsters in the 1920s started out in the children's choir, singing easy songs like "Yes, Jesus Loves Me." But not Rosabell. "Most of her singing was alone," says Musette Hubbard, explaining that, because she could accompany herself, Rosetta performed as a soloist from the start. "That guitar, I think, did a lot of it for her. See, you know, most of the times it's a boy. Most of the time, as I said, the boys would be with the guitar and the drums, and the girl did the singing."

Camille Roberts remembers putting a nickel of her own school money into a collection for Rosetta because "I liked to hear her sing." "And when she, you know, picked the guitar particularly she'd sometimes close her eyes and her voice was coming, a little spirit was within her coming out of her mouth," she adds. "You would become so enthralled with it, it was just, I don't know the word to say for it, but she was very spiritual and very good."

"Good" gospel singing was not necessarily a function of training as understood by traditional European art music standards; rather, it reflected the performer's delivery, her ability to interpret the notes in a deeply felt, convincing way, while conveying confidence, security, and well-being.[9] Perhaps as early as age seven or eight, but certainly by ten or eleven, Rosetta had this ability, such that the memories of her singing and playing are still fresh eighty years later. "I can just see her smile," Camille Roberts says, smiling herself. "I couldn't even describe it, but she had a bright smile, *alive*."

Rosetta's debut coincided with one of the most dynamic periods in the history of gospel music, which largely emerged from Chicago churches where Southern migrants worshiped. At roughly the same time she was balancing her adult-sized guitar on child-sized arms and shoulders, gospel was gaining a foothold as the most important black sacred music since the spirituals. Unlike the spirituals, however, gospel was largely a composed music. As a child, Rosetta sang the early gospel hymns of self-taught Baptist pianist-composer Lucie E. Campbell. She also performed songs written by Bishop C. H. Mason and other COGIC preachers, including Samuel Kelsey, the Washington, D.C.–based minister who would later become a friend and officiate at her third wedding.[10]

Before gospel's most prolific and influential composer, Thomas A. Dorsey, and his colleague Sallie Martin made copyrighting and selling gospel sheet music the norm, in the early 1930s, most of these compositions went unpublished. Yet they traveled orally, through church revivals and state convocations, as well as the annual national COGIC convocation, held every November in Memphis, from which a Fortieth Street delegate might return with one or two new numbers for the gospel choir. The simplicity of these songs, with their straightforward melodies and lyrics based upon Biblical verse, not only allowed them to be transported over geographical distances through listeners' memories, but also enabled congregations to put their own distinctive stamps on them. Gospel might have been formally composed, but in performance, gospel feeling prevailed.

Mother Bell's strictness limited Rosetta's exposure to Chicago's booming secular music scene in the mid- and late 1920s, when the South Side pulsed with jazz, blues, and other popular sounds in clubs and speakeasies. "To be sanctified is to set yourself apart," notes Geraldine Gay Hambric, voicing a central COGIC tenet. Ironically, however, this aspect of sanctification occasionally inflamed tensions with the more affluent, mainline Christians, who found Pentecostals snobbish in their self-distinction. Alva Roberts, who married Elder Roberts's first son, Isaiah, remembers how young people in her neighborhood teased each other about their differences. The Pentecostal children, she recalls with a chuckle, would make fun of the Baptist children for singing their church songs *slooooowwww*. Meanwhile, "some of the Baptist kids would point me out and say, 'She *sanctified!* She don't go to shows!' " Indeed, neither she nor Rosabell—nor Musette Hubbard, Camille Roberts, or Geraldine Gay—was allowed to go to the theater or see movies. Even if they could afford them, most of the saints shunned radios in their homes, as well.

On the other hand, urban sanctified people enjoyed a rich and spiritually satisfying musical life within the church. "Outside" sounds were absorbed into the *gospel blues,* exemplified in the music of Dorsey, former pianist for blues queen Ma Rainey and author of such notably unholy compositions as "It's Tight Like That." Camille Roberts suspects that gospel music had much to do with her own mother's attraction to the Church of God in Christ. Even as a small child in Atlanta, Camille says, she could tell that sanctified people "expressed joy, the same as if you were to hear a man sing a record or blues or something, and you would express it with the body, and that's the way [my mother] would.... She'd come home and [through] her prayers she would express joy.... I really didn't understand it until I came to Chicago Fortieth, and then I began to understand that the spirit was within *you;* you expressed it. If a song inspired you or you felt anything, you would express it, the same as a dance floor."

In one of her earliest recording sessions, Rosetta sang "Something within Me," communicating that joy that Camille had observed in her mother. Starting in Chicago, that "something" had become more than just a route to spiritual satisfaction for Rosetta; it had also become a means of survival. "When Rosetta was singing and people from other churches came to hear her, it was understood that the collection—which was not announced, just freely offered—was hers, and belonged to her. They would put it in an envelope and present it to her mother," Camille says.

In Chicago, Rosetta also discovered music as a means of earning others' approval. Although "it was like a leash," recalls Camille, referring to Katie's stringent protection of her daughter, Rosetta nevertheless grew to be outgoing. Raised by a mother who demanded obedience, she became playful and attention-seeking, not through acts of rebellion, but by entertaining others. In playing and singing, she found she could make people "happy," in both the everyday sense and the Pentecostal sense of Holy Ghost–filled. Moreover, unlike other kinds of "acting up," this kind was encouraged and rewarded.

In later life, Rosetta was known as a prankster, someone who would bend over backwards to get a laugh. As a woman among men, she compensated for not being one of the boys by showing the boys up with her boldness. Musically speaking, "Anything you can do I can do better"—the motto of *Annie Get Your Gun*'s Annie Oakley—became her motto, too. Instead of cultivating girlishness, taking a route more available to conventionally feminine and pretty black women, she fashioned an outrageous, fun personality to win others' affection and love.

Brown-skinned and otherwise "ordinary looking" by the Chicagoans' reckoning, Rosetta in childhood discovered the power of the smile Camille Roberts remembers. This instinct for performance was also part of her gift. In later years, she would give fans this smiling version of herself, not, as some might have thought, because she was stooping to stereotype, but because she believed that happiness was what people in or outside of the gospel world wanted in their entertainment.

Soon word of Rosetta spread to people outside of Fortieth Street, who would visit Sunday evening services just to hear her. In some cases, non-Pentecostals saw the saints themselves as objects of pleasurable diversion, but as often as not it was the *sounds* of the Sanctified Church that drew them in. "I was entranced by their stepped-up rhythms, tambourines, hand clapping, and uninhibited dynamics, rivaled only by Ma Rainey singing the blues at the old Monogram Theater," recalled Langston Hughes, who heard gospel in Chicago in his teens, after World War I. "The music of these less formal Negro churches early took hold of me, moved me and thrilled me."[11] Although she probably never saw Rosetta at Fortieth Street, even "Mahalia Jackson . . . when she started, she used to come there and sit in the balcony to listen to us," says Camille Roberts, not without pride.

Although Mahalia would sing with the early gospel group the Johnson Singers and then work with Dorsey at Pilgrim Baptist, she had always been taken with the sounds of the Sanctified Church. Prior to moving from New Orleans to Chicago in the mid-1920s, she had absorbed both the music of Bessie Smith and the music of Pentecostals. "Everybody sang and clapped and stomped their feet, sang with their whole bodies!" she recalled. "They had a beat, a powerful beat, a rhythm we held onto from slavery days, and their music was so strong and expressive it used to bring the tears to my eyes."[12]

Not infrequently, the members of Pastor Roberts's church would welcome a traveling missionary or evangelist-troubadour who also had a "powerful beat." Of these, one made an indelible impression on Camille Roberts. "Along comes a woman, I can't remember her name, but she was blind, and she was from Texas, and she could just make the piano talk, and she'd get so good she could hit it with her elbows, she could *perform* with it," she recalls. Arizona Juanita Dranes (1894–1969), the woman Camille remembers so vividly, was a COGIC musician who combined thumping, barrelhouse- and ragtime-influenced piano with a wailing, unaffected voice that seemed to emanate from her core. In 1926, Dranes, a Texas native, traveled from Dallas to Chicago at the urging of executives at the Okeh label, who wanted to record her. She journeyed with a note from her hometown preacher, Elder E. M. Page, pinned onto her sweater. "Since she is deprived of her natural sight," it read, "the Lord has given her a spiritual sight that all churches enjoy."[13] The note might have added that she had invented—possibly single-handedly—Sanctified piano style. Dranes used the piano as a distinct voice; she didn't merely play chords to back up her singing. The resulting sound was complex and polyrhythmic, its intricacy tempered by the directness of her singing.

When Rosetta heard Dranes, first in Chicago and later at COGIC convocations, she must have been exalted by the sounds of this spirited older woman who needed no accompaniment but her own. As Rosetta matured as an artist, her own playing would come to bear the imprint of Dranes's style, including her physical connection to her instrument. "It was rather like the blues singers," says gospel expert Horace Clarence Boyer, describing self-accompanying gospel musicians. "When you moved, your instrument moved with you." In Boyer's opinion, Arizona was the only woman who "rocked the world like Rosetta," although Dranes's reputation stayed primarily within the Church of God in Christ. Rosetta, in contrast, would burst out of these boundaries. First, however, she once again had to put on her "travelin' shoes."

* * *

"ROCK ME————OOOOOOOOHHHHHHHHH RRRRRRRo ooocccckkkk—m-ee-Rock me in the cradle of Thy Love" sang the ragged little girl in semi-jazzy rhythm while her companions kept time by clapping their hands and stomping their feet. The singer, a girl of some ten or twelve years, rocked and swayed as she sang in her entrancing throaty voice. . . . Her head was thrown back and her eyes closed and she seemed to put her whole soul into her singing—one is tempted to say *the song seemed to be a part of her soul.*

Such was the picture of a Chicago street musician painted by George D. Lewis, a writer researching "Spirituals of Today" for the New Deal–era Illinois Writers Project.[14] The girl singing Thomas Dorsey's "Hide Me in Thy Bosom" is not Rosetta, but Lewis's description of her as she attracts spectators of different races, at the intersection of Thirty-fifth and Dearborn, squares with Rosetta's likely experience in her early adolescence. When she and Katie Bell began their lives as traveling evangelists, they joined a tradition of Pentecostal singer-guitarists, such as Blind Willie McTell, who made their living saving souls at street meetings, house meetings, or storefront performances. The portability of stringed instruments like guitar and mandolin gave such makers of black sacred music, like the itinerant blues singers, a freedom to move about. On the road with her daughter, Katie Bell preached, joining Rosetta in singing and playing. Sometimes a soul would be saved; at other times, they would receive material payment in the form of nickels, dimes, or quarters tossed into a makeshift offering plate.

For Rosetta, joining her evangelist mother meant an end to her formal education. Musette Hubbard can't say for certain, but she doubts that Rosetta moved on with her to junior high; others say she might not have completed the sixth grade. In any case, some time before her twelfth birthday, evangelizing, not school, became Rosetta's full-time work. Alva Roberts clearly recalls how Katie Bell and Rosetta "labored . . . over on the West Side, in that particular area, they used to call it Jewtown." The area Alva remembers was the Maxwell Street Market, a Jewish ghetto where, on Sunday afternoons, street vendors peddled their wares. Inexpensive clothing and a racially and ethnically diverse street-fair atmosphere drew South Siders over to the market. There, among crowds including recently arrived Southern blues musicians and other evangelists, Rosetta and Katie held street meetings, while black families like Alva's milled about, enjoying a weekly Polish sausage. A young Rosetta would have overheard the sounds of early Chicago blues on Maxwell Street, a vibrant urban space where gospel had to compete for people's attention with other forms of musical entertainment.

Although they remained members of Fortieth Street, Rosetta and Katie Bell probably began traveling outside the northern Midwest by the late 1920s—one reason why Rosetta is generally not considered part of the seminal Chicago gospel scene that included Dorsey, Mahalia Jackson, Roberta Martin, Sallie Martin, and so many others. Instead, mother and daughter set out on the nascent "gospel highway," a loose conglomeration of churches, revivals, tent meetings, and convocations. The Depression was no impediment to religious enthusiasm; indeed, the disproportionate economic hardship suffered by black people after the 1929 stock market crash may well have caused many to turn to religion as an anodyne to despair. "People would say, bring that little girl over who plays that guitar. They would give her fifty cents," recalls Geraldine Gay

Hambric. If, on the other hand, Mother Bell *ran* a revival, Geraldine says, she could make one hundred dollars for two weeks, not including the meals and housing that the saints would generally chip in. This at a time when, as Alva Roberts recalls, a black woman making ten dollars a week in domestic service in Chicago was doing "*real* good."

On the other hand, the gospel circuit was sometimes unpredictable, more akin to what secular artists unromantically call "paying dues." The saints could be skinflints, and opportunities abounded for fraud. Once, Geraldine Gay Hambric says, she toured with an aunt who posed as Elder Lucy Smith, a popular Chicago singing evangelist who, incidentally, also claimed to have constructed the city's first "black-built" church.[15] The aunt was not only a charlatan but a cheat, refusing to share her earnings fairly with her niece. At other times, back home in Chicago, Geraldine's gift earned her the "honor" of playing piano from early Sunday morning to as late as ten or eleven at night. If the church was a nice one, she says, she would sometimes allow herself to fall asleep, spent, on the cushioned pews.

Performing at revivals required special concentration and stamina. Unlike staged performances, revivals were unrehearsed events, sometimes throwing together performers unaccustomed to each other's routines. The preacher would say "It's nobody's fault but mine," and that would be Rosetta's cue to jump into the song. Conversely, Rosetta would have to know when to *interrupt* the preacher, especially if she sensed attention spans flagging. Thus, in addition to developing her distinct musical voice, Rosetta had to hone an intuition for timing and performance, knowing how and when to assert herself musically without undermining a male preacher's authority.

Tent meetings and revivals in the 1930s shaped Rosetta's musical techniques. On the road with Katie Bell, she learned how to project over the cacophony of shouting, crying, and singing worshipers. Following Arizona Dranes on the piano, she developed a Sanctified gospel guitar style that emphasized the picking of individual notes as a counterpoint to her voice. This, too, was a strategy for being heard, for acoustic guitars, unlike pianos, possessed little if any resonance. A note was played, and as quickly as it became audible, it vanished. Plucking individual notes, and plucking them quickly, served not only as a form of visual entertainment, but also as a way of filling the otherwise dead space between vocal phrases. Rosetta also worked on the technique of embellishing a song with improvised lyrics or vocal interpolations, something which later became one of her trademarks. For example, when she got to the line "I ain't gonna study war no more," in "Down by the Riverside," she would make audiences whoop and holler with her "no no no no no no!"

Rosetta's talent for moving an audience arose from feeling as well as showmanship—a word that has no feminine equivalent in the English language. Every aspect of her playing and singing was Spirit-driven, and yet consciously calculated at the same time, just as the saints at Pentecostal services act in ways that are simultaneously spontaneous and scripted by custom. In church, the women tend to "fall out" at particular moments—not, for example, at the beginning of the service, but in the middle of the preacher's sermon, supplanting his voice with their own. As such moments show, sincerity and convention in religious experience can and do go hand in hand.[16]

Rosetta and Katie Bell traveled together through Rosetta's late teenage years. It was likely on the Pentecostal Church circuit that Rosetta met an itinerant COGIC preacher, Thomas J. Tharpe, whom she married in Chicago on November 17, 1934. Not much is known about Tommy; some say he was from St. Augustine, Florida, others New York. Whatever the case, Camille Roberts knows that he was a stranger to Fortieth Street when Pastor Roberts performed the wedding ceremony. By then married herself, Camille stood with Rosetta as she swore before God to honor and obey her husband. "She didn't have a big wedding," Camille recalls. "It was not that popular at that time. We couldn't afford weddings, and *she* couldn't, because I don't remember a father; it was just she and her mother."

Rosetta's name on the official marriage license—"Rosie Etta Bell Nuben"—suggests that by the time of her daughter's betrothal, Katie had herself remarried, although the absence of what Camille calls "a father" suggests that he was absent, or, more likely, that the marriage itself had ended, either through divorce or death. Nevertheless, Katie Harper went by the name Katie Bell Nubin (with an "i") for the rest of her life.

Elder Thomas and Rosetta Tharpe made a compelling husband-and-wife team. He preached, and she sang and played guitar; occasionally, he joined her on the ukulele. Most of the time they traveled with Katie Bell, but occasionally they journeyed separately, as Mother Nubin set out on her own evangelizing. Largely because of his wife's gift, the two became a familiar presence on the gospel highway. They were an especially popular attraction in southern Florida, where they ran revivals at Miami Temple, the area's most prominent COGIC church in the 1930s. Miami was an attractive base not only because of the number of COGIC congregations in the region, but because itinerants like Rosetta and Tommy could sit out the long Northern winters there.

"People talked about how [Tommy Tharpe] lived a pretty clean life," says Reverend Isaac Cohen, whose father, the Reverend Amaziah Melvin Cohen, established Miami Temple. "He was a great preacher.... He looked serious to me. He looked like a man who meant business." Others who knew Rosetta later in life take Isaac Cohen's commercial metaphor literally. Ira Tucker Jr., son and namesake of the legendary lead singer of the Dixie Hummingbirds, characterizes the marriage as a business transaction. "It was a deal, it was a deal," says Ira Junior, who grew up around Rosetta and Ma Bell in the 1950s and '60s. "And see, I think that's what influenced [Rosetta] throughout her life, was that it was very hard for her to separate her personal life from a deal. Do you know what I mean? It was a deal with Russell [Rosetta's third husband]. And I think most of the time, the men in her life, it turned out to be some type of deal, you know, an arrangement, some situation that, you know, if it's going to work for you, then it's going to work for me too." Marie Knight, Rosetta's singing partner in the 1940s and '50s and one of her closest confidantes, suggests that Tommy Tharpe wanted to attach himself to Rosetta's rising star. "He was a young minister and he had no publicity about him," she says, suggesting a pattern according to which Rosetta, however savvy, allowed men to use her for their profit.

Zeola Cohen Jones, a cousin of A. M. Cohen and a member of Miami Temple, says Tommy Tharpe was a tall, good-looking man reputed to be a good preacher. Even so, according to Zeola, Ma Bell didn't approve of Tommy, seeing him as a man who didn't live according to his words. Others soon grew wary of him as well; the Miami Temple grapevine had it that he was "seeing" someone in a different state. As a child, Zeola was an unwitting witness to Tommy's cruelty. "I was seeing him chase Rosetta down the street [at night] and fight her," she recalls. "And then the thing that was amusing, he would get up in church [the next day] and preach, and she would sing like nothing happened. Some things get embedded in a child's mind. I knew how he would beat her, but she *loved* him."

Roxie Moore, who met Rosetta at a revival Tommy and Rosetta ran at Rehoboth Beach Church of God in Christ, in Baltimore, corroborates Zeola's memories. Like Zeola, Roxie had an early suspicion that Tommy Tharpe had a girlfriend on the side. When Rosetta finally came around to realizing this, she was shattered—nothing in her life to that point had prepared her for such a blow. Because Tommy was a preacher, his deceit posed a fundamental challenge to her belief in the sheltering haven of her church.

Tommy and Rosetta stayed together, however—at least initially. As late as 1937, when Roxie met them, their home base was still Miami. "The people came really to hear her sing, not to hear him preach," says Zeola, recalling how Rosetta would get them going with her rollicking version of "Hide Me in Thy Bosom," in which she trilled the "r" in "rock me." "In the 1930s, Rosetta was the most popular singer there," says Isaac Cohen. "People noticed and responded to her playing." He particularly recalls her version of "Sit Down," an uptempo favorite about being so filled with the Holy Spirit that you *can't* stay in your seat.

Rosetta's stardom in south Florida only increased when the Reverend Amaziah Cohen began broadcasting Sunday night programs on WKAT, a white station that featured news and pop music. Rosetta's voice and guitar quickly became a leading attraction on the radio, and soon white people began attending live broadcasts at Miami Temple. "The people at night would come from all areas; sometimes, we had more whites in the church than blacks," recalls Isaac Cohen. The visitors, including many Jews, sat in a horseshoe balcony, while church members gathered on the main floor, up front. Eventually, Elder Cohen says, the church established a policy of a mandatory offering, "because we didn't have room for everyone." Some guests dressed in accordance with church convention, others in ways that church members found disrespectful—the women wearing pants or showing up without stockings.

Frictions between black members and white guests surfaced in other ways. The members of Miami Temple viewed the Sunday night broadcasts as entertaining religious worship, especially when Rosetta Tharpe was singing, but the visitors often treated the worship itself as entertainment. Zeola Jones remembers feeling discomfort with the arrangement:

> The Jews from Miami Beach would come to our church every Sunday night to hear [Rosetta] sing. It would be packed with the win-

ter Jews [vacationers from up north].... They came in *droves* to our church. Buses and limousines. They didn't mind parking in the ghetto for that. They weren't afraid.

When the saints would shout they would throw money down at them. It was, let's go see these niggers. It was amusement to them.

The memory of it still angers her. "When they would see them shouting they would just laugh and carry on and throw money." Moreover, when the church started charging admission to take advantage of all of the outsiders who came on Sundays, "the poor people couldn't attend"—although she recalls, laughing, how some black members of Miami Temple made a point of coming to Sunday-night broadcasts just to catch that money. "You *know* they would come out on Sunday. They would *jump* to get that money!" What is bittersweet about Zeola's memories of those days—the whites throwing money were also funding church renovations and an active college fund—cannot compensate for their ugliness. "I didn't like it," she says emphatically. "They wouldn't do that now."

Around 1938, Rosetta decided to step off the path that had been laid for her by her marriage, her church, and social convention. She made the radical decision to leave the church for a secular career. Zeola attributes the move in part to marital problems, in part to the enticements of white people who came to Miami Temple with "money and promises."

The next time the members of Fortieth Street or Miami Temple heard word of Rosabell, she was "Sister Rosetta Tharpe," Decca recording artist. "The church was hurt that she would leave the church and go into the world," says Zeola Jones. Camille Roberts and Alva Roberts also felt let down. "We knew she went out of the church, as they called it," says Camille. "That was the word that was coming back to the church, that she was mixing popular songs with church spirituals." Alva recalls, "When I heard her I said, my goodness, you mean she's gone into the world playing music like the *world* music?"

Camille can only speculate, but she suspects that Rosetta may have felt that worldly pull all along. "She would sing a line, and she would put a little *hmmmm* into the end of it, and it just look like you could just feast off that little *hmmmm*. I think that's why she moved out into the world, because she couldn't [help but] put a little oompf into the song. Now they're doing it, but when she started it, that was when you were getting away from religion."

Rosetta's gift would indeed "make room" for her—lots of room. But by 1938, it would also begin to estrange her from the very communities that had looked after that gift as their own.

3

FROM SPIRITUALS TO SWING (1938–1940)

Rock Me *(v.): send me, kill me, move me with rhythm.*
The New Cab Calloway's Hepster's Dictionary

We will probably never know exactly how Rosietta Atkins Tharpe—as she was then calling herself—made the leap from a COGIC church in Miami to the stage of the Cotton Club, New York City's most renowned nightspot. Certainly Rosetta was acutely aware of the feelings of disappointment, bewilderment, and betrayal her move stirred among the Pentecostal saints; indeed, regret might explain why, in later years, she tended to gloss over the details of this second "great migration" in her young life. Like her first migration from Cotton Plant to Chicago, the move from Miami Temple to the Cotton Club involved geographical dislocation, but it entailed cultural dislocation of an altogether different order. In the 1920s and 1930s, hundreds of thousands of black Southerners collectively took a gamble on "the North" as a land of freedom and opportunity. Only one—Rosetta Tharpe—had the boldness to bring gospel, the sacred musical expression of that migration, from the churches and street meetings where it developed to the stages of New York concert halls, ballrooms, and nightclubs.

For Rosetta, leaving the church to pursue a secular career was inseparable from leaving Tommy Tharpe; she knew that her husband couldn't pursue his career and condone her move. And yet her unhappiness in her marriage may not have been Rosetta's only motivation. To someone who had grown up wearing secondhand shoes and donated clothes, the promise of money must have been powerfully seductive. Rosetta apparently "thought the [Cotton Club] management was kidding" when, after her initial success, it proposed to pay her a weekly salary of five hundred dollars.[1] With few such lucrative opportunities open to black performers, the sacrilegious thought may well have crossed Rosetta's mind that some worldly opportunities were worth pursuing.

Accounts of Rosetta in those early years provide only the vaguest outline of the circumstances of her "arrival" (as the newspapers called it). According to the *Chicago Defender,* "She was induced to come to New York, where she cast her lot with a large Holy Roller church. One day some one suggested that she might try her talent in one of the amateur shows. She did and from that time on she has been going places." A slightly different version of this story appeared in the *New York Amsterdam Star-News,* Harlem's major newspaper, which reported that Rosetta had been "discovered" in the summer of 1938, while she and her husband were working at A. M. Cohen's church. As for who exactly had done the discovering, the *Star-News* cited Rosetta as saying that "Blanche Gabbie, a white woman," had heard her on A. M. Cohen's radio broadcasts and live at Miami Temple. "Why, she talked me right into Broadway," Rosetta is said to have quipped.[2]

As Rosetta became more accustomed to celebrity, she occasionally offered more farfetched accounts. In a 1941 interview, she claimed that "her agent" had "interested her in coming to New York," but only after she had rejected a scholarship to Alabama State Teachers College after graduating from high school "with highest marks." A different *Defender* piece than the one that had her entering "amateur shows" explained that she had been "brought up" for an audition before Cotton Club stage manager Herman Stark "by a booking agent who had learned of her singing through an office worker who happened to pause in front of the church [in Harlem] where Miss Tharpe was singing."[3]

Rumors also circulated that a "famous" male musician had plucked Rosetta from obscurity. "Several big shots along Broadway and in Harlem . . . claim her discovery," one article suggested. "Among them are two of the best known band leaders in the business." A couple of accounts credited Cab Calloway with signing Rosetta after her heard her singing (one locates the "discovery" in New York, the other at Miami COGIC), although Calloway, vocal about his role in jump-starting the careers of Lena Horne and Pearl Bailey, never confirmed the story.[4]

It's likely that Rosetta was not the only source of such inconsistencies, given the low music journalism standards of the day and the tendency of agents and managers to promulgate stories merely for publicity's sake. And yet, taken together, the elisions, ambiguities, and occasional flat-out implausibilities of these stories point at the failure of Rosetta or the press to come up with a viable "crossover" narrative for her—a way of presenting her as an authentic Pentecostal while explaining how she had turned up at the Cotton Club. Once, Rosetta told a reporter that "when she was a little girl, she dreamed of a theatrical career,"[5] and if this is true, then her move outside the church represented the realization of an old, if suppressed, desire. In general, however, Rosetta portrayed herself as being lured to take a bite of the Big Apple. She may indeed have felt forced to choose between two equally impossible outcomes: divorce from Tommy Tharpe or leaving the church.

Yet Rosetta did choose; no husband or mother forced her to sing in nightclubs where the patrons smoke and drank, and the dancers wore little more than G-strings. Perhaps this is why, in an early interview, she called herself Rosetta *Vashti* Tharpe.[6] The name came from the Old Testament book of Esther, in which Queen Vashti, wife of King Ahasuerus, refuses to obey her husband's command to parade herself before his guests at a banquet. The king's sages determine that Vashti's refusal not only has insulted the king, but has endangered the stability of the entire society, which obliges women to "give honor to their husbands, high and low alike."[7] The reference to Vashti—a name she would periodically return to over the years—hinted at Rosetta's awareness of her "disobedience" to Tommy Tharpe and to the Church of God in Christ itself.

From Cotton Plant to the Cotton Club. The juxtaposition of the racially and socially stratified Arkansas town of Rosetta's birth with the racially and socially stratified New York nightclub where she debuted was more than a little ironic, considering that the entertainment concept behind the latter was the antebellum plantation of "Swanee River" nostalgia. Yet the image of bucolic slavery days was precisely the source of the Cotton Club's charm. Indeed, the name *Cotton Club*, and all that the South's most important cash crop once stood for—national economic prosperity, the promise of industrialization, the expansion of the U.S. empire —appealed to white patrons during the lean and joyless years of Prohibition and the Depression, even to Northerners who had never seen a cotton plant.

The admissions policy of the Cotton Club—no blacks allowed, with rare exceptions for visiting celebrity-performers, whose parties nevertheless sat in tables at the rear—mirrored the ambiance and themes of the shows. The original bandstand, as Calloway recalled, "was a replica of a southern mansion, with large white columns and a backdrop painted with weeping willows and slave quarters."[8] The Duke Ellington Band in the early days played "jungle jazz" to complement "African" set pieces, in which the "jungle" sounds sometimes derived from the horn players' use of modified toilet plungers in the bells of their instruments.[9] Meanwhile, advertisements boasted "tall, tan and terrific" chorus girls as staples of Cotton Club revues. For all of its elegance, the club had a distinctly vaudevillian streak, mixing song, dance, comedy, and novelty acts, from conga numbers to contortionists.

The club's performers took umbrage at its perpetuation of racial stereotypes and its racially discriminatory policy at the door. Yet "some of the proudest Negro musicians in the world played there and adhered to that policy of racial segregation," recalled college-educated Calloway in 1976. Stars of the Cotton Club revues in the 1920s and '30s included Ellington, Jackie "Moms" Mabley, Ethel Waters, the Nicholas Brothers, and Bill "Bojangles" Robinson. "So far as we were concerned," wrote Ellington, whose band began playing there in late 1927, "the engagement at the Cotton Club was of the utmost significance, because as a result of its radio wire we were heard nationally and internationally.... The Cotton Club was a classy spot. Impeccable behavior was demanded in the room while the show was going on."[10]

The Cotton Club that has entered popular legend of the twenty-first century is the glamorous nightspot portrayed in Francis Ford Coppola's 1984 The Cotton Club, with its colorful cast of high-society types, burly mobsters, striving black musicians, and exacting white stage managers. Located at 142nd Street and Lenox Avenue in Harlem, the original Cotton Club was established in 1923 as a place where well-heeled white audiences could venture "uptown"—in those days, a code word for the neighborhoods above 110th Street. In 1935, however, Harlem erupted in riots caused by frustrations over unemployment, high housing costs, and poor public services, and the owners of the Harlem club closed its doors, since its white clientele now considered the neighborhood dangerous. Undaunted, they reestablished the club in a top-floor room in a building at Forty-eighth and Broadway, which, in a former incarnation, had been the Ubangi Club, a short-lived nightspot where popular black lesbian entertainer Gladys Bentley performed in male drag, complete with top hat and cane.

The Cotton Club where Rosetta appeared thus was located in the relatively more humdrum heart of the Great White Way, as the illuminated Broadway theater district was known. That didn't affect the quality of its clientele, however. Among those who caught Rosetta's act in the opening nights of the fall 1939 revue were Mary Martin, J. Edgar Hoover, and Nate Blumberg, president of Universal Pictures.[11]

Much nevertheless had changed in popular music between the 1923 unveiling of the Harlem club and its relocation to Broadway in 1936, years that coincided with Rosetta's development from a child prodigy to a highly sought-after performer on the Pentecostal circuit. For one thing, the meaning of "swing" had changed. Originally, musicians considered swing a quality of musical performance; as Ivie Anderson, singing for the Ellington band, had put it, "It Don't Mean a Thing (If It Ain't Got That Swing)." By the time the Broadway Cotton Club launched its first show, however, swing itself had become a thing. Whereas formerly one might describe a band with a good rhythm section as "swinging," now it was much more common to read and talk about "swing bands" and "swing musicians."

The Swing Era, as it became known, coincided with relatively productive and progressive years in U.S. popular culture, a time when the political left, most notably the Communist Party, exerted unprecedented influence on everything from music to drama to literature. Yet even amid a general cultural move leftward, the new Cotton Club continued to trade on the myth of the Old South.

It was a myth fortified by the 1939 Hollywood blockbuster *Gone with the Wind*, which left generations of Americans pining for a mythical plantation called Tara, even as it made Hattie McDaniel the first black winner of an Academy Award.

More to the point, amid trends toward integration within popular music culture, increased liberalism on race issues, and mounting domestic concern about the rise of Hitler and Nazism—a topic of particular alarm among African Americans after Germany invaded Poland in September 1939—the club persisted in enforcing a racially exclusive admissions policy. Indeed, the club's setup only reinforced whites' social license to regard black bodies, especially scantily clad women, as spectacles—and to do so at a time when analogous acts of "looking" not infrequently got black men lynched. Like the nineteenth-century minstrel stage, the Cotton Club offered whites proximity to black people, but did little to change the terms of the racial hierarchy. Nowhere was this better illustrated than in the mural commissioned for the opening of the Broadway club. It imagined the popular white swing bandleaders of the day—in blackface.[12]

Sister Rosetta Tharpe, as she was professionally billed (the "i" in Rosietta having been permanently dropped), was not supposed to be a highlight of the fall 1938 Cotton Club revue, a fast-paced affair headlining Calloway and the Nicholas Brothers, young dancers who thrilled audiences with their acrobatic elegance. Originally she was just a gamble, signed by Herman Stark for two weeks. Like another new attraction, the Dandridge Sisters—a singing group that included a promising fourteen-year-old named Dorothy—Rosetta constituted one part of a huge supporting cast, performers who largely filled time between the big numbers. Early print advertisements did not mention her name.

Yet from the outset, audiences were thrilled by Rosetta's unusual sound and style. Unaccustomed to the emotionally expressive music of Pentecostals, newspaper reporters, white and black, struggled for the right words to describe her. Most used some variation of "swing" to convey the rhythmic quality of her music, calling her a "swinger of spirituals," a "spiritual swinging favorite," a "hymn swinging evangelist," and a "hymnswinger." Others, drawn to the novelty value of a Pentecostal performer, christened her a "religious shouter," a "Holy Roller Singer," and a "Holy-roller entertainer." The *Chicago Defender* called her "a swingcopated manipulator of loud blue tones" and noted that "she handles the guitar rather creditably in accompaniment."[13]

Still others compared Rosetta to Bessie Smith, the blues singer whose career was cut short by a 1937 car accident.[14] Like Smith, Rosetta presented a compelling picture of black female self-assurance and vigor when she performed. Indeed, her "gospel blues" and Smith's secular blues were not all that distinct. Musically, both sprang from sources in slave culture, and both confronted the harshness of the world with determination to "make a way outta no way." For gospel singers, this "way" was through God; for blues singers, it was through self-reliance.

Shortly after her name began appearing in the newspapers that October, Rosetta acquired a talent manager. He was Moe Gale, born Moses Galewski, influential head of Gale management, a top talent agency, and owner of Harlem's famous Savoy Ballroom. Gale arranged to have Rosetta photographed by James J. Kriegsmann, official photographer to the Cotton Club stars, with offices at the Actors' Equity Building at 165 West Forty-sixth Street.

Rosetta showed up with her National resonating guitar and her own gown. By Cotton Club standards, which practically mandated sequins, feathers, rhinestones, and midriff-exposing outfits for women, it was modest. It featured a quiet print, billowy shoulders, and sweet, pleated detailing around the neckline and down the bodice. Her hair had been curled with a hot iron, in a cute rather than come-hither style, and she wore no jewelry. Kriegsmann, who used overhead lights to illuminate her face, casting sharp, visually arresting shadows behind her, posed Rosetta smiling, hands on the strings of her guitar, glancing upward with wide-open eyes. The only elements undermining the image of Rosetta as a Pentecostal singer appear in the form of carefully plucked eyebrows and subtle traces of makeup—a touch of lipstick and perhaps a bit of defining kohl around the eyes.

Kriegsmann took many photographs of Rosetta during their session, but this one—or variations of it so similar that the differences are barely perceptible—would be the most reproduced. It also established Rosetta's guitar as an indelible element of her image. In the late 1930s and early 1940s, the picture of Rosetta looking at ease with her instrument carried special significance. As the scholar Sherrie Tucker has shown, most images of the women swing musicians who came to prominence as members of "all-girl" bands in the 1940s pictured their instruments as ornaments, rather than as drums, saxophones, trumpets, or trombones they actually played.[15] In contrast, even if Rosetta was not actually picking a note at the moment Kriegsmann snapped the photograph, she was definitely not holding her guitar as decoration, like a bride awkwardly holding a bunch of lilies to her cheek in a wedding photograph.

A very different picture taken by Kriegsmann during that photo session occasionally did appear in the press, but never came close to enjoy-

James J. Kriegsmann publicity photograph of Rosetta
Tharpe, circa late 1938 or early 1939. Photograph courtesy
the Schomburg Center for Research in Black Culture.

ing the same iconic status as the photograph of Rosetta with her National
steel resonating guitar. It was an alter ego to the image of Rosetta as the
cheerful ingénue: a shot in which a determined, even somber-looking
woman stares off into the middle distance, closed-lipped and unsmiling.
That photograph, too, would be a harbinger of things to come.

From October to December 1938, events of profound and lasting
significance to Rosetta's career occurred almost weekly. The first involved
the copyrighting of her material. Irving Mills, at one point the agent of
Calloway, Ellington, and a group called the Mills Blue Rhythm Band—
later to become the band of one Lucius "Lucky" Millinder—approached
Rosetta in mid-October and soon had her signed to an "exclusive publishing contract" with Mills Music. A company with an international

distribution network, Mills Music quickly published *Eighteen Original Negro Spirituals,* an impressive booklet (with the smiling Kriegsmann portrait on the cover) containing songs "with an original and appealing religious quality set down exactly as sung by Sister Tharpe since infancy in Negro churches all over the country." Encompassing such titles as "I Look Down the Road and I Wonder," "My Lord and I," "Saviour, Don't Pass Me By," "That's All," and "This Train," *Eighteen Original Negro Spirituals* would serve as a crucial source of Rosetta's repertoire for the next thirty-five years.

Music publishing was important—as early gospel entrepreneurs such as Dorsey and Sallie Martin well understood—but it didn't have the glamour of sound recordings. Some of that glamour became Rosetta's when she signed a contract the same month with Decca Records. J. Mayo "Ink" Williams, head of the label's "race" division, managed such Decca notables as Louis Armstrong, Count Basie, Chick Webb, and Ella Fitzgerald. In 1938, however, the label was better known to the masses of record buyers as the label of white musicians Bing Crosby, Connie Boswell, and Guy Lombardo. It was also known for undercutting the competition, charging thirty-five cents per disk at a time when the going rate was seventy-five.

Decca had recorded four sides by Mahalia Jackson in May 1937, but they did so poorly that the label dropped her and didn't venture back into the gospel field until it took a chance on Rosetta seventeen months later. With her bell-like voice, winning smile, and Cotton Club notoriety, Rosetta had the combination of the musical goods and showbiz flair that Mahalia had lacked. Her first 78s, recorded in a single session on October 31, 1938, with Rosetta accompanying herself on guitar, were instant successes. How successful they were in hard numbers is difficult to say, but successful enough to bring Rosetta back for a second session in January 1939 and to keep her in Decca's employ, without interruption, until the mid-1950s. It's also likely that her early recordings did well with white record buyers, since Decca did something it normally didn't do with black artists: after she had produced four hit 78s, the label collected the shellac disks together in a deluxe boxed "album."

Rosetta's first session reveals a young woman capable of finding and communicating the emotional core of a song through exquisite phrasing, inventive vocal technique, and guitar playing of originality, confidence, and grace. Her years of using her gift in live performance had taught her how to make a listener *feel* a song, not just hear it, by making use of vibrato, trills, enunciation, dynamic variety (variations in loudness), and melisma, a gospel hallmark in which the vocalist sings several notes within the space of a single syllable. Like a blues or jazz singer, Rosetta tended to sing around the beat rather than on top of it, allowing for rhythmic complexity and improvisation. Like a blues singer, too, she was capable of covering material of enormous topical and emotional variety. Her first four cuts for Decca range widely in tone, from the sassy satire of "That's All" to the wistful contentment of "My Man and I" to the extroverted exuberance of "Rock Me" and the longing of "The Lonesome Road." All bore the mark of a singer-player of extraordinary control and personality.

As a first recording, "Rock Me," the Dorsey song Rosetta had been singing since her Chicago days, and the one Zeola Cohen Jones remembers as a favorite at Miami Temple, was a logical choice. Presumably following the way she was singing it at the Cotton Club, Rosetta made a single significant change in the lyric on the record, substituting the word "swinging" where Dorsey had written "singing." That single added "w" —in the very first line of the very first song that would introduce Rosetta to the wider world—signaled an important shift in her identity. To "swing" was to revel in rhythm, to feel the beat in your body, an experience that facilitated proximity to God in the context of Pentecostal worship—but in the context of a popular record, it belonged to what Rosetta's old Chicago church called the "worldly world."

Moreover, although Rosetta had been putting her signature stress on the words "rock me" since at least the mid-1930s, the juicy growl she produces on the Decca disk—on which "rock me" comes out as "rrrrrock me"—opens up the meaning of the phrase to various secular interpretations. In Dorsey's lyric, the phrase is a prayer addressed to a parent-deity who cares for His child, but as Rosetta sings it, "rock me" is an appeal to the gods of rhythm. The white trade magazine *Variety* took "rock me" as a reference to intercourse, saying her lyrics had "a slay-'em innuendo." Rosetta was not a stranger to sexual double entendre—no one working at the Cotton Club for so long as a week could have been—yet "rock me" makes more sense as a call for delivery from worldly cares through music.

It's tempting to read the other three songs Rosetta recorded during that first session as expressions of her emotional turmoil regarding

Tommy Tharpe. In "That's All," Rosetta rewrote Washington Phillips's "Denomination Blues" as a funny take on religious poseurs, people who claim to "have religion" but never quite walk the talk. To make her point, she daringly rhymed "well" with "hell," describing ministers who would let their congregations go to the Devil if it served their self-interest. "My Man and I," a tender version of her "My Lord and I" from *Eighteen Original Negro Spirituals*, is a paean to romantic love based on camaraderie, shared values, and gender equality. And in her version of "The Lonesome Road," she sang in a lower part of her soprano register, conjuring the sound of the blues women, who similarly sang about lost romance with a compelling mixture of grief and grit.[16]

Notable gigs followed closely upon Rosetta's 1938 Cotton Club engagement and the release of her first records. In early December, although still under contract to Stark, she did a week-long "by courtesy" stint with the Count Basie Band at the Paramount Theater in midtown. Later that month, she appeared at the Apollo Theater's Christmas fundraiser, an annual event that brought together everyone from Fats Waller and Lionel Hampton to Fredi Washington, the Four Ink Spots, Noble Sissle, Artie Shaw, and Hazel Scott. And on December 23, she appeared before a sold-out Carnegie Hall audience for From Spirituals to Swing, one of the most historically significant musical events of the first half of the twentieth century.

John Hammond, the force behind the concert, was the son of a Vanderbilt, but he was also a Yale dropout who maintained open ties to the Communist Party. He possessed an excellent ear, and had curated the concert to reflect a preference for music that had little exposure among cultural tastemakers, the white elites as well as the black "talented tenth," who were often more comfortable with Bach than with the blues. Hammond himself tended to equate a lack of commercial exposure with musical authenticity. The detailed program handed out to ticket holders promised an evening of "the music nobody knows," and the concert was dedicated to Bessie Smith.

To Hammond's mind, From Spirituals to Swing had a vital social mission that went beyond its basic concept of presenting a diverse lineup of African American performers to an integrated audience at a high-culture venue. Indeed, Hammond had a vision of the concert as a sort of "populist challenge" to racism.[17] His only problem, initially, was that no organization—not excepting the NAACP—would go near it. Eventually, he got sponsorship from the Communist Party organ *The New Masses* for a show that included blues shouters Jimmy Rushing and Joe Turner, the North Carolina–based quartet Mitchell's Christian Singers, boogie-woogie pianist Albert Ammons, jazz soloist Sidney Bechet, and a star-studded swing band led by Count Basie, a Hammond favorite.

Rosetta appeared before the sold-out Carnegie Hall crowd in an early segment titled "Spirituals and Holy Roller Hymns," which followed an introduction featuring African tribal music as well as a number by Count Basie and His Orchestra. She sang two songs, "Rock Me" and "That's All," accompanied by her guitar and boogie-woogie piano provided by Ammons, a Chicagoan known for his "hot" sound. (The program noted that he "doesn't read a note of music.") Preserved for posterity, these songs are as close as we will ever get to hearing what she might have sounded like on the Cotton Club stage. And indeed, she is even better on these recordings than on her 78s, projecting an ease and a joy in performing that studio disks could not match. Her voice that night was huge and clear, and she had no trouble keeping up with Ammons, trading finger-picked guitar riffs with his bursts of pulsing piano. She even had the confidence to play with the audience, which spent the entire performance eagerly straining forward in their seats, moving in time to her rhythms. She began "That's All" with a bit of fancy picking. Then she stopped, abruptly, when the crowd didn't expect her to. Her reward was laughter, and at that moment, when she was assured of everyone's attention, she and Ammons launched into a fast-paced rendition of the song. She got a second laugh when she omitted the anticipated "well/hell" rhyme of the lyric, as though to say with a wink, "This *is* Carnegie Hall, after all."

By popular consensus, the performance was a triumph. As Basie remembered, "She sang some gospel songs that brought the house down. She sang down-home church numbers and had those old cool New Yorkers almost shouting in the aisles. There were a lot of people out there who had never heard that kind of singing, but she went over big." The memory of Rosetta remained fresh a half-century later to Harry "Sweets" Edison, trumpeter with the Basie band. "I also remember Sister Rosetta Tharpe," he said. "She was one of the greatest spiritual singers you ever heard . . . and a good guitar player!" Looking back, even Hammond himself seemed to marvel at his good judgment at recruiting Rosetta: "Except for one fleeting appearance at the Cotton Club," he wrote, "she had never sung anywhere except in Negro churches. She was a surprise smash; knocked the people out. Her singing showed an affinity between gospel and jazz that all fans could recognize and appreciate."[18]

The cliché about overnight celebrity does not feel far-fetched in describing Rosetta's experience in late 1938. It's difficult to know how she experienced stardom, however, partly because she wasn't forthcoming about her feelings. Publicly, of course, Rosetta smiled and beamed, learning early on to tell reporters what she thought they wanted her to say. However, there's no reason to doubt Rosetta's happiness at her success. Like a lot of people who take to the spotlight, Rosetta loved to be loved. Her trick at Carnegie Hall—ceasing to play when the audience least expected it, just to get a laugh—illustrated that desire to a T.

On the other hand, just as the "serious" Kriegsmann photograph captured a lesser-known side of Rosetta, so a part of her worried about what she had gotten herself into when she signed with Herman Stark. Occasionally she would confess her misgivings to Roxie Moore. Zeola Cohen Jones remembers her returning to Miami at some point—it may have been later in the 1940s—conceding regret. " 'One of the worst things I did was to leave the church. Because I thought people in the church were kind and loving.' Now she said that to me," Jones says.

Rosetta had reasons to feel uncomfortable. Notwithstanding its whiff of racial romanticism, From Spirituals to Swing had given her a dignified setting, at least in comparison to the stages of New York theaters in 1939 and 1940, as her career continued to expand. Years later, her obituaries would tout Rosetta as the first gospel act ever to headline the Apollo, and yet few probably cared to remember the circumstances of her original appearances there. Before a predominantly black audience, Rosetta appeared in a burlesque of Pentecostal religion, making her a party to the mockery of her church. At From Spirituals to Swing, Rosetta had appeared on a chaste stage wearing a modest dress that buttoned up to the neck; at the Apollo the following summer, she made a stage entrance in the midst of a "holy-roller meeting" as *Variety* put it, complete with "gals dressed in bright-colored old-fashioned dresses," a male quartet "dressed in reds and greens," and house comics doing "preacher stuff from a rickety rostrum and with a telephone book for a bible." It is safe to say there were no practicing Pentecostals in the room. Perhaps because Herman Stark had set contractual limits on what she was allowed to perform outside the Cotton Club, Rosetta did insipid secular fare rather than the versions of "Rock Me" and "That's All" that had earned her raves on Broadway. "Out of [the spiritual] idiom," *Variety* concluded, in language so boorish it stands out even by pre–World War II standards, "she's nothing more than another shoutin' colored gal with a guitar."[19]

The situation was no better at the Cotton Club; indeed, the Apollo's white owners probably derived their idea of what would please black audiences by copying what was popular with the white crowd on Broadway. (Black audiences, meanwhile, might have clamored for access to the type of entertainment they were denied on account of race.) In one Cotton Club revue that ran through the summer of 1939, Rosetta performed in a similar "Pentecostal Meeting" set, backed by dancers and singers playing the roles of worshipers, evidently to encourage the audience to "jitterbug" to her "revival songs." In fact, she was playing at actual Pentecostal churches in New York on Sunday mornings, while "playing church" on stage in an irreverent fashion during the rest of the week. The contrast drew the attention of the editors at *Life* magazine, who arranged for a one-page piece devoted to the singer who "Swings Same Songs in Church and Night Club."[20]

The *Cotton Club Parade* of spring 1940—in which Rosetta shared a billing with the Andy Kirk Orchestra, featuring Mary Lou Williams on piano and Floyd Smith on "the electrified string instrument"—went a step further. At one point in that show, Rosetta entered the stage riding a mule with a phone book strapped to it. The wisecracking comedian Alan Drew played the role of a jive-talking preacher. As *Variety* put it, he "aids the sister in conducting her meetin'."[21]

Given the multiple ways she had violated her church's teachings, it seems curious that in September 1939 Tommy Tharpe showed up to chastise Rosetta—for forgetting to wear her hat during one performance.[22] Where had Tommy Tharpe been this whole time, and why did he publicly admonish his wife for this seemingly minor infraction? Perhaps he thought it best to assert his authority on doctrinal matters so as to undermine Rosetta's authenticity, the quality she was selling on nightclub stages. Zeola Cohen Jones recalls that Tommy stayed behind in Florida when Rosetta first went north, but by late 1939 he apparently felt the need to distinguish himself from her by trading on his power as a man and a minister. By publicly reproaching Rosetta, Tommy created the necessary distance from her to continue with his own work as a COGIC minister in Brooklyn.

Even without her husband's reprimand, it's not surprising that Rosetta could sing "I Looked Down the Line (and I Wondered)" with such conviction in late 1939, or that she sometimes longed publicly for a return to the days before her theatrical stardom. "You know," she told reporters just before Tommy Tharpe's public censure, "there was something about the work as soloist in the church that I cannot seem to find as a star on Broadway. Guess I just learned to love the folk I was associated with and miss them more now that I don't see them anymore."[23]

While Rosetta was contemplating the consequences of her choices, debates raged in various sectors of the black press about the morality of swinging the spirituals. (Typically these took place among members of mainline denominations, excluding entirely the voices of black Pentecostals or adherents of other Holiness churches.) In Pittsburgh, George W. Harvey, pastor at New Hope Baptist Church and associate religion editor at the *Pittsburgh Courier,* gave a "stirring address" urging responsible black Christians to "stamp out the wanton practice of desecrating the songs of our fathers and mothers." As an example of a primary offender he cited pianist-singer Fats Waller, whose uncle happened to be a deacon at New Hope Baptist, and who had performed "When the Saints Go Marching In" in "a fast swing time in places of business conducted by or for the race."[24] The implication was clear: black entertainers who "swung" the spirituals were rendering the sacred music of their ancestors into music for social dancing, and everyone knew what social dancing signified. Dorsey himself entered the fray of public debate in a 1941 piece in the *Chicago Defender,* making essentially the same point. After noting that "some of our churches are so high-tone now that they are above singing spirituals"—a dig at those institutions that rejected his own compositions as unholy—he continued: "I have written more than three hundred gospel songs and spirituals. I do not object to them being used on the air, but they must not be desecrated or used for dance purposes."[25]

Others, especially black intellectuals, also chimed in. In "Spirituals and Neo-Spirituals," an essay from 1934, the anthropologist and novelist Zora Neale Hurston, *enfant terrible* of the New Negro establishment, took a stance rooted in her own fieldwork among Sanctified churches in Florida. "The great masses [of black people] are still standing before their pagan alters and calling old gods by a new name," she observed. "As evidence of this, note the drum-like rhythm of all Negro spirituals. All Negro-made church music is dance-possible."[26] Unlike her fellow intellectuals, Hurston rejected the terms of the "swinging spirituals" debate as established by organs such as the *Courier*. Instead, she reframed the entire question according to her belief that the spirituals were a *living* music, not a fossilized legacy.

The writer Arna Bontemps, a leading light in Chicago and Harlem literary circles, took a similar tack. In "Rock, Church, Rock!," a 1942 article from the left-leaning journal *Common Ground*, he sketched two dilemmas: a generational battle over the new rhythmic sounds emerging from Northern urban churches, and a brewing resentment among churchgoers over the dissemination of this music as secular entertainment. While Bontemps sympathized with those who liked their church songs "lively," he also commiserated with those who were aghast at what Rosetta was doing. Noting that "Georgia Tom"—Dorsey's name when he was with Ma Rainey—lurks in songs like "Hide Me in Thy Bosom," he concludes: "It is not surprising that the swing bands fell for this stuff, nor that a church singer like Sister Thorp [*sic*] could join Cab Calloway without changing her songs. Neither is it surprising that the church folks resented this use of their music and complained bitterly. They have their case, and it's a good one."[27]

The same month *Life* pictured Rosetta as a performer who precariously bridged the sacred/secular divide in black popular culture, it sent photographer Charles Peterson out on assignment to do a feature spread that would never make it into the pages of the magazine. The idea was to illustrate a jazz jam session, and toward that end, *Life* had recruited the white jazz guitarist Eddie Condon and promoter Ernie Anderson to organize a by-invitation-only party at the Riverside Drive apartment of Burris Jenkins, a pioneering black political cartoonist. Along with record producer Harry Lim, the guest list included Calloway, Ellington, Rex Stewart, Max Kaminsky, Ivie Anderson, Hot Lips Page, Pee Wee Russell, Chu Berry, Johnny Hodges, Billie Holiday, Cozy Cole, Clyde Newcombe, Bud Freeman, and Dave Tough.

Before long, it seems, everyone at the party had lost all self-consciousness about the fact that they were being photographed for *Life;* there was too much pleasure to be had drinking and smoking and making music. Rosetta had brought along her guitar, and took turns with Ellington playing it. At one point, she looked on as he strummed and Calloway messed around on the keyboards, and one can only imagine

Rosetta jams with Duke Ellington (at piano), Cab Calloway, and trombonist
J. C. Higginbotham at a private party arranged by *Life* magazine, August 1939.
Trumpeter Hot Lips Page looks over Duke's shoulder. Photo by Charles Peterson.
Courtesy of Don Peterson.

what they were playing, since everyone in the photograph, including
Ivie Anderson, is laughing. At another point, Rosetta, wearing one of the
men's striped suit-jackets, with a glass of beer beside her, sang and played
guitar while Ellington sat at the piano. In the photograph, her eyes are
closed in concentration as she plays, using a finger pick on her right
thumb. Duke, his tie undone, and drenched in sweat, regards her with
what looks like wonderment, while Calloway and trombonist J. C. Higginbotham lean in for a better listen. Trumpeter Hot Lips Page, meanwhile, gazes toward Ellington, with a smile that says, "Well, isn't this
something?"

Rosetta stayed on the payroll of the Cotton Club until it closed in
June 1940. By that point, she had not merely played in New York, but
throughout the country and in Canada, as part of Calloway's popular
traveling show. In a little less than two years, she had not only endeared
herself to a variety of New York audiences, but managed to meet, if not

work with, most of the notable black entertainers of the day. (She even did a brief stint opposite Louis Armstrong in the Cotton Club's waning days.) The intimacy of Peterson's photograph hints at the high regard with which many secular musicians regarded Rosetta. Yet as a gospel entertainer, a Pentecostal, and a woman, she was never part of the inner sanctum of jazz in the 1930s or '40s. Indeed, Rosetta's turn at the Cotton Club, although relatively short-lived, set a tone for the rest of her career. The "swinger of spirituals" moniker would stick, outlasting the Swing Era itself.

4

SHOUT, SISTER, SHOUT (1940–1946)

*Everything she did, she did well. Even when she was singing
blues with Lucky Millinder . . . whatever she did, she always
put her heart [into it]. She was great whatever she did.*
Gospel singer Clyde Wright

In a 1971 *New Yorker* interview with jazz journalist Whitney Balliett, Barney Josephson explained how he had been inspired to open a nightclub
at Sheridan Square in Greenwich Village. He liked what he had seen of
the European political cabarets of the 1930s, and hoped to open a New
York nightspot that would similarly alternate satire with "serious" music.
"But there was an even more important reason why I wanted to start a
club," he said. "My fondness for jazz often took me to places like the Cotton Club in Harlem, to hear Ethel Waters or Duke Ellington. Well, the
Negro Club patrons were seated at the back, in a segregated section—in
a *Harlem* nightclub! . . . I wanted a club where blacks and whites worked
together behind the footlights and sat together out front. There wasn't,
so far as I know, a place like it in New York or the whole country."[1]

Thus was born Café Society, the satirically named anti–Cotton Club,
a place where, as Josephson told Balliett, "one could sit at the bar, nurs-
ing a single beer, for an entire evening." Josephson knew what music
he liked, but he lacked the business connections to book acts, which is

how he joined forces with John Hammond. Hammond immediately produced Albert Ammons, Meade "Lux" Lewis, and Pete Johnson, musicians from the "Boogie-Woogie Piano Playing" segment of From Spirituals to Swing. So, too, did he produce Sister Rosetta Tharpe, who began a run there in October 1940, joining a lineup that variously included pianist Art Tatum, trumpeter Henry "Red" Allen, trombonist J. C. Higginbotham, and Lady Day herself—in short, many of people Rosetta had been pictured with in the canceled *Life* magazine "jam session" spread. Rosetta came to know—although how well is unclear—all of these performers, as well as Hazel Scott and Lena Horne, women who were also part of the Café Society circuit in the 1940s.[2]

The crowd at Café Society was distinct from those Rosetta had previously experienced. Habitués of the club included members of the black cultural and political elite, including NAACP executive secretary Walter White; Howard University professors Ralph Bunche, E. Franklin Frazier, and Sterling Brown; writers Richard Wright and Langston Hughes; and performer-activist Paul Robeson.[3] White intellectuals mingled with them, along with those of any race or ethnicity drawn to the club for its music and openness. "Village people came, and so did uptown types and college kids," Josephson recalled to Balliett. "On Friday nights, the place looked like Princeton, Yale, and Harvard rolled into one."[4]

Not only did Café Society afford Rosetta access to a different audience than that at the Cotton Club, but it provided her with a stage on which she could perform and promote her Decca material—including "Rock Me," "This Train," and the majestic "Beams of Heaven"—without the unbecoming props of mock Holy Roller revivals. Café Society was not a utopian space of sexual and racial equality, however; nor did its clientele necessarily view Rosetta in a radically different fashion than audiences at the Apollo, the Paramount, or the Cotton Club. To the world at large, Rosetta was still a swinger of spirituals, her smiling, exuberant style contrasting with the more studied and self-conscious artistry of performers such as Robeson and Holiday.

Rosetta's initial Café Society engagement, like her first run at the Cotton Club, exceeded box-office expectations, keeping her in the employ of Josephson until the end of October 1941. Meanwhile, Rosetta became embroiled in a public spat with Thomas Dorsey over her version of "Hide Me in Thy Bosom." In an open letter to the press and radio, Dorsey said she had claimed authorship of his song during a January 1941 ap-

Rosetta singing at Café Society on Sheridan Square, December 11, 1940.
Photo by Charles Peterson. Courtesy of Don Peterson.

pearance on a *We the People* radio broadcast. Rosetta had taken advantage of the show to clarify, or perhaps repair, her reputation as a "hymn-swinger," explaining "that her mission is to save souls, and that she sings in a night club because she feels that there are more souls in the niteries that need saving than there are in the church." Whether Rosetta actually claimed songwriting credit, as Dorsey alleged, or more likely merely was talking about a song she had been singing for years, the public argument illustrated ongoing tensions provoked by Rosetta's crossover moves. For its part, the *Chicago Defender* seemed to take Dorsey's side, referring to him as "Prof. Dorsey," while characterizing Rosetta as a defector to New York nightclubs.[5]

While she was still in the midst of her Café Society engagement, Rosetta was reunited with her old friend Roxie Moore. Since Rosetta's departure for New York in 1938, Roxie had occasionally seen her when she did shows with the traveling Cotton Club Revue at Baltimore theaters; sometimes, Rosetta would stay with Roxie and her husband and daughter, instead of at a hotel. But like Rosetta's marriage to Tommy Tharpe,

Roxie's own marriage had soured, to the degree that in early 1941 she and her daughter moved in with Rosetta and Katie Bell in New York. The stay was just for a few months, enough for Roxie to get some breathing room. The four of them lived in a two-bedroom apartment at 55 West 129th Street with a living room, a single bathroom, a Pullman kitchen, and a big closet where Rosetta kept her wardrobe trunks.

Rosetta appreciated her friend's presence and took Roxie into her confidence. Roxie was the only outsider present when Rosetta finalized her decision to work with Lucky Millinder as featured singer with his recently formed band. Born in 1900 in Anniston, Alabama, but raised in Chicago, Lucky had much in common with Cab Calloway, Rosetta's old boss. Like Calloway, Millinder was not an instrumentalist but a handsome, dapper showman with a fine ear and a knack for shaping a group of talented musicians into a smooth-playing swing band—a crucial, if underappreciated, talent. Like Cab, Lucky began his career working with other bands before forming his own outfit. And he, too, was managed by Moe Gale, the agent who had the original idea to pair him with Rosetta, according to Millinder drummer Panama Francis.[6] Word in the gossip columns was that Gale hoped a Millinder-Tharpe pairing could compete with the indomitable duo of Chick Webb and Ella Fitzgerald, whom Gale also represented.

Bill Doggett, pianist with the Millinder band, remembered the circumstances somewhat differently. "I think that Lucky heard Sister Tharpe singing down at the Cotton Club," he recalled. "And Lucky was a good judge of talent. And he saw in Sister something that he could use in conjunction with Trevor Bacon, who was doing the ballad singing in the band at the time. And Sister coming in doing the spiritual type of thing, and playing her guitar was *new* to show business and especially a swing band."[7]

Rosetta and Lucky sealed their deal privately at her apartment, on February 24, 1941, with Roxie their only witness. According to Roxie, Rosetta agreed to a several-year deal and made it clear at the time of the signing that she was agreeable to performing spiritual material in upbeat arrangements, but not straight-out blues.[8] Yet it wasn't a year before Rosetta would be dipping deep into the well of secular music, most notoriously with the hit "I Want a Tall Skinny Papa." Like "It's Tight Like That," Dorsey's famous blues composition, the title spoke for itself.

Before Rosetta got to such material—popular songs both loathed (by conservatives) and loved (by the likes of future rhythm-and-blues singer Ruth Brown)—she and Millinder collaborated on big-band arrangements of several of the songs she had done in her first solo Decca sessions. In September 1941, they recorded a big-band version of "Rock Me." It swung at a slower pace than the 1938 recording, and featured Rosetta singing over a smooth horn section with an easy, bouncy rhythm. Playing the role of "girl" swing-band vocalist, Rosetta dropped the preacherly locution of her earlier recording for a smoother, more evened-out sound. Although the lyrics of the song are more supplicating than happy, she delivered them with a lusty, vocal cheer, replacing her personal, idiosyncratic performance of the late 1930s with the more familiar sounds of commercial "personality."

From the viewpoint of a mainstream swing aesthetic, these changes would almost certainly have been regarded as marked improvements on Rosetta's 1938 version of the song. While that "Rock Me" possessed an undeniable intimacy, Millinder's big-band version was highly danceable in a way Rosetta's solo version, for all its touted swing, simply was not. Rosetta's solo performance conveyed the loneliness of a speaker cast upon the storms of life, looking to God for her comfort. But the Millinder band version of "Rock Me" packed a different punch precisely because Rosetta was so obviously not alone, but instead buoyed by the lush sounds produced by three trumpets, three trombones, two alto saxophones, a tenor and a baritone saxophone, a piano, a guitar, a bass, and a drum kit. Lost in this big-band version of "Rock Me" was the aura of self-sufficient black femininity that evoked comparisons between Rosetta and Bessie Smith; gained, however, was a wider audience, since even more than her initial solo work, the 1941 "Rock Me" brought Rosetta to a wide multiracial public looking for fun sounds amid rising social and political anxiety.

Indeed, less than three months after the recording session that produced "Rock Me" and "Shout, Sister, Shout!"—a light, upbeat call-and-response song in which the band members played the ragged chorus to Rosetta's "Sister" persona—the Japanese attack on Pearl Harbor spurred the United States to enter World War II. Even before the nation officially declared war on Japan, the escalating conflict in Europe affected the music industry, primarily in the form of the 1940 peacetime draft, which took male musicians away from their jobs for yearlong stints in the military. After December 7, 1941, however, the war took priority in virtu-

Rosetta recording at Decca Records with the Lucky Millinder Orchestra, summer 1941. Lucky is to Rosetta's left, agent-manager Moe Gale to her right. Photo by Charles Peterson. Courtesy of Don Peterson.

ally every sector of American life. Blackouts, curfews, and entertainment taxes darkened many ballrooms and theaters. The diversion of supplies of shellac and gasoline to the war effort led to cutbacks in record production and reduced the mobility of swing bands, particularly those of black musicians, who traveled by bus to avoid Jim Crow trains in the South. "All-girl" swing bands that had long been active suddenly came into greater prominence, filling the gap left by absent male musicians. The U.S. military remained segregated, but in the course of the war, nearly a million black men and women were either drafted or volunteered to serve (notably, Pentecostals were among the conscientious objectors). For the majority of black Americans in the '40s, military service made a potent antiracist statement, both internationally and at home. It was a means of affirming the freedom America stood for but had not yet realized.

Amid the growing disquiet of 1941, Rosetta and Roxie enjoyed being at the center of the New York entertainment world. For Roxie, living with Rosetta was a backstage pass to the shows of all her favorite musicians.

"She was very busy, and I followed her around, her mother and I both followed her around. When she would go and perform we'd be backstage with it, and then I got to meet everybody. It was fun for me. It took my mind off my problems. And we had a good time!" Like Roxie, Rosetta had come to love big-band jazz; their favorites included Earl Hines, Don Byas, Lester Young, Coleman Hawkins, Johnny Hodges, and Harry Edison. Katie Bell was decidedly less enthusiastic about her daughter's activities, but she never stood in Rosetta's way. "Ma Bell would never say [that she was proud of her]," Roxie remembers. "She followed her, she would go where Rosetta went if it was local and if she could go she would go, and be right backstage with me. She would sit there and wait till Rosetta was finished performing." Bill Doggett understood Katie's relative permissiveness regarding her daughter's ventures into secular entertainment. "You know," he recalled, "before I became a professional I wouldn't play jazz songs on a Sunday. That was my upbringing, and I think that most of the artists . . . their parents . . . looked upon the stage as a no-no. And then they began to see how their son or daughter was performing up there . . . making more money than their parents were making. And then you know you sort of accept this as something big."[9]

At home, however, Mother Bell attempted to enforce some semblance of sanctified standards of living. Although Rosetta had made hit records, Mother Bell would not allow a machine into the apartment to play them. But Roxie and Rosetta were allowed a radio. They weren't "big dancers," Roxie recalls, but they both loved the syndicated radio show *Make Believe Ballroom* and would sometimes dance around the apartment to the songs they liked. "They played all the hits," Roxie recalls. "They played everything."

When it came to performing, however, Rosetta didn't have to "make believe." Soon after she teamed up with Millinder, the band began a regular gig at the Savoy on 140th and Lenox, then billed as the "World's Finest Ballroom." The Savoy, with its enormous mahogany dance floor, was a Harlem institution and the place where really good dancers went to show off their moves from week to week. Musicians liked it for the challenge to keep the dance floor full. "Now, the Savoy Ballroom was strictly big-time," Cab Calloway remembered. It had its own theme song—"Stomping at the Savoy"—and regular radio broadcasts. A young Detroit Red, later Malcolm X, fondly recalled doing the Lindy Hop at the Savoy, where Thursday night in the early '40s was dubbed Kitchen Mechanics'

Night and dedicated to black female domestics. "I'd say there were twice as many women as men in there," he recalled, "not only kitchen workers and maids, but also war wives and defense-worker women, lonely and looking."[10]

"When Sister Tharpe opened up at the Savoy with Lucky Millinder's band people just went *wild*," Bill Doggett recalled. "Everybody loved Sister. Because she knew how to mingle with people, and she just had that, the charisma. Of course they weren't calling it [that] then, I guess they were just calling it 'show business,' but that's what it really was. Sister really had it." That "show business" edge that Doggett remembers made Rosetta game for the playful musical competition at the Savoy, where shows typically featured two big bands alternating sets. When she wasn't working, meanwhile, Rosetta and Roxie had plenty of time to mingle with some of the biggest musical names of the day. Sometimes, Roxie recalls, they would sit in one of the booths that lined the ballroom and chat with Rosetta's friends while watching the dancers and listening to the music. At other times, musicians—Roxie particularly recalls Dizzy Gillespie—would visit them at Rosetta's apartment on 129th Street. Although, as Pentecostals, they had been raised to regard alcohol as sinful, Roxie and Rosetta even treated themselves to a nip now and then. "We weren't drunkards, but if we wanted a drink, we would take one," Roxie says. "The only thing we did was hang out with the show business people, because both of us loved music, and we would go where the music was." When Katie Bell got wind of their doing something she didn't like, she would scold them: " 'Girls, you girls, you all ought to be ashamed of yourselves!' But we would always say, Ma Bell, you don't understand! She said, 'Yes I do.' . . . But then, she would still go with Rosetta because they had been together all of Rosetta's life."

After several months with Rosetta, Roxie returned with her daughter to Baltimore. Meanwhile, Rosetta continued putting out records, both on her own and with the Millinder band. Rosetta's solo work in the early 1940s leaned in the direction of gospel; in December 1941, for example, she put out two solo 78s, one pairing "Precious Lord," Dorsey's signature song, which Rosetta performed at a quicker than average tempo, with "Nobody's Fault But Mine," a song that seemed to address Rosetta's own drifting away from the Pentecostal Church. Within the space of three years, already it was becoming clear that Rosetta had carved out a definite repertoire for herself consisting of contemporary gospel compositions (both her own and others') and adaptations of songs from oral tradition.[11] It was clear, too, that she would return to this repertoire—much as people return to the same songs every Sunday in church—to mine the meaning of different songs at different moments in her life. Rosetta's "Precious Lord" of 1941, when she was still considered a popular entertainer, would not be the "Precious Lord" of, say, 1948, when she had forsworn popular music for the church. Nor would it be the "Precious Lord" she would perform as a mature musician, for young European devotees of the music in the 1960s.

When she played with the Millinder band, however, Rosetta exercised considerably less control over her repertoire; her role was that of female vocalist. A few Millinder disks combined one side featuring Rosetta with another side on which she didn't appear, producing peculiar juxtapositions. The most notorious of these was "Big Fat Mama" opposite "Trouble in Mind," released in November 1941. On the latter, Rosetta proved that she was just as adept at delivering a blues lyric as a gospel lyric; when she sang the lines, "When you see me laughin' / I'm laughin' just to keep from crying," she made the listener feel the tears that poignantly communicated black struggles in a white world. A fan of Rosetta's might have been surprised to turn the record over to find Millinder's paean to big women, a bawdy companion piece to "Tall Skinny Papa." So popular was "Big Fat Mama" that, a month after the song's release, the Apollo played host to a "Big Fat Mama" week, during which women weighing over 250 pounds were admitted for free. At the end of the week, a fifty-dollar prize was awarded to the "most versatile 'mama.'"[12]

In 1941, fans of the Millinder band had a chance to catch a show at the Apollo, the Regal in Chicago, the Royal in Baltimore, or the Paradise Theater in Detroit. Short of live performances, however, audiences had no way to *see* the Millinder band. That changed around 1941, when large wooden machines called Panorams began appearing in bars and clubs. Fitted with 16-millimeter projectors inside, the machines played "soundies," jukebox music films of three minutes apiece, which could be viewed for a dime each. As the *Amsterdam News* explained to readers, " 'Soundies' are machines which include small screen[s] so that musicians, vocalist, etc., may be seen as well as heard when coin is dropped in slot."[13]

Soundies translated theatrical spectacle to a film format, anticipating music videos in concept and execution. Dorothy Dandridge, for example, the teenager Rosetta had appeared with at the Cotton Club in 1938, did a soundie of "Zoot Suit" that had her singing and dancing in a sequined bikini. Male big-band musicians, predictably, didn't have to strip down to be seen and heard; instead, they presented dapper displays of musical prowess highlighted by camera closeups of their fingers skipping across the ivories or the keys of their horns.

Roxie is emphatic that had Rosetta appeared in public dressed like Dorothy Dandridge, "Ma Bell would have had a fit. Ma Bell would have said, Now Sister, you go and put some clothes on! You're not going out of here like that!" Hence, in the "Lonesome Road" soundie, Rosetta stood to the side while light-skinned dancing girls dressed in white feathers did a modified cancan. Next to the dancers, Rosetta, wearing a long skirt and long-sleeved jacket with a high-collared blouse, appeared saintly. And although she struck moves that would have made sense in a nightclub, snapping her fingers, clapping her hands, and gently rocking her body from shoulders to hips, these came straight from the Pentecostal Church.

"With a million young men swinging guns and war the interest of the day, orchestra leaders find that there is also a demand for distinction in dance bands of a new type," announced the *Pittsburgh Courier* in August 1941. Among its predictions: "Sister Tharpe who rocks 'em with an aboriginal wail will come into a new power with her string instrument in the new musical order."[14] Indeed, by year's end, it was clear that the addition of Rosetta as female vocalist and occasional guitarist had boosted Millinder's popularity, making his one of the most in-demand big bands of the war years. Radio exposure from the Savoy Ballroom broadcasts helped immensely, as did admiring notices from *Billboard* radio columnist Dick Carter. "Sifting through our fondest memories, we are unable to recall a more sensational slice of sustaining radio time than that consumed by Sister Rosetta Tharpe in singing 'Rock Me' as she sang it on this band remote," he wrote in January of '42. "Every third number or so Sister Tharpe takes over with one of her vocals, giving an unbelievable lift to the proceedings."[15]

A "lift" was what many people clamored for in 1942. Rosetta and the Millinder band did little in the way of recording that year or the next, largely because of a dispute between the American Federation of Musicians and the record companies, including Decca.[16] But squabbling within the music industry didn't make much of a dent in Rosetta's career. The Millinder band was busier than ever in 1943, doing shows that took it from Jacksonville, Florida, to Charleston, West Virginia; from Indianapolis to Galveston to Tulsa; from Flint, Michigan, to Dayton to Utica, New York. As drummer Panama Francis remembered, "We used to have, like a string of one nighters, three straight months without a night off— I mean we played all of the chitlin' circuit, we used to call them, because it was all black dancers, all except maybe one or two white dancers who were thrown in on a Saturday night."[17] In between one-nighters, which included stops at U.S. Army camps, the band "rested" during one-week stints at places like the Savoy, the Fox Theater in Brooklyn, or the Regal in Baltimore, where the advertisements for Lucky Millinder promised: "featuring the spiritual rockin' rhythm singing of Sister Rosetta Tharpe and Her Guitar"—the instrument now getting its own billing. In September, Rosetta appeared with Lucky Millinder and the Four Ink Spots in a show at the Apollo, where, as "the prize of Lucky's band," she sang both "Rock Me" and "Tall Skinny Papa." Released that June with "Shout, Sister, Shout," "Tall Skinny Papa" earned favorable notice in the *New York Times* (the *Washington Post* called Rosetta "a bit shrill and not her old self"). In August, Dizzy Gillespie joined Millinder's band, cementing a friendship with Rosetta and Katie Bell that would bear fruit in unexpected ways in 1960.[18]

Rosetta was a particular hit with the troops on both sides of the color line. In late May 1942, she and the Millinder band entertained black soldiers at Fort Custer, Michigan, where the crowd included "approximately 86 young women and 12 additional chaperones, [who] contributed around $6 and sandwiches towards the boosting of morale." The *Chicago Defender,* which gave ample coverage to the Fort Custer ball in its society pages, listing the name of every chaperone and female guest, referred to Rosetta as "the beloved Sister Rosetta Tharpe" and the "belle of the ball"—quite a turnaround from its pre-war coverage of the somewhat disreputable "swinger of spirituals."[19]

But the war had turned people's minds elsewhere, away from debates about the ethics of rhythmic music—although these continued periodically to flare up—and instead toward the welfare of the troops and the war effort at large. Asked in a 1988 interview if Rosetta had gotten "flak" for performing gospel music with a commercial big band, Doggett responded, "Well, I don't know, I didn't hear too much about it.... Somebody might have been against it, but it didn't raise that much [controversy] because people weren't paying that much attention to it anyhow. A lot of people were coming to the Savoy Ballroom in New York and enjoying it. Then when we went out to play the theaters like Chicago, Baltimore, and the Apollo and the Paradise Theater in Detroit, they were enjoying it."[20]

Rosetta played at least three different roles as an entertainer in the early 1940s when she was working with Millinder. On the one hand, she was the popular dance-band attraction Doggett remembers, playing a new acoustic instrument and cultivating a more polished look. She was also a darling to the troops, enjoying special status as one of a very few black "religious" musicians both to make V-disks (government-manufactured 78s shipped overseas during the war) and to appear on the Armed Forces Radio Service's *Jubilee* program, an all-black variety show. Rosetta's *Jubilee* performances paired her with Noble Sissle and His Orchestra, as well as the band of fellow Arkansan Louis Jordan.

At the same time, Rosetta kept alive her reputation as a spiritual singer, making recordings that appealed to a public that increasingly consumed gospel music in the 1940s. When she wasn't in the studio with Millinder, Rosetta did solo recordings of songs such as "Precious Lord," "Just a Closer Walk with Thee," "All Over This World," and "Pure Religion." Along with "There's Something within Me" and "Stand by Me," this religious material was especially popular among black Southerners, who heard it on jukeboxes (amid blues and other popular fare) in places like the Chicken Shack, the Dipsie Doodle, and Lucky's in Clarksdale, Mississippi, the central Delta town where Muddy Waters grew up.[21] Even in taverns, people didn't necessarily dance to these songs, instead allowing Rosetta's music to take them to church in their imaginations.

Marketed as part of Decca's "race" series, Rosetta's gospel records received less attention in the press than her secular recordings, but they were not necessarily any less important to her as a musician. On "What He Done for Me," for example, a song that made *Billboard*'s list of popular songs of 1943, she sings confidently and with perfect phrasing and elocution about the joys of sanctification in the Holy Ghost, as though the

Rosetta recording at Decca, summer 1941. Katie Bell Nubin holds
her daughter's guitar as Rosetta sings. Photo by Charles Peterson.
Courtesy of Don Peterson.

"Tall Skinny Papa" didn't matter or even exist. Her guitar playing is even
more impressive, little trills and embellishments entwining with the
song's lyrics like ivy on a vine. It may have been "popular," but this was
the music that made Mother Bell proud.

As the war took its human toll, including jazz musicians, performers on
the home front found themselves in even higher demand than in previous years. Indeed, theater and club owners did bigger business in the
1942–1943 season than they had before Americans joined the fighting.
The Millinder band was one of the groups that saw its star rise during the
war years. Along with the Ink Spots, the most popular black quartet of
the era, Lucky and Rosetta embarked on a blockbuster tour in the spring
of 1943. The bill, which also featured dancer Peg Leg Bates, comics Gordon and Rogers, and singer Trevor Bacon, drew more than ten thousand
people to Atlanta's City Auditorium in late May, with the *Afro-American*
estimating the crowd as 40 percent white. Another ten thousand came

out to see the show in June at the Kiel Auditorium in St. Louis. In Philadelphia on a solo gig, the Millinder band pulled in thirty thousand dollars of business at the Earle Theatre, equaling the grosses of the Horace Heidt Band and the Ink Spots.[22]

Notwithstanding such impressive numbers, Rosetta and Millinder were increasingly at odds in 1943, as Rosetta itched to quit the big-band circuit and renew her career as a strictly gospel act. As Roxie Moore remembers, she hadn't wanted to do light fare poking fun at "old-time religion" or worldly material like "Tall Skinny Papa," but found herself bound by contractual obligations. Yet in managing to separate herself from Tommy Tharpe, Rosetta had shown once already that she had her limits, whether the contract was for marriage or for music. When she felt abused or trapped (or both), she could also be forceful and self-protective.

In September, Rosetta walked out on Millinder, during the course of a West Coast stint at the Casa Mañana in Los Angeles, near the Hollywood studios where the *Jubilee* broadcasts were being produced. She did so without giving notice, and showed up at the Streets of Paris café, where she joined a show featuring Jimmy Noone, the Floyd Hunt Trio, and Sonny Boy Williamson. The walkout caused a minor tempest of competing charges among the musicians' union, the owner of the Casa Mañana, and Millinder, who told *Down Beat* that Rosetta had secretly stolen the charts to her numbers when she defected.[23] Lucky threatened to sue, and Rosetta likely had to settle, but the matter was ultimately resolved when Millinder hired Judy Carroll, a West Coast singer, to replace her.

Also in 1943, Rosetta finally managed to wriggle out of the agreement that tied her to Tommy Tharpe. Her resolve to get a divorce was undoubtedly strengthened by the fact that she had fallen in love with a man named Foch Pershing Allen, a native of Omaha born in 1920. Allen was not a minister like Tommy Tharpe, and not much is known about him before his marriage to Rosetta; it's possible they met when the Millinder band appeared in Omaha on February 6, 1943.[24] If so, that would explain why Rosetta officially filed papers against Tharpe in March, charging that he had "wholly disregard[ed] his duties as a husband" and had "been guilty of extreme cruelty," and why she did so claiming Omaha as her legal residence. Thomas Tharpe, then living at 40 Morningside Avenue in New York, was served with a summons on April 5, but failed to answer it. A judge accordingly granted the divorce on May 7.[25] Foch P. Allen of Omaha and Rosetta Tharpe of New York City were officially married on June 3, 1943, in St. Louis, in the midst of the Millinder–Ink Spots tour.

Rosetta was in all likelihood in California touring with Millinder when riots broke out in Harlem on August 1, 1943. A white policeman had shot and wounded a black soldier who confronted him over the way the policeman was addressing a black woman during the course of an arrest. Rumors that the soldier had been killed kindled already smoldering discontent over persistent poverty, police harassment, racial discrimination and—not least, given that a black soldier's life was in question—the segregation of the military. "All through the war, the Harlem racial picture never was too bright," recalled Malcolm X, in his autobiography. The situation was only worsened when, in April 1943, just a few months before the riots, the New York City Police Department filed vice charges against the Savoy Ballroom, alleging it to be a den of prostitution. When Mayor Fiorello La Guardia claimed he was powerless to reverse the decision, the NAACP and other groups organized protests. "Harlem said the real reason was to stop Negroes from dancing with white women," wrote Malcolm X. "Harlem said that no one dragged the white women in there."[26]

"Politics was not a subject about which people whose life was music thought very much," the historian Eric Hobsbawm has written. "For black artists, the savage and pervasive racial discrimination was a deeply resented fact of life, but almost certainly most of them doubted whether politics could do much about it."[27] Hobsbawm's analysis may not do justice to either jazz musicians or politics, but it comes close to describing Rosetta's relation to organized political resistance. On the other hand, Rosetta was not cut off from the political scene that would have been familiar to any Harlemite in 1943. Although, like most musicians, she never spoke out publicly about racial discrimination—she wanted bookings, after all—she, like virtually every black star of the era, participated in a yearly round of benefit concerts to combat poverty, to support the NAACP, and, during the war, to rally black troops.

In the 1940s, too, she took the step—uncommon for an African American, a woman, and a Christian—of speaking out publicly about venereal disease, a cause cited by the police for the Savoy Ballroom's closure. In a public service radio announcement sponsored by the New York

Health Department and directed by Alan Lomax, she sang songs—the program begins with "We're Not Afraid to Be a Witness for the Lord"—and "shar[ed] the good news" about "bad disease." "Although I'm a woman, I'm not afraid," she said, reading from a prepared script. "Syphilis has stricken so many lives...broken up homes, and destroyed innocent children." Like a preacher, she illustrated her thesis with a story about a Mrs. Jones, a good wife, good mother, and good church member, who watched three children die because she didn't know she had passed the disease on to them. And, like a preacher, Rosetta summed up the moral of the story: "Go to a doctor," she told listeners on WINS. "Make sure your blood is clean. Get a blood test."

In retrospect, the public service announcement Rosetta read is both astute and progressive: astute because it argues that seeing a doctor and having a blood test is the Christian way, and progressive because it also urges compassion for the woman "who made the one little mistake." The way of doing God's work on earth was not to condemn people, but to be a friend to them. Syphilis was a false friend, lying and deceitful; it didn't necessarily manifest outward symptoms. Christians, on the other hand, could be true friends, Rosetta argued, "and let him who is without sin cast the first stone." Rosetta was herself a type of Mrs. Jones, someone who had strayed—through divorce, through the rejection of her church's teachings—but who deserved and wanted those true, compassionate friends.[28]

Rosetta began 1944 with a new husband and a reinvented identity as Sister Rosetta Tharpe, gospel soloist. "Last week viewed a new Rosetta Tharpe at Harlem's Apollo," the *Chicago Defender* announced. "Appearing on a bill with the Ink Spots, doing a single, Tharpe was groovingly grand." At the Howard in Washington, she was "a stellar single act" and a "mighty and heighty guitarist" who shared the stage with Erskine Hawkins. Rumors circulated that Rosetta intended to form her own band, but these never materialized; rather, she dropped some of the popular if embarrassing theatrics of her old routines—the "hallelujah stuff," as one *Defender* columnist put it.[29]

Rosetta's recommitment to gospel did not amount to a rejection of secular audiences or popular stages; she would still play the same theatrical venues that she had been playing since her Cotton Club debut in 1938. It didn't even mean an end to sharing a stage with Millinder; in

May 1944 they both appeared at an NAACP Thirty-fifth Anniversary Birthday Ball at the Savoy, and in June 1945, they toured together, albeit as separate acts. And although a lack of reliable records makes it harder to tell, neither did it necessarily mean a self-imposed ban on her performance of "popular" material from the late 1930s and 1940s. Rosetta's self-reinvention in the early 1940s did, however, translate into a change in her recorded repertoire and her tagline, which was now "America's greatest spiritual singer."[30] As soon as the dispute between the American Federation of Musicians and the record companies was resolved, she went into the studio to do "Sleep On Darling Mother" and "I Want to Live So God Can Use Me," released in March 1944. She also laid down the tracks for an album (i.e., several 78s), *Gospel Hymns*, which included her own popular composition "God Don't Like It," a song that might as well have been addressed to the music industry itself.

These songs, featuring Rosetta and her guitar as in the old days, sold well among gospel devotees. But the biggest hit of Rosetta's career came in the form of a composition she recorded in September 1944 with members of Decca's house band. Released in the spring, "Strange Things Happening Every Day" spent eleven weeks on the "race" charts, peaking at number two in late April. Along with "Two Little Fishes and Five Loaves of Bread," a religion-themed song on the B-side, it featured the boogie-woogie piano work of Sammy Price, leading a trio that included Abe Bolar on bass and Harold "Doc" West on drums.

Although "Strange Things" gives the impression of flowing from a happy musical collaboration, Sammy Price disliked Rosetta and found her difficult to work with. By his own account, she "tuned her guitar funny and sang in the wrong key," and Price refused to play with her until she agreed to use a capo, the bar that sits across the fingerboard of a guitar and changes its pitch.[31] (The capo enabled Rosetta to play in what Price called a "normal jazz key," not the "Vestapol," or open, tuning she and other Delta musicians more commonly used.) As he told jazz historian Dan Morgenstern, Price also had anxieties about mixing up a boogie-woogie beat with gospel lyrics. These reservations were assuaged, however, by no less austere a figure than Katie Bell Nubin, sent to Price by Mayo Williams, Decca's talent scout for "race" records, and Milt Gabler, then a Decca executive. She assured him that "if the mind teaching were right," then there was no reason to feel reluctant. Price went along with it, but he still resented the fact that he didn't see profits be-

yond the flat fee of a hundred dollars Decca paid him for the session, and
he charged Rosetta with claiming to have the Sam Price Trio with her on
tour (she didn't). "Rosetta Tharpe never gave me a Christmas card," he
said. "And I made her a lot of money."[32]

In fact, Price's behind-the-scenes influence is one reason "Strange
Things" has often been acclaimed as among the first rock-and-roll songs.
The sound of "Strange Things" is thoroughly modern, not quite gospel, but gospel becoming rhythm and blues. In terms of its arrangement,
it is worlds away from the big-band swing of Lucky Millinder and His
Orchestra. Where Millinder sounded big and brassy, full of bombast,
"Strange Things" is dance music pared down to the essentials, stripped of
everything but a rhythm section and a powerful voice. Like all great popular songs, it has an instant catchiness, as though it had always existed;
and yet that catchiness, however ephemeral, is also durable, even profound.

"Strange Things" opens with a few bars of Rosetta's feisty guitar
picking before Price joins in, playing a romping boogie-woogie piano
line like an Arizona Dranes of the dance hall, using his right hand to
add birdlike warbles to complement a thumping left hand. From the
second "Strange Things" begins, the song jumps, moves, pulses with
rhythm. Rosetta sings in a direct, strong voice, with a minimum of vocal fussiness, holding back and allowing the beat to propel her and the
band along. She gives the title line rhythmic flourish, breaking down the
word "everything" into four syllables, and raising the pitch at the word
"strange," as though to mimic, in sound, the look of rolling eyes. At the
break, she shows off some fancy guitar riffs, alternating between strumming and fast picking, doing arpeggios and plucking the strings hard so
they resonate an extra fraction of a second.

The allure of "Strange Things" comes not just from its rhythm, however, but from its rather impressionistic lyrics, which in retrospect seem
perfectly suited to the times. On the one hand, the "strange things" of the
title refer, however loosely, to those who claim holiness and yet live in sin.
But listeners might also have detected the strains of a somewhat more
subversive, political satire in "Strange Things Happening Every Day."[33] In
1945, there were indeed strange things happening, some wonderful, some
horrific. May saw the German surrender, laying the groundwork for the
end of the war in Europe. August saw the dropping of an atomic bomb
on Hiroshima, as well as the breakthrough talks that led to the signing of

Jackie Robinson as America's first black major-league baseball player. Which events were strange? "Strange" was a powerful word, a word like "Precious" from Dorsey's "Precious Lord, Take My Hand." (According to Dorsey's account of the song's composition, he originally had used the word "blessed," until a friend urged him to substitute "precious." After that, Dorsey said, "something hit me.")[34] "Strange" could mean foreign or it could mean new; it conjured unfamiliarity and discomfort as well as things astonishing or remarkable.

The openness of "Strange Things," as an expression of what it feels like to live in a world of strangeness, may explain the song's extraordinary musical legacy. Although it peaked in sales in 1945, "Strange Things" enjoyed a second life in the early and mid-1950s, when Rosetta's song emerged as a major influence on the young white musicians who coalesced around Memphis's Sun Studio. At the time, recalls white producer Jim Dickinson, the city "had a black station for black people and three or four white stations for white people." According to Dickinson, amid this segregation of the airwaves, only one person—white Memphis deejay Dewey Phillips, who broadcast his wildly popular *Red Hot & Blue* program on WHBQ—"played *music.*" Phillips (no relation to Sun impresario Sam) had no qualms about airing the harmonies of a Memphis or Norfolk gospel quartet on a Friday night, believing the music could hold its own against anything "popular." And in contrast to the wishes of record companies, he paid little mind to whether a record was new. "No matter that Ike sat in the Oval Office," recalls Dickinson, "Dewey would play 'Tell Me Why You Like Roosevelt' "—an a cappella gospel song by the Evangelist Singers of Detroit—and "say it was a hit."

Phillips was newly abuzz about "Strange Things Happening Every Day" when rumors circulated that young rockabilly sensation Jerry Lee Lewis was going to record it. "Man, we've been playin' it the last few nights—I don't know, the last three four nights—and we've been havin' a lot of requests for it," Phillips said in a radio broadcast from the period. "Looks like [unintelligible]"—Phillips was known for garbling the names of his sponsors—"is gonna have to order another fifty of 'em."[35] Although the rumors never panned out, Jerry Lee loved "Strange Things" enough to sing it in his own audition before the intimidating Sam Phillips. The young man who in 1957 would channel his own Pentecostal upbringing in the white Assemblies of God into one glorious, unforgettable yelp—"Great balls of fire!!!"—had also seen Rosetta perform, probably in Natchez, Mississippi. As he told music writer Peter Guralnick, "I said, 'Say, man, there's a woman that can sing some rock and roll.' I mean, she's singing religious music, but she is singing rock and roll. She's . . . shakin', man. . . . She jumps it. She's hitting that guitar, playing that guitar and she is *singing*. I said, 'Whoooo.' Sister Rosetta Tharpe."[36] Rosetta left an indelible mark on Lewis's playing as well. "Listen to his piano," notes the Arkansas-born musician Sleepy LaBeef, a roots musician who was also influenced by her. "His right hand on the piano is quite like Rosetta Tharpe."

So, too, did Rosetta influence Elvis Presley, Johnny Cash, and Carl Perkins—with Lewis, the members of the "Million Dollar Quartet" who jammed informally at Sun Studio in December 1956, warming up with "Peace in the Valley" and "Down by the Riverside."

"Elvis *loved* Sister Rosetta Tharpe," says Gordon Stoker, who clocked thousands of studio hours with Presley as a member of the Jordanaires. "Not only did he dig her guitar picking—that's really what he dug— but he dug her singing, too." In his 1975 autobiography *Man in Black,* Cash, who grew up picking cotton on a farm in Dyess, Arkansas, not far from Cotton Plant, recalled an Air Force friend, C. V. White, "who'd had an album by black singer Sister Rosetta Tharpe. And that song ["Strange Things"] was on the album. C. V. and I'd listen to her sing that song over and over again." Cash was the bigger star when he saw Rosetta live in 1960, and yet in an interview with Guralnick he would remember the concert "as one of the most moving musical experiences of his life." Shortly after he died, his daughter Rosanne Cash confirmed that Rosetta was likely her father's favorite artist.[37]

"['Strange Things'] was always one of my favorite songs," Carl Perkins, the man responsible for the massive 1956 hit "Blues Suede Shoes," said in 1979. "It was my Dad's favorite song. When Sister Rosetta had it out, that's one of the things I'd set there trying to learn how to play. . . . As I say, my Dad, he loved that song. When people would come to our house, which was pretty regular—on Sundays—or we'd go to my grandfather's, I'd always take my little old guitar, that was part of it, I'd always play 'Strange Things Happening Every Day.' It was rockabilly, that was it—it was."[38]

BRIDGE

"SHE MADE THAT GUITAR TALK"

Sister Rosetta Tharpe?

"That girl could *play* that guitar."

"Lord have mercy! She would make it talk!"

"Made that guitar walk *and* talk."

Ask gospel fans, especially those mature—don't say *old*—enough to have seen Rosetta live, listened to her records in their heyday, or even performed with her, and the phrase inevitably comes up: *She made that guitar talk.* The expression praises Rosetta's talents as an instrumentalist, and yet it also speaks metaphorically to how she played and what her playing meant to those who felt moved by her music. *She made that guitar talk* conveys how Rosetta transformed the guitar into an extension of her body, how she could let her instrument speak through and for her.

Within the gospel world, Rosetta's guitar playing was exceptional. "When Chuck Berry came out, I had seen all that," says Chicago gospel singer Geraldine Gay Hambric. Indeed, like more famous male players, Rosetta had an elemental connection with her instrument as well as technical prowess. "You would wonder where she learned to play a guitar like that," remembers Alfred Miller, musical director at Washington Temple COGIC in Brooklyn, where Rosetta's friend Madame Ernestine Washington was First Lady. "She could do runs, she could do sequences, she could do arpeggios, and she could play anything with the guitar. You could say something and she could make that guitar say it. . . . I mean, she could put that guitar *behind* her and play it; she could *sit on the floor* and play it, she could *lay down* and play it. Oh, she was an artist! And that made the people just go berserk, and they just knew that she was alright whatever she did."

"That was her style. Anytime she went on . . . she was *emotional* with her guitar," says Marie Knight, recalling the times she and Rosetta sang together in the 1940s and '50s. Rosetta's guitar "was an extension of her," remembers Lottie Smith, who sang with Rosetta's 1950s-era backup group, the Rosettes, "because you know she just blended so *well* with it. And different chords she'd play she'd have different movements. She was just *bound* into that thing. She just carried it with her. It was something to see her."

"Making the guitar talk" had significance specific to Rosetta's position as a gospel singer and her upbringing in the Church of God in Christ. In musical terms, it paralleled the religious practice of speaking in tongues. Outsiders to Pentecostal faiths often ridicule tongue-speaking as gibberish, or as a performance faked for dramatic effect. But for believers, tongue-speaking attests to the authenticity of the experience of possession by the Holy Ghost.

"Where did rock and roll come from? It came from the music of the Negro churches, definitely," once noted Pearl Bailey, another famously flamboyant performer who grew up in the Sanctified Church. "Just listen to the beat and go to one of the churches and see if you don't hear the same thing."[1] Indeed, rock and roll took not only the beats of the church but, less self-consciously, its mode of ecstatic talking. After Rosetta, rock guitar "gods"—here the metaphor of divinity seems less than incidental—appropriated the euphoric practice of tongue-speaking in their guitar solos. They too made their instruments talk, in the language of a strutting and ebullient masculinity.

"Like the kids say today, she got *down* with it," says Jeannette Eason, Rosetta's friend and the wife of renowned steel guitarist Willie Eason. "Mahalia had a beautiful voice and all, but she couldn't compete with Rosetta Tharpe. . . . When you look at Rosetta, Rosetta got her man in her hand, in a way of speaking. And Mahalia had to depend on other people. She sung beautiful and all. And Mahalia went over what, a million records or something like that? Rosetta never got that far . . . but between the two of them? I mean I liked her singing and all, but Rosetta was it."

Rosetta may have had "her man in her hand," but she never exemplified the stereotypical image of the guitar as a phallic symbol in her playing. Instead, as a black woman with few outlets for public speaking, Rosetta fashioned a distinct means to speak through her guitar. When Rosetta made the guitar talk, she bristled with kinetic energy, especially at the bridge, that portion of a song given over to her instrumental solo. At the bridge, Rosetta didn't need words, because the guitar could do both the singing and the talking for her. Emotionally and musically, the bridge was the climax of a song, giving rise to its most satisfying and thrilling moments precisely because it was free of the distraction of lyrics.

When Rosetta's fans said she could make that guitar talk, they meant she could play the instrument with abandon while still exercising exquisite control. When she made the guitar talk, she gave her audience an opportunity to feel excitement, pleasure, power, and emotional release in the sounds she generated. She loved nothing more than the cacophony of a few hundred—or several thousand—fans yelling out: "Go on, girl! Make it talk, Rosetta!"

Today, we tend to use the term "charisma" in a secular sense to describe the drawing power of everyone from athletes to heads of state. Yet the roots of the word are in the ancient Greek term for "divine gift." Rosetta possessed charisma in both senses. Well before the guitar gods of more recent decades made a fetish of the guitar solo as an orgiastic expression of male sexual libido, Rosetta perfected something both more subtle and more radical: the art of the guitar as an instrument of ineffable speech, of rapture beyond words.

5

LITTLE SISTER (1947–1949)

She had a gift and so did I and the two gifts go together.
Marie Knight

In the spring of 1946, Rosetta attended a program at Harlem's Golden Gate Auditorium, presumably to hear the featured act, Mahalia Jackson, who was to sing her way, that fateful day, to a deal with Apollo Records. At the time, Rosetta was making a point of avoiding nightclub appearances for more traditional gospel programs; that May, in fact, she and Mahalia appeared together in a "battle" of gospel song at Chicago's Eighth Regiment Armory. The concert, which took place less than two weeks after Rosetta wrapped up a recording session in New York with Sammy Price, put the women's distinct strengths on display: Mahalia's magnificent voice and her ability to interpret a lyric, Rosetta's prowess as a self-accompanying singer who could whip a crowd into a frenzy with her guitar.[1]

By chance, Jackson invited a young vocalist to join her on stage at the Golden Gate. Marie Knight has forgotten what she sang, but Rosetta heard her voice and something clicked; it was the acoustic version of love at first sight. "I didn't even know Rosetta at the time," Marie says. "But Rosetta happened to be at the concert, and she saw me on the floor, and right away it jumped into her mind: this is the girl I want to team with me." Rosetta was not merely listening to Marie, but thinking of the sound they could produce together, Marie's rich contralto complementing her soprano. It probably didn't hurt that Marie, then in her twenties, was a handsome young woman with shining, expressive eyes, a slim figure, and a natural elegance.

Born Marie Roach, Marie grew up in Newark, New Jersey, although her family was originally from Sanford, Florida. She claims a lady's prerogative not to dwell on the subject of her age, leaving gospel scholars guessing, although it's likely she was born in 1923.[2] In any case, Marie was younger—young enough for Rosetta affectionately to nickname her "Little Sister," as Rosetta once had been called. And like Rosetta, Li'l Sis was a natural singer whose gift was acknowledged at an early age. Her parents belonged to 210 (pronounced "two-ten) Church of God in Christ"— 210 was the address—and when Marie was five, they lifted her atop a table during service, where she piped out "Doing All the Good We Can," carried along by the congregation. What formal instruction she received was in the youth choir, led by a stern but discerning female director. By age nine, she had been elevated to soloist, singled out for special attention as well as drilling: on how to walk, how to sing, how to present herself. When she was not being drilled, Marie was teaching herself how to play piano. "I used to go into church when I was little because the building where I lived was right across the street from the church, and I used to go into the church in the daytime, because the cleaners or the janitors would be there, and I would go in and just hit one note at a time, to hear that sound on the piano," she remembers. "It was a joy to me just to go in there, to put those notes together, on the piano, just one key at a time."

By the early 1940s, as Rosetta was riding the wave of her commercial success with Lucky Millinder, Marie had found a way to turn that joy into a vocation, touring the revival circuit with the evangelist Frances Robinson. The two women traveled by train, appearing in places such as Chicago and Detroit, and at least once making it as far west as Oakland, California, where they attracted crowds from all over the Bay Area.[3] By the middle of the decade, however, Marie was back in New Jersey, tending to her two young children by Albert Knight, a Texas-born preacher whom she married in Corpus Christi, on Christmas Day, 1941, after a romance of less than a week. ("I met him Monday and married him Thursday," she says, "real quick.") In the meantime, she made her first forays into a recording studio, singing with a quartet called The Sunset Four. Their performances of songs such as "Lift Every Voice and Sing" were charming in their "old-timey" feel, but didn't promise to put Marie on the gospel map.

"I didn't go looking for her," Marie says of Rosetta. "She came looking for me." As Marie sees it, having distanced herself from the likes of Lucky Millinder and wanting to redeem herself in the eyes of the church, Rosetta was in need of someone who could raise her profile on the gospel circuit. In an interview from 1958, however, Rosetta said she met Marie through Foch Allen, thereby omitting the Golden Gate and Mahalia Jackson from the story. (She also called Allen "my first husband"—a fib for modesty's sake.[4]) Whatever the source of their meeting, there's no dispute that once she had decided on Marie, Rosetta acted quickly. Soon after she heard her, she and Allen turned up at Marie's mother's house in Newark, where Marie was living at the time. Rosetta, who arrived with contract in hand, cut straight to the point. Johnny Myers, the big-time gospel promoter, had already given the deal his blessing.

Even a less ambitious and keen young singer than Marie would have found Rosetta's offer to tour with her hard to refuse. Although it meant leaving her two young children at home with their grandmother, Marie was eager for the opportunity to take her talent on the road, and Rosetta was the premier gospel solo draw of the day. During her marriage to Albert Knight, Marie chafed at the limitations associated with being a preacher's wife, and they divorced after eight years. Marie didn't care for domestic life either. It was the freedom of the road she was after. "I'm a born traveler," is how she puts it, "I'm from one place to the other." Initially, Marie's mother was leery of sending Marie off with a woman they didn't even know. In the end, however, Mrs. Roach concluded that it was best to trust in God, who had blessed Marie with that voice for a reason. Maybe this smiling, enthusiastic stranger at their door was part of His plan?

Rosetta paid Marie her surprise visit on a Saturday. Two days later, on a Monday in the early summer of 1946, they took off for previously scheduled appearances in Chicago and Detroit, where Myers, unbeknownst to Marie, had already billed her as an added attraction.[5] After this initial stint on the road, they returned to New York, practicing songs in Rosetta's Harlem apartment until they thought they could convince

Decca to record them as a duo. The neighbors complained more than once about the racket they raised, recalls Marie, but no matter. They were on a mission.

The prospect of singing with Marie surely energized Rosetta, but she may have been eager for her companionship for other reasons. At around the same time she and Marie were beginning their collaboration, Rosetta was finalizing her divorce from Foch Allen, who had shown little interest in Rosetta's career beyond the ways it profited him. Rosetta initiated divorce proceedings in Las Vegas in early January 1946, two and a half years after they married. She spent six weeks there again with a friend in late 1946 and early 1947—enough to establish residency, or at least a plausible imitation of the intention to be a resident—and then returned a final time late that April to testify in the case of *Tharpe v. Allen.*

Like a lot of women at the time, Rosetta may have been perfectly willing to "yes" the judge into granting her a divorce—even if it meant misstating or exaggerating certain facts for the record. The court made it easy, supplying all the necessary language. As Rosetta surely must have known, questions like "Has he beat you physically?" and "It finally got to the point that you were mentally unable to take care of your work?" were rhetorical, a form of official call-and-response. The "correct" answers she provided—"Oh, yes, he has" and "That's right"—were the legal equivalents of a "Yes, Lord" delivered back at the preacher during service. On the other hand, at least one of Rosetta's friends, speaking off the record, gives credence to the possibility that her testimony about Foch wasn't entirely fabricated, and other friends who weren't there but are nevertheless inclined to speculate agree that, particularly in its details of Allen's contempt for her career, the story has the feeling and flavor of truth. Asked in the courtroom whether Allen had perpetrated any acts of cruelty, Rosetta supplied her own definitions. "Well, he was cruel to me," she said. "He didn't ever appreciate anything I do, even in my line of work, and come on my job and he would just argue all the time." Pressed for details, she explained, "I got so sometimes I couldn't hardly remember anything when I got ready to sing."

Having your man stand in the way of your calling was a familiar enough version of the female gospel musician's blues. Mahalia Jackson knew about it, and so did Marie Knight, and so did Clara Ward and many others. In the 1982 film *Say Amen, Somebody,* a documentary about

Chicago gospel from the days of Thomas Dorsey and Sallie Martin to the early 1980s, there's an affecting scene in which Delois Barrett Campbell, a member of the Barrett Sisters, prepares breakfast for her husband as they discuss whether or not she will be "allowed" to travel to a gospel program she clearly wants to attend. Campbell strains against challenging her husband outright and in front of the camera, but she registers her annoyance with his disapproval in the acid way she inquires whether he wants some sausage with his eggs.[6] "Well it was hard," Campbell explains, reflecting back on the scene of domestic tension director George Nierenberg captured on film. "After I married [in 1950], my husband got called to the church. He pastored the church, so therefore I gave a lot of my time to his church." During those years when her husband wanted her close at hand, she only accepted "big gigs, and wherever I went I flew and flew back in for that night." Eventually the two divorced.

For Rosetta, for whom music was both career and calling, Foch Allen's behavior may well have inflicted similar emotional wounds. Yet they didn't stop her from planning a Decca audition with Marie. Once they felt confident enough, the two women went down to the studio to sing "Beams of Heaven" and a few other numbers for label executive Paul Cohen. The songs must have gone over pretty well, since Marie remembers Cohen exclaiming, "That's the girl we want!" from an adjacent room. Without further ado, a contract was prepared, and studio time was blocked out for early July. Marie joined the 802, the New York City musicians' union. Then it was back to Rosetta's place to pick material and rehearse.

Having Sam Price and Rosetta together in the studio again complicated things. "Sam and Rosetta used to clash all the time, *all the time*," Marie recalls. Whereas Sam saw himself as an equal, if not more important, player in the making of their records, Rosetta, who was the star and did all the work of touring, saw no need to take orders from a man whose salary she considered herself to be paying. The mistrust led to testiness on both sides. Sometimes Rosetta would interrupt a take because a band member was playing off-key; at other times, Sam would break in with his own demands. Meanwhile, Marie says, Paul Cohen would stop by and take a conspicuous look at his watch. "Okay, Sam," he would tell Price, "get it together."

Amid such tensions, it's a miracle that Rosetta, Marie, and Sammy

Price made great music. Yet "Didn't It Rain," Rosetta and Marie's first hit as a duet, is the proof that they did. Released that summer to critical and commercial acclaim, the gospel hymn narrates the Biblical story of the Great Flood, in which God punishes humanity for its transgressions. Yet although it recounts an apocalyptic moment in history, the song is upbeat, focusing on the hope that comes with the washing away of sin. Rhetorically speaking, the title phrase "Didn't it rain?" is more a prompt than a question, as in a preacher's "Are you with me, church?" *Of course* it rained, the song proclaims jubilantly, and isn't the Lord *wonderful?*

Coincidentally, a recording of "Didn't It Rain" by the Roberta Martin Singers was released around the same time, but to hear the Chicago group's version next to that of Rosetta and Marie is to hear two very different musical sensibilities at work. The Martin Singers' record, arranged for piano, lead voice, and chorus, features Roberta Martin's sweet delivery of the lyrics over delicate harmonizing and softly rumbling piano chords that conjure storm clouds gathering on the horizon. In the hushed, shimmering intensity of Martin's lovely call to listen to the rain, audiences might almost have heard the pitter-patter of a distant downpour. What drama the recording has comes from the Singers' subtle play with dynamics; when the chorus joins in with Martin, the heightened volume of their combined voices conveys the awesome power of a God who can destroy His own creation through a single, perfect storm.

In contrast, Rosetta and Marie's "Didn't It Rain," with its guitar solo at the bridge and instrumentation that is heavy on the rhythm section (bass, piano, and cymbals), has a distinctly "bluesy" feel. Their lyrical delivery is bluesy as well. The Martin Singers voice the words with the precision of students in an elocution class. Rosetta and Marie depart from the text immediately, embellishing each phrase with little "extras," added syllables that give their phrasing a syncopated, offbeat feel. Flouting gospel convention, they rebound their voices off one another, making it hard to know who is singing lead. The music writer Nat Hentoff would later compare their trading of "swift, crisp choruses" in "Didn't It Rain" to a bebop performance by trumpeters Dizzy Gillespie and Roy Eldridge.[7]

The rhythmic complexity of the chorus carries into the first verse, which begins with Marie narrating the story of the forty days and forty nights and the bird sent out by Noah to bring news of dry land. As she sings, the band shifts into high gear, Rosetta picking on her guitar, Sam playing a tinkling boogie-woogie piano, Harold "Pops" Foster holding down a steady walking bass line, and Kenny Clarke adding the lightest touch of cymbals underneath.

Then Rosetta picks up the lead. She doesn't merely sing; she incants. Like one of the saints speaking in tongues, she empties the word "rain" of ordinary signification, until the sound of her voice communicates a feeling of holy possession. At one point, after a near guitar solo, she conjures the children's rhyme "Rain, rain go away / Come again some other day" —words that bemoan the tedium of a day spent indoors with nothing to do. But there's nothing tedious about this "Rain," which pounds down for a joyful two minutes and thirty-five seconds.

The two versions of "Didn't It Rain" illustrate how in the postwar era different sounds continued to signify distinct social values associated with different branches of African American Christianity. The precision of the Roberta Martin Singers' recording, with its absence of sour notes or ragged entrances, expresses in acoustic form the orderliness and tidiness valued by postwar mainline congregations. Rosetta and Marie's "Didn't It Rain," on the other hand, could have gone over as gospel or secular music, depending on a listener's orientation. "Sam was one of the greatest rock-and-roll musicians out there," Marie says, "and he put a lot of that rock and roll behind the tempo and the tone with our recording. That's why [our record] went like that."

It also "went like that" because there was magic in the combination of Rosetta and Marie. "I thought Rosetta then was at the top of the game when they were together," says LeRoy Crume, "that's the tandem that I really loved." Crume, a member of the gospel group the Soul Stirrers, also remembers Marie as so pretty he could barely take his eyes off her when his quartet played with them. Not a few professional gospel singers admit to preferring what Geraldine Gay Hambric calls Marie's "rich velvety tone" to Rosetta's flatter, more piercing vocals. On the other hand, as one singer says, Rosetta knew how to "do things" with her voice; as with other great singers, it didn't matter that her instrument had technical "flaws." Whereas Rosetta used her voice like a jazz musician, Marie had a more straightforward style.

The two complemented each other in their onstage personae as well. Marie had "a great sense of presentation," says gospel scholar Tony Heilbut; when she sang, "her eyelids seemed to flutter like Camille," the title character played by Greta Garbo in the 1936 film. Marie Knight carried herself like a "grande dame," he continues, whereas Rosetta was playful and melodramatic. Rosetta was also more comfortable with self-revelation on stage. While Marie sang and played, Rosetta talked to her audience, testifying as if she were in church with her mother, or doing it up as she had on the stages of Broadway clubs.

"Didn't It Rain" ascended the *Billboard* "race" charts and put Marie in the national limelight for the first time. Meanwhile, she and Rosetta continued touring. That summer, in a marvelous turn of circumstance, Rosetta and "Golden Voiced Favorite Madame Marie Knight" headlined at the Golden Gate. Four months later, in November 1947, they did a special eleven-thirty evening show with the Sam Price Trio at New York's Town Hall—a prestigious venue for the top jazz and pop artists of the day, and a place that attracted a liberal, multiracial audience—singing their gospel blues as Saturday night quite literally turned into Sunday morning.

The Dixie Hummingbirds, featuring lead singer Ira Tucker, did several tours in the late 1940s with Rosetta and Marie. A typical show with the famous quartet would start with the local warm-up acts, then move on to a slightly bigger attraction, then culminate with the Hummingbirds and Rosetta and Marie. As Tucker recalls, the two women would switch between solo songs and duets, trading places at the piano on those numbers when Rosetta wasn't playing guitar.

The Hummingbirds and Rosetta did tours of Biblical proportions, including a forty-nighter that diminished to a thirty-six-nighter, but only because of four rainouts. They broke records, especially in the South. "We did about three thousand people at the Textile Hall in Greenville, South Carolina," remembers Tucker. "Oh, we were packing just about every place we went to."

At other times, Rosetta and Marie toured on their own, playing a mix of auditoriums, theaters, and outdoor venues such as Atlanta's Ponce de Leon Park, where relatively lenient noise ordinances made it possible for Rosetta to turn the amps up on the electric guitar she was now regularly touring with. (Recordings with the electric instrument emerged around late 1947.) Some weeks found them doing two shows on Sunday, at three and at eight, and five other late weeknight shows. If bookings allowed, they combined theatrical and church performances in a single day, playing, for example, Newark's Laurel Garden, a former boxing arena, in the afternoon, and then Washington Temple COGIC at night.

Rosetta's Northern following was always strong, particularly among African American audiences, but Southerners, including whites, went crazy over her, recalls Marie, perhaps because they saw the Arkansas girl in her. While the most urbane New Yorkers sometimes viewed her as "country," these Southern audiences harbored a deeper appreciation of her particular combination of down-home sincerity and look-at-me glamour. What was déclassé in Manhattan might be debonair in Memphis. When in early June 1947 she and Marie appeared in St. Louis, Missouri—touted today as the gateway to the Midwest, but in the 1940s and '50s still a city of Southern black migrants—crowds of handsomely dressed admirers, young and not so young, turned out to hear and see the visiting celebrities. Rosetta and Marie had decked themselves out like churchwomen after a Hollywood shopping spree, in fancy white dresses, sparkly earrings, and fur stoles, a brown one for Sister Rosetta and a grayish-white one for Madame Marie.

A local photographer captured Rosetta after the show, autographing the sleeves of her 78s, her dimpled face flushed with pleasure and excitement. She and Marie stand out in the photograph as stars, and yet they appear to be buoyed by the community, not isolated at all. They look young and alive enough to live forever.

Looking good was an important aspect of Rosetta and Marie's performances. It was particularly significant to their audiences, who might see in their radiant appearances the realization of their own aspirations. "Oh we had fabulous things," remembers Marie. In the 1950s, Clara Ward would give Rosetta a run for her money as most glamorously bedecked gospel singer; as one old-timer on the gospel circuit puts it, you could tell when the Ward Sisters had preceded you into a hotel because the lobby carpet would be sparkling with the glitter that had rained down from their towering wigs. Still, the Ward Sisters nodded to church propriety by wearing robes—grand ones, to be sure, but robes nonetheless (later, they switched to sequined gowns). Such attire made sense for gospel groups, but for Rosetta and Marie, it was neither practical nor desirable. They preferred coordinated gowns or suits, usually white, worn with matching earrings and heels. If the fancy struck, or if they had full pockets, they added wigs, hats, furs, and decorative flowers à la Billie Holiday's famous

Rosetta and Madame Marie Knight (in fur stole to her right) signing autographs after a program in St. Louis, June 3, 1947. Photograph by Karl's Photo of St. Louis. From the collection of Mrs. Annie Morrison.

garland. For a while they paid a woman, Bessie Henderson, to travel around with them as their stylist. (In those days, of course, the term didn't exist; she was just Bessie who did their hair and helped them lay out their dresses.) But when Bessie returned to her family in Virginia, they went back to doing each other's hair, or visiting local salons.

Rosetta, conscious of a scar on her forehead, always insisted on short bangs, which Marie curled under, using a hot iron. A lot of women who knew Rosetta remember that hairstyle, which she wore through the 1960s, with only slight variations. "She would wear them bangs!" laughs singer Inez Andrews. "And I always thought that anybody that wore bangs was some kin to Mamie Eisenhower. Every time I saw her she had them bangs and I used to call her Mamie Eisenhower!"

Not all of life on the road was glamorous, of course. Racial segregation imposed particular inconveniences and insults in the South, where Rosetta and Marie could not dine at most restaurants, use public facilities, or stay in "white" hotels. Well-dressed black women driving a nice car with New York plates were at best objects of curious ogling, and at times targets of harassment by police or locals, usually white but sometimes black. Like other black female entertainers, Rosetta and Marie developed an arsenal of tactics to deal with potentially ugly situations. In the 1950s, when they were traveling by bus, they took to getting around with the help of their white bus driver, "because in the South," as Marie explains, "a white man and a black woman is the charm; they can get anything they want. But you gotta keep your mouth closed, you got to know what to say and when to say it. Because down there in that period of time...like it was then, [people] would say 'Yes, Ma'am' to you as quick as you would say 'Yes, Ma'am' to them. As long as you mind your own business."

What Marie calls "the charm" is an allusion to the sexual and racial double standard that policed relationships between black men and white women, but permitted white men to engage in sexual liaisons with black women. The grip of such slavery-era conventions had abated little by midcentury. Neither had navigating places like Mississippi become any less perilous. Mississippi is a "gorgeous" state, Marie says, "but it's one of the most *dangerous* states in the world.... The sheriff was in there with the guns up on our shoulders while we were working."

Gospel performers were no safer in this respect than their secular sisters. Ruth Brown, the Virginia-born rhythm-and-blues singer whose career took off in the late 1940s, remembers, "It was hard for *all* of us at that time, because you could not stay in hotels. And then you would have to go into town to look for what they called a motel, and if you couldn't find one of those you had to . . . go to the barbershop or the beauty parlor and ask if they knew a place to stay." In Mississippi, she adds, "we always had to stay at someone's house. Or you lived on that bus."

Like their male peers, Rosetta and Marie doubled as their own roadies, traveling with their microphones as well as backup batteries for Rosetta's "tone box" (amplifier). Unlike the men, however, they carried the extra burden of having to appear on stage looking as if they hadn't lifted a finger all day. Male gospel quartets could show up at programs from week to week wearing the same matching suits, but for the women this added labor of glamour—which paradoxically entailed creating the impression of *not* working—precluded the recycling of evening gowns.[8] "It's not easy for a woman—especially changing your clothes and doing your makeup," Ruth Brown remembers. Lacking water, she learned how to bathe with alcohol; lacking a proper dressing room, she learned to dab on lipstick and eyebrow pencil in the swath of light cast by the high beams of an automobile.

Ira Tucker Jr. recalls hearing Rosetta tell stories about times when black funeral homes were the only places gospel singers could find to stay, or when she and Marie were treated with cruelty and disrespect. "A lot of white women took them for granted in terms of just being like ho's, you know, on the road. And they were out there making money *legitimately* and *professionally*. And she didn't like that aspect of it, she didn't like the fact that, you know, she was getting hit on a lot, too, you know, especially by ministers who were supposed to have been a certain way."

A typical performance, circa 1949, billed as "Sister Rosetta Tharpe featuring special guest Madame Marie Knight," might have gone like this: Rosetta comes out on the stage first, dressed in a white satin gown with sequins on the sleeves. She straps on an electric guitar and launches into a few of her Decca hits, audience pleasers such as "That's All," "This Train," or "Strange Things Happening Every Day." Marie, dressed in a gown of complementary color and cut, joins her on stage and together they slow things down, doing a contemplative "Oh, When I Come to the End of My Journey," a hopeful "Stretch Out," and perhaps a soulful "Precious Lord" or "Precious Memories," with Marie at the piano. As befits a "spiritual" concert, there isn't much in the way of secular dancing in their routine, but there is meaningful movement nonetheless, Rosetta strutting about, Marie swaying elegantly and illustrating vocal phrases with her hands, hips, shoulders, and eyes. Next Rosetta switches with Marie, taking the keyboard and giving Marie the chance to perform a few solos of her own. The audience cheers to see Rosetta, a guitarist, showing off her chops on an instrument she isn't known to play.

After a few more solo numbers by Rosetta, accompanied by occasional storytelling in between, to contextualize the songs, the audience is ready for a little something on the lighter side. This is when they segue into their "Saint and Sinner" act. Marie plays the sinner, Rosetta the saint. Rosetta enters the stage in a gown carrying her big guitar, followed by Marie on the "sinner side," dressed like a yokel in a big straw hat and jeans and playing a tiny ukulele. The audience erupts in laughter to see the contrast between the high-toned, urbane "saint" and the low-down country bumpkin, with their differently sized instruments. Rosetta and

Marie ham it up awhile, until Rosetta, sensing that the joke has been milked to its fullest, strikes up the notes to a big number like "Up Above My Head"—Marie's cue to run backstage for a quick costume change. When she rejoins Rosetta onstage as her regular elegantly dressed self, they really let loose, building and building the intensity of the emotion until everyone in the hall is whooping and applauding. Rosetta might well sing all night but for a piano cue from Marie that says it's time to quit. The audience goes mad, stomping and calling for more. Even as the MC comes out to say goodnight, Rosetta and Marie are out of the building.

Trips back to the studio punctuated Rosetta and Marie's touring. Some time in July 1947, the same month they did "Didn't It Rain," they recorded a couple of tracks for the Down Beat label as "Sister Katty Marie," a pseudonym that fooled no one. By the end of the year, Decca had won a court order to have the masters and existing copies of the record destroyed. Around the same time, Rosetta and Marie recorded two songs that joined "Didn't It Rain" as top request-getters in the 1940s. "Beams of Heaven," by the Reverend C. A. Tindley, a Philadelphia Methodist preacher who was a major influence on Dorsey, turned out to be magnificent material for Rosetta and Marie. Marie regards it as their best work together. "There was something about that song," she says, "it did something for me." Isaac Hayes can remember his grandmother listening to it, "glued to her radio." It was around the time he heard Rosetta playing electric guitar, a sound that would leave an indelible mark on his own developing musical sensibility.

Rosetta and Marie had another big commercial hit with "Up Above My Head," a familiar church song that became their signature duet and reached number six on the "race" chart on Christmas, 1948. Recorded in the same November 1947 session as "Beams of Heaven," "Up Above My Head" engages the listener in an ear-popping display of vocal fireworks. The record begins with a few introductory boogie-woogie piano phrases by Price, joined after a few notes by Rosetta on guitar. Then Rosetta, still strumming as a walking bass line kicks in, sings the opening line, *"Up above my head,"* her delivery so fierce and smooth at the same time that it anticipates 1960s soul. A fraction of a beat later, Marie answers, repeating the phrase while digging deep into the rich lower part of her register. Again Rosetta sings: *"I hear music in the air"*—and again, after an almost imperceptible pause, Marie answers, the contrast in their voices giving their call-and-response an appealing texture. The second time around, Rosetta sings the line again, changing the words slightly so that the revision has a jauntier, more emphatic feel: "Now *up above my head* / You know *I hear music in the air.*" After a final run-through of these phrases, they merge voices in a syncopated conclusion that works through the tensions built up in the previous three lines: "*I really do believe there's a heaven somewhere.*"

Especially in the driving instrumental bridge between verses, "Up Above My Head" leaves the Sanctified Church behind and charts a straight course toward rhythm and blues. Rosetta *works* the guitar, alternately plucking and strumming up a storm, while Sam Price provides the tinkling piano line underneath her. On some of Rosetta's recordings, the guitar solos can sound a little like perfunctory displays of virtuosity—as though to say to the listener, "I'm Sister Rosetta Tharpe, and here are a few bars just to prove it to you"—but in "Up Above My Head," Rosetta plays her heart out.

Like "Beams of Heaven," "Up Above My Head" had an undeniable energy that paralleled the collective optimism of black people in the postwar years. As "Beams of Heaven" spoke of freedom, both worldly and otherworldly, so it captured people's budding hope that the late 1940s and early 1950s would bring about sorely overdue change.

It was some time during those early years of their collaboration that word began to get around the gospel circuit that Rosetta and Marie were something more than "just friends." These were not rumors that either woman would have welcomed, especially since their livelihoods depended on their legitimacy as religious performers. Many black churches of the day, not only Pentecostal denominations, found ways to look in the other direction when a member transgressed, as long as the transgressor repented—or at least kept her sins out of public sight. In such a way, out-of-wedlock births, extramarital affairs, and occasional dabbling in alcohol, cigarettes, and other forbidden pleasures, shameful as many felt them to be, could be efficiently forgotten even as they were noted.

Homosexuality ranked as a different order of sin, however, reflecting broader social and cultural prohibitions on sexual identities that violated, at least by some Biblical interpretations, the natural, God-given order of things. (In this respect, African American Christians differed little from other American Christians in their understanding of homosexuality.) For many black people, homosexuality threatened to hinder the progress of "the race" as a whole, insofar as they believed progress to be predicated on mainstream acceptance.

It's difficult to say for sure how church audiences might have reacted to hearsay about Rosetta's bisexuality, although it's easy to imagine that as a woman she would have been treated more harshly than outwardly gay men like Richard Wayne Penniman, who, as Little Richard, imitated elements of Rosetta's animated style of singing. Rosetta had even given Richard a hand-up in his career when, in 1945, at a show at the Macon City Auditorium in Georgia, she invited him onstage to sing with her. "Everybody applauded and cheered and it was the best thing that had ever happened to me," Richard recalled. "Sister Rosetta gave me a handful of money after the show, about thirty-five or forty dollars, and I'd never had so much money in my life before."[9]

Richard, who had come from the church and would return to it, was recognized as a gay man from the start. "I loved him," recalled rhythm-and-blues singer Etta James. "He had the guts to be a king and queen all at the same time."[10] Although male homosexuals were more visible, there is evidence that lesbians and bisexual women were a recognized presence within black gospel circles. In her as-told-to autobiography, Willa Ward-Royster, Clara's sister, writes about how Clara "revealed" to her that she had "engaged in a clandestine affair" with a female gospel performer. The scene of Clara's revelation is a meeting of the National Baptist Convention, the largest and most important black Christian gathering in the country, but also, as Willa portrays it, an event that included plenty of after-hours partying.[11] That evening, at the home of one of the members of a gospel quartet appearing at the convention, Willa saw preachers "who had inspired the people to holy dancing and shouting" days before "now doing their own inspired thing—with other men." She also overheard a gay male friend address Clara. "I know this sharp young child who'd just love you," he was telling her, "she's a Stone man, Honey."

Willa, apparently, knew plenty of gay men in the church—"it was easy to admire their creativity and wit," she writes—but the information that her sister "had dabbled in homosexual activities" came as a bolt from the blue. Clara attributed such "dabbling" to the strictures on dating men imposed by their mother, the daunting Gertrude Ward. The combination of loneliness and vulnerability rendered Clara "open to anything that filled the void in her life." When Willa asks Clara to tell her more about "liking girls," Clara's reply is evasive: "Willa, you know my thing is men," she says, "but Mom gets between me and any man I decide to get tight with." Then she switches subjects. "Never again did we approach that topic," Willa writes, and likewise, after this brief anecdote, her own book drops the subject as well.[12]

In passing on the story of her sister's reticence to discuss her bisexuality, Willa nevertheless makes visible within the gospel world what had long been talked about in the blues world by such openly lesbian performers as Ma Rainey, who sang a defiant "Prove It on Me Blues" in 1928. Rosetta did not deal with questions of her sexuality so publicly, and the ongoing wariness of most insiders to talk about it, even decades after her death, indicates how sensitive a subject her—or other gospel performers'—sexuality continues to be. Some, however, offer their own knowledge as evidence. Barney Parks, a founding member of the Dixie Hummingbirds, who later had an affair with Rosetta, says she and Marie were "intimate." Speaking anonymously, one of Rosetta's closest friends states—albeit with palpable discomfort—that Rosetta had female as well as male lovers. Gospel scholar Tony Heilbut, who came to know Rosetta in the 1960s, recalls times when she would comment on the attractiveness of women in her audiences. Of her sexuality, he says, "Rosetta belonged to the Whosoever Will Church, as in Whosoever Will Let Him (or Her) Come." Another gospel insider (who will speak only off the record) says that he heard over the years about various women gospel singers having women lovers, but understands why the rumors were quickly hushed up, given that "segment of the church that was ready to dismiss you if you *coughed* the wrong way." And Allan Bloom, who as a young man worked with one of Rosetta's promoters, says he saw Rosetta and Marie in flagrante delicto with a third woman, the Prophetess Dolly Lewis, when he was sent to fetch them from their hotel room during Rosetta's 1951 "honeymoon tour" after her third wedding.

Marie rejects these stories about Rosetta and herself as so much hokum. The gospel world is full of liars, she says, and it's best not to believe the rumors and gossip other people pass off as truth. In a different conversation, she recalls instead her role as caretaker to Rosetta the grown-up woman-child. Since Rosetta "couldn't count money the way it's supposed to be," Marie says, she took care of their finances on the road. She indulged Rosetta when she wanted to play little-girl games like jacks, or when she would stay up at night accompanying herself on the piano. And she defended Rosetta, with her inherently trusting personality, against prowling men looking to take advantage of her for her money and celebrity.

Notwithstanding the question of their truth, rumors contain meaning, especially in the insular world of midcentury gospel. Like other artistic realms, the gospel circuit had its own protocols of private and public behavior, of what could be said out loud and what could only be whispered about or not said at all. Many gospel musicians could and did party like their jazz and pop counterparts, but such behavior was carefully compartmentalized and, unlike that of many secular performers, it was understood to be off-limits as a subject of inquiry by the Negro press. On his early trips with his father on religious missions, a young Marvin Gay (before he added an "e" to his name to ward off associations with homosexuality) noted that sometimes "I'd see things which weren't always purely religious." "The gospel circuit was filled with temptations," he continued, and even if their religious devotion was authentic, "many of the performers fell to sin."

"Gospel performers were as human as anyone else and did not live apart from any aspect of [popular] performance culture," writes Nick Salvatore in his biography of C. L. Franklin, Aretha's famous minister-father. In her autobiography, Etta James recalls attending a particularly wild Philadelphia party with Little Richard and Professor Alex Bradford. "When it came to partying," she writes, "the gospel gang could swing all night."[13]

The circulation of this and other lore indicates that the gospel world had its own legends of outlaw identities and behaviors: of sissy men and bulldagger women, of philandering evangelists and pilfering prophets, of hypocrites who boozed up backstage before singing in front of the curtain about the virtues of Holiness living. For homosexuals in her audiences, rumors about Rosetta might have been liberating, an invitation to look for telltale signs of affirmation of their own veiled existence. Or perhaps Rosetta and Marie, performing together, might illustrate alternative possibilities of intimacy in a world where lines of gender and sexuality were religiously policed.

In 1948 Rosetta bought a house where she, Marie, and Mother Bell could live when they weren't out on tour. It cost $7,500, and was located at

2306 Barton Avenue in Barton Heights, an early suburb of Richmond, Virginia, then considered a desirable neighborhood for middle-class African Americans. Although the racial composition of the neighborhood was rapidly changing, at the time Barton Heights was home to a mix of blacks—among them teachers, principals, and postal workers—and white immigrants, primarily Latvians and Slavs. Rosetta, who had rented in New York, was proud to bursting at having purchased in the "Heights," a name that itself announced status.

By 1949, Rosetta had things a small-town Arkansas black girl wouldn't dare dream about: a swanky home, fine clothes, her own cars, famous friends, and a string of hits on one of the country's premier record labels. All the same, there were clouds on the horizon. Slightly and yet perceptibly, the rising national popularity of Mahalia Jackson was dimming Rosetta's stardom. Beginning in 1949, the press—music publications and African American newspapers alike—increasingly played the two off each other, contrasting Rosetta's Broadway background with Mahalia's renunciations of opportunities to cross over. Indeed, the angelic "Mother" Mahalia who emerged in the 1950s couldn't have been more different from Rosetta, who remained "Sister" throughout her career—a small but telling point, insofar as her image was always more sexualized, more *flamboyant*. (The word, used frequently in the '50s and '60s to describe Rosetta, referenced her flashiness and hinted at the sexual impropriety of homosexuals.) Rosetta played clubs, while Mahalia stuck to nontheatrical venues. Rosetta played blues, Mahalia (mostly) didn't. Rosetta played guitar, Mahalia sang along to the accompaniment of a piano or an organ, the traditional instruments of the church. Mahalia had greater vocal authority, Rosetta had zing. Once in circulation, it was difficult for Rosetta or anyone else to challenge the dualities that hardened into received wisdom.

The situation was exacerbated when, in January 1949, Decca had Rosetta do a copycat version of Mahalia's monumental hit "Move On Up a Little Higher," a song that had changed the gospel landscape utterly upon its release a year earlier. Producers at Decca barely made an effort to stamp Rosetta's "Move On Up" with any originality; even the instrumental accompaniment was similar. Not only that, but Rosetta's "Move On Up" was released on the front and back sides of a single 78, just as Apollo had released Mahalia's version.

To listen to Rosetta's "Move On Up" is to hear that rare occasion when her heart was not in it. One can only speculate, of course, about the source of the missing "flavor," but Rosetta knew that Mahalia owned "Move On Up"—even if she didn't own the copyright—by virtue of her definitive performance of it. Yet even when she produced uninspired music, Rosetta in the late 1940s was one of the hardest-working women in the business. Jerry Wexler, then a writer for *Billboard,* estimated that in March 1949 alone she grossed $24,000. Her yearly take he guessed at about $200,000.[14]

Soon things started to go terribly wrong, however. While Rosetta and Marie were on tour in California, Marie received a telegram saying her mother and two children, ages four and six, had died in a fire in their Newark home. She and Rosetta flew to New Jersey so that Marie could bury her loved ones. Two days later, they were back in Nevada for a show.

Until then, Marie had taken care of Rosetta, but now it was time for Rosetta to take care of her. "I got you from your mother—your mother gave me permission to take you out there with me—" she told Marie, "and I'm gonna stick with you, whatever happens. You'll always be my little sister. And as long as anybody on Broadway has got a dime, we're going to survive."[15]

Yet despite Rosetta's promises of protection, their professional relationship faltered. Perhaps it was Marie's desire to get out from under Rosetta's wing and see if she could fly as a solo artist; perhaps it was boredom or the stress of touring; perhaps it was the weight of all the grief Marie was suffering over the loss of her babies and her mother. By the end of 1950, they had split up as a duo. "She went her way, and I went mine," is how Marie puts it. A 1951 press release from the Taps Agency tells a more attention-grabbing story. Noting the "terrific" response to Marie's solo recordings—produced when she was still teamed up officially with Rosetta—it announces that she has "decided to work alone to gain recognition on her own merits.... It is also a known fact that she has composed many religious songs, and hopes to record all of them, someday."

The tone of an item Rosetta sent to the *Pittsburgh Courier* late that November was more businesslike, even curt. "I would appreciate your placing an announcement in your newspaper, that Madame Marie Knight is no longer associated with Sister Rosetta Tharpe," it announced. She "now appears with the Rosettes, formerly known as the Angelic

Queens, her own pianist and musical director, James Roots Jr., and also with one of the most outstanding personalities of the church, Sister Rosetta Tharpe's Mother, Katie Bell Nubin."[16]

One door had opened, while another—for the time being, at least—had closed.

6

AT HOME AND ON THE ROAD (1948–1950)

She wasn't a groveler, and she didn't let us grovel.
She said, Hold your head up. Even if you had a headache
and you had to hold it down you had to hold it up.
Rosettes singer Lottie Henry Smith

In moving to central Virginia in the late 1940s, Rosetta bucked the usual pattern of twentieth-century African American migration. But leaving Harlem for Richmond made personal and professional sense. In Richmond, she was comfortable and content, familiar with the rhythms and rituals of daily life. At the same time, Richmond afforded Rosetta easy access to the places where she enjoyed the greatest popularity. Atlanta and Baltimore were a day's drive. So was Decca's new Nashville studio, as well as, for that matter, her hometown of Cotton Plant.

Just as it afforded her the ability to travel, so Richmond also represented stability. Before she bought the house on Barton Avenue, Rosetta had never really enjoyed a rest from a life of unceasing movement. "She grew up without a home, so home was important to her," says Roxie Moore. The Barton Avenue house was the structure with which Rosetta repaired such childhood deprivation. Furnished according to the lavish standards of a girl who had grown up poor, but still not too grandiose, it wasn't on the scale of Graceland, Elvis's baroque monument to a poor white country boy's ideal of home, but it served the same palliative function. It was where Rosetta did ordinary things: cooked meals, watched *Ed Sullivan,* or listened to records by silky-voiced Nat "King" Cole. When fellow musicians stopped by, she would settle in at her white baby grand piano or break out her guitar, play a few bars of something she had been working on, and solicit their feedback. "Does this work?" she would say. Or: "Listen to this."

Because of Rosetta's celebrity, 2306 Barton Avenue was something of a legend among neighbors. Modest-sized by the standards of today's suburban McMansions, it had a foyer graced by white ionic columns and mirrored walls and ceilings. The basement had knotty-pine floors and walls. The outside featured a substantial lawn, a rose garden, and a three-car garage, which served for some period of time as a makeshift stable for Rosetta's horse, Margaret.[1] There was also a shedlike structure in the back, although no tool had ever seen its interior. Lined with cedar shelving and insulated to protect against heat or cold, it instead served as an extra-large closet where Rosetta and Marie stored their dresses, shoes, hats, and other accessories. When future Rosettes Sarah Brooks and Lottie Henry first laid eyes on the interior of 2306 Barton Avenue, they were awed by its luxury. "Her carpets were so thick your foot went down in it," Sarah remembers, illustrating with her hand. "Televisions had just come out and she had cabinets with a television. Just a little one, but it was beautiful, it was amazing to us." Robert Allen, who lived at 2401 Barton Avenue as a child, never saw the inside of 2306, yet he does remember seeing Rosetta outside in all her finery. "The women [Rosetta and Marie] used to wear fox fur things," he says, grasping for the right description of the macabre fur stoles then in style—the sort with "clips in the fox's mouth. . . . They were sharp. As a little kid I thought it was cool. It was almost like they were wearing costumes."

As well as a refuge from show business, the Barton Avenue home was Rosetta's stage for creating her self-image in the conservative 1950s. Amid postwar political retrenchment, especially concerning women and gender roles, the Richmond house proved an ideal place for her to massage her public image as a respectable female gospel singer and a domestic woman. A publicity photograph from the era, which turned up in the photo morgue of the *Richmond Times-Dispatch,* shows Rosetta standing in her yard next to a rosebush in full bloom, wearing a formal, satiny gown with a high collar and ruffled cuffs, her hair piled in loose, feminine curls on top of her head. Her gaze is modest rather than direct, her eyes cast downward at a small piece of paper that she holds in her left hand. The image has a nostalgic air; take away the chain-link fence, and you would think it belonged to an earlier era. A caption imprinted at the bottom of the photograph reads, "At Home in Her Garden, Richmond, Virginia."

Unlike the vast majority of images of Rosetta produced during her career, this one is introspective and serious in a way that resembles contemporary images of a pious, contemplative Mahalia Jackson, who was often pictured wearing a robe, her eyes closed and her face a knot of prayerful contemplation. Most striking of all, it departs from virtually every other publicity photograph of Rosetta in showing her reading rather than performing. Instead of being accessible, she is lost in a realm of private thoughts that viewers can't share, just as we can't know exactly what is written on the piece of paper she holds. The outdoor setting of the photograph underscores the naturalness of this captured moment, especially in contrast to the more obviously staged, artificially lit images of Rosetta from earlier days. The natural Rosetta, the photograph says, is a woman of feminine grace and intellectual refinement, not "primitive" spiritual enthusiasm.

The picture of Rosetta engaged in a leisurely, intellectual pursuit was significant in other ways. At a time when most black women still worked as maids, it illustrated a dream imagined by a burgeoning civil rights movement. Like Billie Holiday, who as a child scrubbed the stoops of homes in Baltimore, Rosetta had only her gift to fall back upon as a way out of a life taking care of other people's things or children. The phrase "in Her Garden" on the photograph conveyed powerfully the importance of freedom from such domestic labor.

Because Richmond had a substantial black middle class and was a key Southern transportation hub, black residents of the city in the 1930s and '40s took to calling their hometown the Harlem of the South. On a mild Saturday night in 1943, leisure-seeking rail workers, domestics, teachers, cooks, and tobacco factory laborers would have gone out to the Booker-T theater to see *Stormy Weather,* the movie musical starring Rosetta's Broadway friends Lena Horne, Cab Calloway, and Richmond native son Bill Robinson. The next day, the same audience might have found musical edification of a different variety at one of Richmond's many established Baptist and Methodist churches, or at an evening gospel program at a local auditorium. Although dwarfed by New York in population, Richmond had a richer gospel music culture than Harlem. Indeed, although unrivaled as a mecca of jazz and swing, New York had never quite fostered the distinct gospel scene or sound of much smaller cities.[2] Virginia, however, had a grass-roots gospel tradition, especially of the groups known as "jubilee" quartets.

Jubilee quartets were vocal harmony groups, and in the 1930s and '40s, as modern styles were developing, they sprang from churches, schools, neighborhoods, tobacco factories, veterans' associations, and trade unions—in short, wherever there were voices to harmonize. People in Richmond were "gospel oriented" according to Reverend Franklin G. Pryor, associate minister at the city's First Baptist Church, and jubilee singing satisfied a need for "clean" leisure. Even working-class families, he says, placed value on a musical education, especially for girls. "Most of your southern black homes had two things in it: a sewing machine—that was for the girls to sew and make clothes—and you also had a piano. All black young girls, it was almost mandatory that they take piano lessons at fifty cents a lesson." Future Rosettes Sarah Brooks and Lottie Henry, musically inclined and admonished by their strict parents to stay out of trouble, discovered in harmonizing an enjoyable, adult- and church-sanctioned means of passing the time. "Back in those days we couldn't do much going out," says Lottie. "So we'd sit around on the front porch and, you know, amuse ourselves with [singing]."[3]

Rosetta herself had worked closely with Richmond quartets even before buying the Barton Avenue home. In 1947 and 1948, she released three Decca 78s with the Dependable Boys, a five-member group with a nimble, effervescent sound.[4] Their recordings of "Everybody's Gonna Have a Wonderful Time Up There," "Down by the Riverside," and "My Lord's Gonna Move This Wicked Race" delightfully paired Rosetta's expressive lead vocals and plucky guitar stylings with the quartet's suave harmonizing. One of their recordings—"My Lord and I"—stood out as a striking reversal of the move Rosetta had made in her Decca debut a decade earlier, when she sang the song as "My Man and I." Another, "Little Boy How Old Are You," demonstrated Rosetta's agility with the electric guitar, an instrument that she probably had been playing since the late 1930s. At the bridge, she unleashed a thrilling solo, reaching for the top of the instrument's range and squeezing out unexpected notes. In such recordings, you can hear the palimpsest that is twentieth-century black popular sound: gospel merging with blues merging with something about to be rock and roll.

The Dependable Boys was a virtuoso group, but not a major name outside of the Southeastern orbit of jubilee singing. In contrast, the Harmonizing Four, the pillars of the Richmond scene, had a following that stretched from Pittsburgh to St. Petersburg and beyond. One of the longest-lived quartets in gospel history, the group debuted in 1927 at Richmond's Dunbar Elementary School and recorded its first 78s on Decca in 1943.[5] By the mid-1940s, Rosetta (and Marie) had begun touring regularly with the Harmonizing Four, whose members became good friends with Rosetta. Especially after she bought property in Richmond, she frequently visited the singers' homes. Donald Liston Smith, son of quartet member Lonnie Smith, remembers Rosetta stopping by one day when he was five or six with a gift of a miniature white guitar that she had seen in a store window and spontaneously bought for him, perhaps because it brought to mind pleasant memories of her own childhood. Yet the little white guitar, although unforgettable, failed to make a lasting impression. Like his brother, Lonnie Liston Smith Jr., Donald grew up to become a jazz pianist instead.

In 1949, around the same time that she presented Donald Smith with his own guitar, Rosetta was preparing to celebrate her first Richmond "anniversary" concert, marking one year of official residence in the city. Flyers advertising the event, which was to include several guest performers, were printed up and distributed around town—at the two black high schools, Armstrong and Maggie Walker; at various churches, and at Globe and Archer's record shops. Those who were so inclined could purchase tickets directly from Lonnie Smith. The venue was the Mosque, a popular auditorium that featured several balconies, a basement-level ballroom that could be rented out for dances, an impressive gold-leaf-covered dome, imported mosaic tiles, elegant chandeliers, and a massive pipe organ. Its name came from its architectural inspiration in the mosques of India and the Middle East.

Such grand surroundings called for grand performances, which is partly why no one in Richmond that season looked forward to the anniversary with quite as much nervous anticipation as the Twilights, a local quartet scheduled to appear on the program. Formerly known as the Bluebirds and then as the Twilight Female Gospel Singers, the Twilights consisted of four young women: Lottie Henry (lead), Sarah Brooks (tenor), and Lottie's first cousins Oreen and Barbara Johnson (alto and contralto). Later, a friend, Erma Wallace (bass), would join, bringing the group to five. At sixteen, Barbara was the baby, followed by Lottie and Sarah, both nineteen and graduates of Armstrong; Oreen and Erma, in their early twenties, were the "older" ones. At the time, all but Erma were unmarried.

The Twilights began their front-porch harmonizing on Twenty-eighth Street in Richmond's Church Hill neighborhood. Their musical world was diverse, filled with spirituals and hymns in church, jubilee singing at gospel programs, and hillbilly and popular music—from Bing Crosby to Dinah Washington—on the radio. Inspired by the Ward Singers of Philadelphia, by the late 1940s, the Twilights had developed a "good radius," according to tenor Sarah Brooks, a tall woman with a round, handsome face. They had stayed busy doing programs in most of the Virginia counties and cities as far north as Baltimore, and had also amassed significant broadcast experience, especially on Richmond radio stations WANT and WLEE. [6]

Until that night at the Mosque, however, the Twilights hadn't sung on a program with anyone as famous as Sister Rosetta Tharpe. The thought of appearing before her gave Lottie, diminutive and fine-boned, the jitters. "That big star?" she thought, "We can't get up in front of her!" But her father, who managed both the Twilights and the Dependable Boys, was unrelenting. In the end, Lottie and the other girls complied. They trembled inwardly, but they sang with steady self-assurance. And that, Lottie says, is when Rosetta "fell in love with us."

Ever since it had looked like her partnership with Marie would end, Rosetta had been scouring the gospel landscape for singers to be part of her regular traveling act. Now, it seemed, she had found them, and in circumstances not all that different from the ones in which she had "discovered" Marie. Once again, too, she had the task of convincing wary parents to entrust their daughters to her. Lewis Warren Henry, Lottie's father, knew the terrain of the professional gospel world, and he made his expectations exceedingly clear. "I want you to bring each one of them back here like you take her away. I don't want nothing to happen to any of them," he instructed Rosetta. Only after she had given him her solemn promise could the Twilights go into rehearsals with her on Barton Avenue.

Next to Rosetta—who was undiminished in vitality, and yet approaching midlife—the Twilights were young and new. Their sound was fresh, too. Whereas Rosetta's background in the Sanctified Church had bequeathed to her an earthier, more dynamic approach to melody and rhythm, the "girls," the products of strict Baptist upbringings, sang with a precision and purity that resembled the refined, sweet sounds of the Roberta Martin Singers (although they could get happy, too). When they harmonized, every individual tone was audible, and yet their voices blended together with a shimmering seamlessness. Theirs was the sound of the heaven pictured in Victorian engravings, complete with white-robed angels, golden harps, and God on His celestial throne.

Rosetta dubbed the group the Angelic Queens Choir and quickly set about rehearsing them to sing with her. Rosetta "had a voice that she could carry up," remembers Lottie. "Her range was beautiful. She could sing high or low. She had come out of the Sanctified Church. And you know they belt their songs. Our [sound] was more...melodious." They rehearsed constantly—sometimes for two or three hours at a time, sometimes for two or three days on end—to ensure that every part in the Angelics' harmonizing was audible. As a background group, they worked hard to figure out how to complement Rosetta without overpowering her.

Rosetta and the Angelics began touring together in June 1949, just as the verdant Richmond summer was settling in. Their first stop was Macon, Georgia—not that far away, and yet well beyond the perimeter of their previous experience in what Lottie calls the "close-in" states. The "Deep South" was to them a forbidding place. "We were scared to death to go to Georgia because we had heard so many terrible things about it," says Sarah. Rosetta, however, made sure they traveled comfortably and in style. In Macon, they stayed at a place called the Crystal White, which seemed so luxurious to the teenagers that they regretted leaving.

Hitting the road with Rosetta was a little like being called up from the Richmond jubilee farm team to sing for the gospel major leagues. In short order, the Angelics had not only whipped themselves into singing shape, but bought matching suits and heels, practiced their moves, and rehearsed their theme song, "Pass Me Not O Gentle Savior." Rosetta was meticulous down to the finest detail. She insisted that their out-fits, like their voices, blend with hers, and she was as exacting as a ballet mistress when it came to their routines. "She'd set aside an hour just for one hand movement," recalls Sarah. As "her girls," moreover, the An-gelics (and, later, the Rosettes) always had to be dressed just so, and not repeat outfits too often.

Rosetta paid each of her singers in cash—fifteen dollars per day, or as much as thirty dollars each on a Saturday or a Sunday, when they did two programs. She also lived up to the promises she had made to Lewis Henry, fussing like a protective mother hen over her baby chick-ens. When one of the Angelics required medical care, she took her to a doctor. When the group had to shop for something as mundane as a new pair of stockings, Rosetta ensured an appropriate chaperone. In their presence, Rosetta never drank or cursed. "The whole time we were with her she conducted herself as a lady," Lottie recalls. "She didn't have men running around the hotel. And when we finished our program, *we* were hustled back to the hotel." Her motto was "Keep a smile on your face and your big mouth shut"—pragmatic advice for well-dressed black girls traveling through unfamiliar Southern territory. Sarah admired Ro-setta's passionate commitment to her fans. "In gospel music if you can't reach the people they just sit there," she says. "But her audiences were usually very animated and they enjoyed her singing. And then she would stop singing and just pick that guitar, and sometimes they'd go *crazy!*"

Mother Bell attempted to exercise her own discipline, but to less ef-fect. "Yes, Lord! She was *very* old-fashioned," declares Sarah, in the man-ner of someone recalling spankings that never stung. "We did a lot of one-night stands. A lot of times we had to go in the [segregated] bath-room that we weren't supposed to go in and wash off. And Ma Bell would have a fit. She'd say [doing an imitation of Katie Bell's voice and diction] ... 'See those girls in there putting water all over theyself!'"

"Mama's like all moms," remembers Clyde Wright, then a young singer with the New York–based Selah Jubilee Singers, who toured peri-odically with Rosetta and the Rosettes. "She was watching us, the young people on the bus. We were the young guys, the girls they were so nice, and traveling after the concerts, usually, you know, sometimes we had to travel at night, and at that particular time . . . you know, we would try to smooch with the girls, but no way. She would [say], 'Boys, get back in your place!'" And they would respond: "Yes, Mama, we going back."

The young people could laugh secretly about Mother Bell's strictness, but no one could deny her power as a singer of the old-time variety. Whenever she opened her mouth to sing "Ninety-nine and a Half Won't Do," her trademark number, she *had church*, Sarah and Lottie recall. The popularity of her performances of "Ninety-nine and a Half" on the road was buoyed by the success of a mother-daughter duet of the song released by Decca that same year, with the backing of the Sam Price trio (Price, bassist Billy Taylor Sr., and drummer Herbert Cowans). Katie Bell didn't possess Rosetta's range or tonal clarity, but she had a flat, moaning delivery that imbued her singing with spiritual authenticity, even on shellac. The 78 clocked in at under three minutes, but in concert Ma Bell drew the song out as long as she could, especially in its emotionally propulsive section of counting up from one to ninety-nine and a half, until she was satisfied that she had squeezed from it every last drop of holiness feeling.

Rosetta had chosen an innocent-sounding name for her group, but her motivations may not have been so pure. The moniker, or at least one close enough to it, had already been claimed by a Philadelphia group, the Angelic Gospel Singers, who had a hit at the time with the song "Touch Me Lord Jesus." When the incumbent Angelics found out Rosetta had appropriated their name to draw publicity to her new group—in effect, tricking crowds into thinking they were seeing the Angelics of "Touch Me Lord Jesus" fame—they demanded she put an end to it. "She felt as though [using the name] would help to draw a crowd for her," remembers Angelics lead singer Margaret Allison, who later became a friend. "She apologized for it later. I accepted her apology." Hence it came to pass that seven years before Ray Charles named the female vocal group formerly known as the Cookies the "Raelettes," Rosetta dubbed her angelic backup singers the "Rosettes," after herself.

The name change was finalized just in time for the group's triumphant return to Richmond with Rosetta in late 1949 for another concert at the Mosque. Billed as Rosetta's "homecoming," the program featured local supporting musicians, with one unusual exception: a group billed as "The Jordonairs of Nashville, Tenn.—Nationally Known White Quartet."[7] Later, the Jordanaires (with an "e") would sing backup for Elvis Presley, providing the famous "oohs" and "ahhs" on hits like "Hound Dog" and "All Shook Up." At the time they toured with Rosetta, however, they were a white group partial to African American gospel and spirituals, and they had found modest success on the stage of the Grand Ole Opry. Gordon Stoker, who joined the Jordanaires as pianist in 1949 and became lead tenor in 1950, says his group admired Virginia jubilee quartets like the Golden Gates and the Harmonizing Four, as well as soloists like Rosetta. "We dug black artists singing spirituals," Stoker recalls, "and...what attracted us to her was the way she sang spirituals."

Although Rosetta's first concerts with the Jordanaires predated Stoker's membership in the group, he speculates that "we were the first white quartet" to tour with an African American gospel musician, or at very least one of Rosetta's prominence. Like the Rosettes, the Jordanaires admired Rosetta's work ethic and her business savvy. Stoker recalls supporting her on tours of Arkansas and Tennessee, where they played three or four shows a week in filled-to-the-brim high-school auditoriums "because that's all there was in those days." Rosetta, he says, would work the crowd to a frenzy by doing one song "over and over and over," stretching it out so fans would get maximum spiritual value for their money. As with the Rosettes, with the white Jordanaires Rosetta presented herself as a model of propriety and respectability—not an easy feat considering their schedule and the circumstances of their travel. Stoker remembers hearing that Rosetta "didn't draw a line" when it came to alcohol or swearing, and yet, "I never heard her say a dirty word and I never ever heard a curse or anything like that...around us, she was always beautiful."

Rosetta's 1949 concert was a "homecoming" because, together with the Rosettes and arranger-pianist James Roots Jr., she had been on the road for five straight months. Thanks to her New York–based booking agent, David Taps, many more months of travel, especially through the West and Midwest, lay ahead. Sarah and Lottie, who traveled with Rosetta in each of the forty-eight states except for Washington and Maine, remember feeling as though they barely had time to change their clothes and say a quick hello to their parents before heading out again.

For their second tour, Rosetta had bought a bus, a refurbished number from Groome's, a local tour company. James Boyer, the gospel singer and scholar who saw it when Rosetta made her annual visits to Florida in the early 1950s, remembers that it had "ROSETTA THARPE—DECCA

RECORDING ARTIST" emblazoned across its length in an impressive script. The bus was impressive inside as well. In the back, the seats had been ripped out, making room for a dressing area with mirrors and closets, one for each of the Rosettes. Toward the front it had seats for riding and sleeping. Their road manager and Jimmy Roots occasionally did the driving, but mostly the bus was handled by a white driver whose name has slipped into oblivion.

Their first stop on this second go-round was the Jordanaires' home base of Nashville, where Gordon Stoker got his first glimpse of the bus. It struck him as highly desirable; for one thing, he thought he had seen some bottles of alcohol on it. He didn't then consider that the bus, which did triple duty as sleeping, eating, and changing quarters, might have been more of a necessity than a luxury for Rosetta and her touring ensemble. In retrospect he sees this as almost comically naïve. Why the Jordanaires never traveled with Rosetta, and why Rosetta might have required her own bus in the first place "didn't even enter into our minds," he says. "We didn't even *think* about us staying in one hotel and her staying in another. Isn't that funny? . . . I know we would go into the restaurant sometime and get a bag of food and bring it out. But even *then* I didn't think about the fact that she couldn't go in that restaurant and eat with us."

In fact, Rosetta had her driver for emergency food runs when restaurants serving "coloreds" weren't available. A white chauffeur of black musicians at a time when blacks typically chauffeured for whites, he was a secret weapon in Rosetta's anti–Jim Crow arsenal. When Rosetta or one of the Rosettes had a craving that needed instant gratification, and when the only places for miles were Jim Crow establishments, their driver bought and delivered their food. Sometimes light-skinned Jimmy Roots could get service if he acted the part of a white man. Occasionally, Barbara or Oreen "passed" with a head scarf and a foreign accent.

Compared to the bus Rosa Parks would board in December 1955 on her way to becoming the public face of the civil rights struggle in Montgomery, Rosetta's tour bus may seem a historical footnote. But as a symbol of black female independence, it was perhaps no less important or inspirational. At the time when few hotels in the entire country welcomed blacks, having a bus meant having a place to sleep no matter where you were. It meant not having to eat at the restaurants at the back of Greyhound Bus stations. Those who saw it—from Gordon Stoker and James Boyer to Rosetta's neighbors on Barton Avenue in Richmond—have never forgotten it.

Soon after partnering with Rosetta, the Rosettes had a string of Decca recordings to their name. Some they did as the Rosette Gospel Singers, without Rosetta. On others, they sang backing vocals on "Sister Rosetta Tharpe" releases. One of these—"Silent Night" and "White Christmas," released on flip sides of a single 45 rpm—became a surprise hit. *Billboard* gave high marks to the single, released just in time for the 1949 holiday season and the beginning of a new decade: "Miss Tharpe's evangelical fervor and the choir backing make a sock Christmas side for the rhythm and blues outlets."[8] Some more conservative radio stations, on the other hand, found Rosetta's singing about the Baby Jesus with a bluesy lilt in her voice a bit too racy, and banned her record from the air. "She just couldn't keep it in," laughs Rosetta's friend Georgia Louis, referring to Rosetta's failed attempts to "discipline" her voice.

Notwithstanding what was probably a mismatch between singer and material, however, the record went over big with buyers. Bing Crosby had rendered the standard version of "White Christmas" for Decca in 1942, breaking every previous sales record in the history of the industry and making him the first white performer to chart on *Billboard*'s Harlem Hit Parade.[9] Since then, it had become a Christmas tradition to cover "White Christmas," and every year new versions had their five minutes of fame. In early 1950, record buyers sent Rosetta's record—which had two Christmas classics on it—to number six on the recently dubbed "R&B Hit Singles" chart.

The record also paved the way for Rosetta's first national television appearance, a coveted spot on the January 1, 1950, Perry Como *Supper Club* show.[10] The opportunity to perform on TV thrilled everyone, not least Rosetta. Yet when she, Jimmy Roots, and the Rosettes arrived at the CBS studio in New York for rehearsals, they found that the show's producers, for reasons unknown, had envisioned the stage set for "White Christmas" as a country hayride, complete with horse-drawn wagon. This was puzzling, but not outside the realm of the imagination, so they let it slide. Then they discovered that as part of the country theme, the Rosettes' heads were to be covered in bandanas.

That was when Rosetta put her foot down, recalls Sarah, who had put off college to join the Rosettes. The bandanas suggested gratuitous stereotypes of the type Rosetta herself had confronted, and according to both Sarah and Lottie, they triggered a rage they didn't often see. Perhaps Rosetta was thinking of her own "Four or Five Times" soundie with Lucky Millinder, in which she had hammed it up in gingham and painted-on freckles. In any case, Rosetta threatened a walkout if the Rosettes were made to wear the bandanas. She "would not let people demean us in any way," Sarah recalls. "She said, Over my head."

In the end, the show's producers gave in to Rosetta's stipulations, and the Rosettes made their first and only TV appearance "riding" in a hay-filled wagon that didn't obscure their cute hairstyles and smart new red, white, and black plaid jumpers with matching white blouses. With the television cameras rolling, they, Rosetta, and Jimmy Roots performed "White Christmas" for an all-white studio audience. Back in Virginia, Sarah's and Lottie's families, full to bursting with pride and excitement, couldn't witness it firsthand; none of them yet had a television. Downstate in Newport News, however, a lucky cousin got to watch the flickering, black-and-white images of the Richmond Rosettes perfectly coiffed, singing in perfect harmony.

Rosetta's experience on Perry Como's *Supper Club* show provides some indication of the constant struggles she continued to wage over how others—from television producers to music journalists to her own record label—categorized and represented her. Her argument with Como's people was less over costuming per se than over the professionalism of her entire enterprise. Yet white television producers weren't the only ones to typecast Rosetta. Through the late 1940s and early 1950s, the black press continued to describe her as a "former Broadway star," defining her by work she had done a full decade earlier. The phrase had a powerful anchoring effect, securing Rosetta to a frozen place and time, even as she sought to move on as a musician and a person. It was particularly burdensome as she faced the ever-ascending star of Mahalia Jackson.

Five months after the success of "Silent Night"/"White Christmas," Marie returned to work with Rosetta on an occasional basis. Had this taken place three years earlier, the reunion of the dynamic duo of gospel might have made headlines, but attention spans in the world of professional entertainment were notoriously short. Where gospel was concerned, moreover, Jackson's was the name in the air that spring and

summer of 1950. Black news outlets regarded her favorably for her refusal, especially after the million-selling "Move On Up a Little Higher,"
to give in to offers to record blues. "Mahalia Jackson Rejects 10G Bid,"
said a piece from the *Richmond Afro-American*. It was typical in its take
on Mahalia, and yet noteworthy for the way it used Rosetta to define
Jackson's persona. Rosetta, it reported, had unleashed an " 'R' bomb" in
"theatrical circles" by performing a program of "Spirituals with a Modern Touch" at an unnamed Harlem location. In fact, Rosetta had been
singing at the Apollo Theater, whose managers were trying every trick in
the book to get Mahalia to do a joint concert there with her. Mahalia,
however, refused. "I have informed the manager of the theatre and the
public in general that I do not appear in performances in theatrical places
or on any kind of program wherever theatrical artists appear," she told
the *Afro-American*. "I am a religious singer and very true to my religious
belief."[11]

Once again, Rosetta's indifference to the distinction between "sacred" and "secular" had given offense. "That's the thing, she was the kind
that didn't limit herself to the *doctrine* that came with the music," says Ira
Tucker Jr. "She allowed herself to be involved in other things, and she'd
listen to anything. She wasn't like her mom, she wasn't tuned in and
locked on to just one thing." As someone who wanted to have it both
ways, Rosetta represented a crack in the dam many black people had
erected to preserve the church as a space apart: away from white eyes as
well as free from commercial meddling. Dinah Washington (the former
gospel singer Ruth Jones) could sing in clubs about being "A Slick Chick
(On the Mellow Side)," and Mahalia could proclaim her principled refusal to sing at the Apollo in church halls across the nation, but Rosetta
was a threat because she dared to bring Mahalia's repertoire into Dinah's
territory.

Neither Jimmy Roots nor the Rosettes ever questioned Rosetta's authenticity or sincerity as a gospel singer. They cherished their two Apollo
appearances with her, keeping the club's trademark collage-style photo
souvenirs in scrapbooks they carefully preserved upon their return to
Richmond. Lottie and Sarah remain staunchly protective of their mentor
and big sister. "She was a *gospel* singer," says Lottie. "I would defend her
anywhere."

Rosetta and Mahalia were on better terms than newspaper reports
suggested. As photographer Lloyd Yearwood puts it, they were "good

bosom friends," linked as successful black women gospel singers, even if distinguished by different styles. Yet comparisons of the two, as well as gossip about their rivalry, proliferated until Rosetta's death. A rumor would later circulate that Mahalia had refused to attend Rosetta's funeral, although Jackson predeceased her by the better part of two years. Others would say Mahalia was jealous of Rosetta, or vice versa. Still others would resent the way the industry had thrown its weight behind Mahalia, not Rosetta. As Rosetta stepped into the second half of the twentieth century, however, one thing was clear: she needed some *good* publicity for a change, something that would lift up her career. Little did she know it, but a couple of unlikely gospel promoters just north in Washington, D.C., had the very thing.

7

"THE WORLD'S GREATEST SPIRITUAL CONCERT" (1950–1951)

Gospel singer Sister Rosetta Tharpe is a big girl with
a big voice who believes in doing things in a big way.
Ebony magazine, October 1951

Irvin and Israel ("Izzy") Feld, the Maryland-born sons of Jewish immigrant parents, were the reigning kings of gospel music promotion in the region extending from Baltimore to Norfolk when Rosetta met them around 1949. Allen Bloom, who worked for the Felds, remembers Rosetta walking into Super Cut Rate, their drugstore-turned-record-store in Washington's Seventh Street shopping corridor, to propose a business deal with his bosses. Tim Stinson, who worked for Irvin Feld in later years, heard just the opposite—that the Felds sought out Rosetta's business because her music sold so well among their customers.[1] Either way, it was a match made in heaven: Rosetta, the singer-guitarist who was always and forever looking to reinvent herself, and the brothers with good ears and marketing instincts to match, who had created a miniature music empire before Irvin Feld's thirtieth birthday.

Initially, the Felds promoted Rosetta in places like Turner's Arena, a ratty two-thousand-seat auditorium at Fourteenth and V Streets, NW, then primarily known for hosting boxing and wrestling matches. But in 1950, Irvin and Israel, in concert with Rosetta, ratcheted up their ambition several notches. Especially when she toured with Marie, Rosetta was no stranger to huge shows with impressive profit margins. Once, the two women had played to a crowd of seventeen thousand at Atlanta's Ponce de Leon park for a gross of $7,800, then played the same venue ten days later, for an additional $4,200 take.[2] Surely if it could be done in Atlanta, it could be done in the District of Columbia, with its substantial population of Southern migrants?

With that challenge in mind, the Felds set their sights on promoting Rosetta at Griffith Stadium, the ballpark then home to the American League Washington Senators and the Negro League Washington Grays. A little more than half a mile east of Turner's, the stadium stood in the heart of Shaw, black Washington's most historically significant and vibrant neighborhood. Geographically and socially, Shaw occupied a crossroads. Just up the hill to the north was Howard University, the nation's preeminent historically black institution of higher education. Directly to the south stood the Gospel Spreading Church of God, home base of Elder Solomon Lightfoot Michaux, a charismatic preacher whose CBS radio shows and socially conscious ministry had made him a national celebrity during the Depression. South of the church was a large residential area, home to blue-collar workers as well as large numbers of the relatively privileged, including Duke Ellington, who once had a job selling peanuts at Griffith Stadium. The area was a literal crossroads, too. Just in front of the stadium, the streetcars that ran up and down Seventh Street changed power from overhead trolley line to underground third rail.

Although Clark Griffith, owner of the stadium, was infamous among African Americans in the region for his resistance to integrating Major League baseball, Griffith Stadium "was sort of like outdoor theater for the black community," resident historian Henry Whitehead recalled. In segregated Washington, where black people could see the white-domed Capitol reflected back at them in the windows of establishments they were forbidden to enter, it was considered an important civic space. "Griffith Stadium was, putting it uncharitably, a dump," sportswriter Dick Heller noted in a 2001 remembrance. "But it was our dump."[3]

In setting their sights on Griffith Stadium for a gospel concert, the Felds unashamedly replicated precedents established by Elder Michaux. Like Rosetta, Michaux was famous for mixing piety with pageantry, often to the detriment of his reputation for religious sincerity. No one could deny his popularity, however. In 1938, he began renting out the ballpark for what he called "spectaculars," outdoor events that featured singing, mass baptisms, and plenty of the Elder's unconventional preaching. Michaux occasionally drew crowds numbering twenty thousand, mostly African American, although through the years his audiences included white notables such as First Lady Mamie Eisenhower. On one day in 1949, more people came out for Elder Michaux's annual spectacular than for the Nationals/Tigers doubleheader, which had been played at the stadium earlier in the day.[4]

In planning their 1950 concert for Rosetta, the Felds took their cue from such colorful, theatrical, and resoundingly profitable affairs. Like Michaux, who used fireworks and other devices to dramatize Bible scenes, they hired a fireworks company to produce a state-of-the-art display. To ensure a varied, top-notch lineup, the Felds hired the Golden Gate Quartet and Elder Smallwood E. Williams, activist pastor of Bible Way Church, who had won a 1948 *Afro-American* newspaper contest for "most popular preacher in the District" by a whopping margin of thirty-three thousand votes.[5] Since Marie and Rosetta had recently returned to the studio together to record "When I Take My Vacation in Heaven," backed with "You Gotta Move"—a record racing up the chart of Top Spirituals—the Felds billed the show as a special reunion concert. "SISTER ROSETTA THARPE and Madam Marie Knight, Together Again for This Performance Only!" trumpeted radio advertisements and print headlines.

In fact, the Felds had plans for future shows that would bring the two stars together again, and they started preparing for the second as soon as the July 1950 show ended. The "reunion concert" featuring Marie and the Golden Gates did well, according to Israel's wife, Shirley Feld, who played a key role in running the business. But it did not succeed on the order they had imagined. Allen Bloom recalls that the very night of the 1950 concert, "Irvin said, 'Rosetta, next year we've got to do something bigger and better.'"

That was when Irvin Feld got to thinking. Unlike her mother, Rosetta wasn't an evangelist, so she couldn't conduct a revival in the stadium, à la Michaux and other celebrity preachers. Then it hit Feld: perhaps they could combine a musical concert with a wedding, with Rosetta playing the star of both events? What was more attention-getting than a bride in her wedding gown? Didn't everyone love a wedding, particularly a celebrity wedding? And weren't weddings inherently theatrical, social rituals? Irvin considered the possibilities of a wedding at which the bride could entertain her own guests. If Michaux could administer the sacrament of baptism in the ballpark, then could not Rosetta follow his lead in using a baseball stadium for the sacrament of marriage? A practical man, Feld put the proposition to Rosetta without a lot of beating around the bush. Recalls Shirley Feld, "My brother-in-law said, Rosetta, find a husband. We'll promote the wedding."

Rosetta needed little convincing to sign on to Feld's idea. That very night, she signed a contact with Irvin and Izzy, promising to produce a groom in seven months, by the beginning of the new year.

By the following spring, Rosetta had found her future husband. He was Russell Morrison, a handsome man two years her junior. Born in Pittsburgh to seventeen-year-old Allene Owens Morrison, a migrant from South Carolina, Russell, like Rosetta, had grown up without a father's steady presence. Unlike Rosetta, however, he didn't have the benefit of a protective mother to soften the blows life would deal him. According to his widow, Annie Morrison (whom he married after Rosetta died), Russell suffered through a difficult childhood. His only sibling, a younger sister, died before her twelfth birthday, and Allene, battling her own demons, drank heavily. During the Depression, she found solace in being what people in those days called a "good-time woman," Annie says, often leaving Russell to make do alone. As soon as he graduated from high school, Russell lit out for Harlem.

Russell wasn't musical himself—he couldn't sing or play an instrument—but he was drawn to the glamour of the jazz life. As a young man, he did what he could to make himself useful to musicians. He found money doing odd jobs, and eventually landed a position as valet with the Ink Spots in 1941.[6] It's likely that Rosetta met Russell while on the road.

A lot of people who knew Russell call him lazy, and perhaps he was, but from another perspective, it's possible to see him as someone who refused to let his ambitions be boxed in by reality. If Ralph Ellison's Invisible Man, who also roamed the streets of Harlem in the thirties, was a "thinker-tinker," "kin to Ford, Edison and Franklin,"[7] then Russell was a dreamer-schemer, part of a less celebrated, but equally American, tradition. William Gittings, Russell's younger cousin, recalls that when he came back to Pittsburgh to visit family in the late 1940s, Russell would talk about his life among New York's musical stars. He would boast that "it was a toss-up [for marriage] between Rosetta and Mahalia." At the time, no one paid him much mind. Imagine the surprise of everyone back in Pittsburgh, then, when they found out he might not have been 100 percent hot air after all.

Russell's marriage must have fulfilled his most grandiose hopes. On the other hand, Russell had a way with women. "He was the slickest dude you ever wanted to meet," recalls Ira Tucker Jr. "In the day, when [Rosetta] married him, he was *bad*. I mean he had the process, he had his hair processed all pretty. He was light-skinned, which meant a lot at that time. He was thin, and he dressed well."

It wasn't just his looks, however, that drew women to Russell. A cigar smoker (he would eventually die of emphysema), he also had a rakish quality that, combined with a natural reserve, gave him an air of quiet confidence and invulnerability. Especially once he and Rosetta married, he carried himself with the insouciance of someone to the manner born. Although he stood no more than five foot nine in his socks, Russell seemed a bigger man. "He was quiet, but you better not cross him," is how Annie Morrison puts it.

It seems that few people shared Rosetta's excitement about her husband-to-be. Marie, who had always been savvier than her partner, was not amused; she took one look at Russell in her coolly knowing fashion and figured, rightly, that he was after Rosetta's money. Young as he was at the time, Allen Bloom shared Marie's feelings. So did Irvin Feld, but he stayed out of it, figuring that, although he was throwing Rosetta the wedding, the groom was none of his business. Even Annie Morrison, who never knew Rosetta personally, concedes that Russell probably married Rosetta for economic security. Certainly, she says, her husband had no particular interest in gospel and was not a religious man. "Russell always liked working around the nightlife," she said, but "he never talked about the church. I only got him to go to church a couple of times with me."

Other people emphasize Rosetta's interest in the marriage. Georgia Louis, Rosetta's friend from the 1960s, speculates that Rosetta needed Russell as much as he needed her. "You want someone to go ahead and do things for you," Rosetta had told her once, in a heart-to-heart. "You needed a forerunner because you needed help. And then you became dependent on that person" and fooled yourself into mistaking dependency for love. Roxie Moore similarly notes that a part of Rosetta had always placed a premium on male "protection." Like a lot of resourceful women, Rosetta made her own way in the world, and yet she still conceived of herself as deeply fragile, incapable of self-support. "She had no stability of her own," Moore observes. "She needed a backbone. She needed a strong man." Shirley Feld lays the matter out in practical terms. Rosetta "was a showman, that's why she wanted this wedding, too," she says. "It wasn't exactly a love affair, but it was a good way of having a husband and a wedding."

Rosetta's marriage to Russell throws into relief her own complexities and contradictions. "She couldn't imagine anyone would hurt her, and every husband attempted to steal a little of the light in which she shined," says photographer Lloyd Yearwood. Unlike Marie, who never wed again after her divorce from Alfred Knight, Rosetta attached importance to being someone's wife, even as she pursued a career that made traditional domesticity impossible. The Christmas cards she and Russell sent to friends in the early 1960s, when they had resettled in Philadelphia, captured this ambivalence. On the outside, the card features a cheerful image of a Christmas wreath against the background of a bright red front door. Inside, the card reads: "Wishing You a Merry Christmas and a Very Happy New Year. Mr. and Mrs. Rosetta—Tharpe—Morrison."

Rosetta at once believed in romantic love and treated the wedding as a performance, perhaps because two previous marriages had taught her as much. The idea of turning her wedding celebration into a huge party appealed to that side of Rosetta that loved entertaining others. Indeed, she recognized life itself as something of a performance, where the fun lay as much in breaking the rules as in adhering to them.

In the spring of 1951, a few months before her nuptials, Rosetta met her half-brothers and -sisters from her father, Willis Atkins. Willis's offspring took great pride in the blood connection they shared with one of gospel's First Ladies, although, until then, they had known Rosetta only through her music or family lore. For her part, Rosetta suddenly went from being an only child to being part of an extended brood of eleven.

Rosetta became friends with her half-sisters Emily and Elteaser, but took a particular liking to her young half-brother Donell. When she returned to Camden in 1954, on another swing through her home state, she asked the sixteen-year-old to accompany her on a summer concert tour up and down the East Coast. Traveling with Rosetta was especially exciting for Donell because of the chance it gave him to meet other stars on the gospel circuit. A singing contest between the Bells of Joy and the Five Blind Boys of Alabama made an impression on him that has lasted more than fifty years. "They had a great gettin' together, and there was so many people there, and there was people trying to outsing each other, and that was a great time," he recalls vividly. On a few occasions, he even got the chance to "bring Rosetta on," or introduce her to the crowd.

Donell remembers a particular incident from that summer that demonstrated Rosetta's playfulness. One day, he said, Rosetta challenged him to climb a flagpole in a park where they had stopped to rest, betting him that he couldn't do it. He appraised the situation and advised Rosetta to withdraw her bet unless she wanted to lose her money, but she refused. Realizing they were playing a game, Donell climbed the pole. When he arrived back on solid ground, Rosetta promptly paid up, in the form of a crisp hundred-dollar bill.

Irvin Feld's dare to Rosetta—*Find a husband, and we'll promote the wedding*—was something like that challenge to Donell. Just as Donell knew that Rosetta used the flagpole dare as an excuse to give him money, so Rosetta knew that the Felds understood the wedding as a vehicle for publicity and profit—theirs and her own. As Shirley Feld had intuited, it was a good way to have a husband and a wedding. It was a means of playing a game for the pleasure of others. It was certainly a way of having fun, and of showing her audience a good time. It might even prove to be the publicity stunt she needed to keep pace with the rapidly changing gospel world.

Janis Joplin, the white blues singer who came to prominence for her whiskey voice and gutsy performances à la Bessie Smith and Etta James, is usually credited as being the first American woman "stadium rocker." The phrase itself suggests the degree to which this grand setting became synonymous with rock and roll after the Beatles' wildly successful 1965 appearance at Shea Stadium in New York. Yet the phenomenal success of Rosetta's 1951 wedding concert at Griffith Stadium demonstrates how incomplete popular memory can be, especially when it comes to gospel, which has never enjoyed the broad popular appeal of other black musical forms, such as jazz or rhythm and blues. Rosetta wasn't a rock performer by any conventional definition. Her music never specifically targeted a youth audience, and despite her excursions into secular music, she primarily conceived of herself as a religious performer.

Yet if there is any doubt that she deserves the title of "stadium rocker," consider that on that July 3, 1951, a balmy summer evening, when trolleys and buses in Washington sat idle because of an ongoing mass transit strike, she outsold the hometown Washington Senators in a regular-season game.[8] Estimates of the crowd who came out to witness her nuptials vary. Decca, which made a live recording of the wedding concert, put the official number at twenty-two thousand, although it speculated that thirty thousand and upwards would have come had traffic not been snarled. The *Afro-American,* which featured the story on its front page, put the number at fifteen thousand, whereas *Ebony* magazine guessed twenty thousand. Shirley Feld, who worked the box office that night, can't say definitely how many people showed up, although she knows "we had *some* big sale."[9]

No expense had been spared for the event. Whereas usually they publicized concerts through posted signs or radio, the Felds took out display advertisements in area newspapers, calling out to readers with carnival-shouter flamboyance:

WEDDING BELLS RING OUT FOR...

SISTER ROSETTA THARPE

WITNESS THE MOST ELABORATE WEDDING
EVER STAGED! EVERYBODY IS WELCOME!
PLUS WORLD'S GREATEST SPIRITUAL CONCERT!

That last line made the music seem a bit like an afterthought, although the Felds had booked an impressive lineup: Marie, her protégée Vivian Cooper, the Rosettes, the Harmonizing Four, Katie Bell Nubin, James Roots Jr., and the Prophetess Dolly Lewis, a "spiritual advisor" and relatively recent addition to Rosetta's touring ensemble. Advance admission ran from ninety cents, for seats in the nosebleed section of the ballpark, to two dollars and fifty cents, for prime real estate in the first-base dugout. Not even Rosetta's half-sister Emily, who came up from Camden for the event, got a free ticket.

Reverend Samuel Kelsey, a popular COGIC pastor and recording artist, had been tapped to perform the ceremonial honors. Rosetta knew him well, having made visits to Temple Church of God in Christ a regular habit whenever she was in town. The congregation there opened their hearts to her, just as they had to Reverend Kelsey, who had a vivacious, outgoing personality. "People, they enjoyed him, because usually a minister of that caliber is so starchy that you're afraid to go up and say hi, that sort of thing," recalls May Ethel Holmes, who joined Temple COGIC in 1944. Consistent with his liberal approach to the pulpit, Reverend Kelsey encouraged a liberal approach to music in his church. When Rosetta had time, she would do freewill services at Temple COGIC or even work with the choir. Everyone loved her guitar playing, recalls Mother Holmes. "She could, as we said, make the *hair* rise up on your head in our church, 'cause we are very emotional. And she had something to offer in her music. Her music wasn't just words. They were words that meant something to us, as Christians. And that's one thing that Bishop [Kelsey] was very fond of, that she never stopped doing that gospel."

Temple COGIC was in the midst of celebrating its annual youth congress in early July, when Rosetta arrived in Washington for the wedding. She visited the congress, May Holmes remembers, but gave no indication that she was in town for her own marriage. That news leaked out through the Reverend Kelsey. "He told me, you know I'm gonna marry Rosetta tomorrow, so I was able to come in [attend]," May says. "I went with two or three other members of the church. We were dressed in what we call our Sunday best, so we didn't have to go home and get dressed up for the wedding." From high up in the stands, they had a clear view of the entire ballpark.

What Mother Holmes and other paying "guests" witnessed that evening, on the eve of the annual celebration of national independence, was a crowd-pleasing spectacle that merged church and state, secular and spiritual. In an amusing tweak on ceremonial conventions, the Felds had assigned all of the musicians supporting roles in the ritual of the wedding itself. Marie beamed in a colorful gown as Rosetta's maid of honor, and the Rosettes (reduced to four, since Sarah Roots was home sick in Richmond) sparkled as her rainbow of bridesmaids, each Rosette in a gown of a different color. The perpetually dapper Lucky Millinder, whose career had come upon hard times in the early 1950s, put in a guest appearance as Russell's best man. Theodore LeMar Summers—known to everyone as LeMar—a boy who lived with his mother and siblings in a small apartment above the Felds' Super Cut Rate store, served as ring bearer. Together with Mother Bell and the others, they formed a procession that began at the third-base dugout and led to a stage at second base. Last out, and marching regally to the tune of the "Bridal Chorus" from Richard Wagner's opera *Lohengrin*, was Rosetta.

Her entrance into the ballpark was greeted with gasps of admiring pleasure. From the upper deck, women leaned forward and squinted to get a look at her outfit. Rosetta had spent a small fortune on it—about $1,500, the average price of a new car in 1951, or roughly one-fifth of the cost of the house on Barton Avenue. In addition to $800 on the dress itself—a white lace nylon gown with a five-foot train, a scoop neck, and sheer lace sleeves that narrowed to a diamond shape and attached by a loop to the third finger of each hand—she had spent $350 on a magnificent sequin-trimmed veil that hung from a rhinestone- and pearl-encrusted tiara, and $400 on an extravagant bouquet of white orchids interspersed with white ostrich feathers.[10] Matching white satin heels peeked out from under her hem.

Backstage, the dress made an impression, too, and not just for its lofty price tag. It had been driven up to D.C. earlier that day from Thalhimer's, the Richmond department store where Rosetta had purchased it, in its own car. The Rosettes were used to Rosetta's fine things, according to Lottie Henry, but in their opinion, this one detail proved that Rosetta had outdone herself. "Nobody rode with the gown but the person driving the car and the lady that was going to arrange it," Lottie recalls. "But they sent their station wagon *just* for that gown with all this trail and stuff."

What Shirley Feld recalls most vividly is the race of the woman sent up from Richmond to fit Rosetta: she was white. "Thalhimer's was the leading department store, and [at the time] they didn't even want to *see* a black person walk in," Shirley recalls. "But because it was Rosetta Tharpe and she bought this expensive wedding gown, they sent the bridal consultant [to D.C.] with the gown to get her in it. And that wasn't easy!" she laughs. "It had like a thousand little buttons down the back. And the white bridal consultant from Thalhimer's had the job of getting her in it. . . . She was nice about it. But it was a big thing for a white to have to button a black into something."

The unusual "courtesy" extended to Rosetta may well have been compensation for an earlier incident that had caused the store some embarrassment. In 1949, according to Lottie and Sarah, Rosetta decided to go on a shopping spree at the Thalhimer's anchor store at Seventh and Broad Streets. "This was in the latter part of the segregated years," Lottie recalls, "and she had gone and bought a mink coat. And by her buying all this stuff, spending all this money and stuff, they might have thought she was criminal or something. I don't know what they thought."

They speculate that the situation might have been prompted in part by Rosetta's casual attire. Normally, Rosetta didn't leave the house without paying careful attention to her appearance. ("Oh, that thing could dress! Yes, she could!" Lottie testifies.) But that day, she set out in a cropped, "inexpensive-looking" fur coat, jeans, and comfortable boots, a scarf covering her hair. In any case, Sarah continues, "They asked her how she's going to pay. And she said she's going to pay cash. And they made a call to the [police] and they came and took her downtown. And later when they found out who she was and that she could afford to pay cash, then they apologized and she got all that stuff for nothing."

Over the years, word of the incident morphed into something of a legend. Drink Small, the blues singer and guitarist from South Carolina, was a friend of Rosetta's in the 1950s. He saw her on a number of programs, including one with the Harmonizing Four and the Swan Silvertones, and another with the Five Blind Boys and the Soul Stirrers. In the version of the story he knows, Rosetta wasn't just arrested; she *charmed* her way out of the clutch of the Richmond police. "I heard it said that she was in jail," he says, "and that she played so good the jailor let her out." Even if it has a "Robert Johnson at the crossroads" quality, the scene is tantalizingly imaginable: Rosetta, in street clothes rather than her usual glorious getups, surprising a dubious white police officer and using her guitar skills as a get-out-of-jail-free pass. It would have been a satisfying resolution to an unpleasant affair.

It took a full twenty minutes for the wedding procession, including Rosetta and her dress, to assemble at the altar, which had been decorated with a white wooden lattice draped with white gladiolas and American flags. Reading in a solemn voice from the District of Columbia marriage ceremony, Reverend Kelsey asked the crowd of twenty thousand whether anyone knew of any reason why the couple couldn't be married: "Speak now," he warned, as Shirley Feld and the others backstage cracked up. "Don't talk tomorrow!"

By the time he got to the portion of the ceremony in which vows would be exchanged, Kelsey, known for making wisecracks at weddings, was fully in his element. He referred playfully to the possibility of divorce, and teased the groom about his authority over his bride. He delivered the admonishment to both parties to "forsake all others" with a winking tone, and drew an audible crescendo of giggles from the women in the stands as he instructed Rosetta to "obey," "serve," and "love" her husband. Allusions to Russell's semiornamental role in the affair received the biggest reaction, however, and the crowd broke into outright laughter when Kelsey asked, mock-innocently, "*Do* you have a ring, Russell?"

The concert part of the evening followed immediately after the vows. The Sunset Harmonizers did "Gospel Train," the Harmonizing Four "Thank You Jesus for My Journey." Rosetta, still in her wedding dress, sang and played electric guitar. Accompanied by the Rosettes—no longer scared girls, but experts at performing before large crowds—she did "So High," a familiar song at Reverend Kelsey's church, as well as "God Don't Like It," her song about the sinfulness of alcohol, which mixes two parts Louis Jordan cheekiness with one part Wings Over Jordan holiness. She and Marie also performed several of their recently recorded songs, including "Revival Telephone," which picks up on the longstanding Pentecostal metaphor of a "telephone to heaven."

The wedding concert concluded with fireworks. In addition to the "lifelike reproduction" of Rosetta strumming on her guitar, guests were treated to "a huge display of Cupid's hearts pierced with arrows," as well as luminous simulations of Niagara Falls and a duck laying eggs. (These constituted a visual allegory of the couple's progress, from falling in love, to celebrating their marriage, to having children). By the time the last of the sparklers in the stadium fizzled out, it was practically midnight.[11]

Like Elder Michaux's "spectaculars," the wedding concert thumbed its nose at middle-class conventions of piety and flaunted the marriage of religion and commerce. From Rosetta's perspective, the event was an undisputed triumph, melding her overlapping entrepreneurial, spiritual, and artistic ambitions into one unforgettable evening. No single concert had ever put her in such high spirits. "I am happier than I've ever been in my life!" she gushed theatrically to the small band of reporters gathered outside her dressing-room door.[12]

It is fitting that the Griffith Stadium show is the best-remembered achievement of Rosetta's career, the one that gets a specific reference in all of her obituaries. Rosetta made memorable recordings, but the essence of her gift and her art lay in her ability to communicate with an audience. "Rosetta was more than a guitarist, she was an instrumentalist blessed with wonderful technique and feeling," says Swiss music promoter Willy Leiser, who befriended Rosetta in the 1960s. "Above all, she had an exceptional stage presence."

The huge crowd that turned out for her wedding concert was the proof Rosetta needed—at a crucial time in her career and her life—that she could still rely on her gift. The event also allowed her to combine blushing-bride modesty with uninhibited musical authority. Because these roles implied such disparate expressions of female sexuality, Rosetta, like other women musicians, rarely got to inhabit them simultaneously, without disharmony. But the wedding concert momentarily created a space where the good and the bad woman, the domestic goddess and the guitar goddess, could coexist.

Rosetta's wedding and concert embodied feelings of community and hope that took her audience of primarily black women outside of their everyday lives. In a testament to the closeness they felt to her, and out of respect for the occasion, these fans came to Griffith Stadium dressed for church. Some came with dates, others with children who were expected to sit still and behave. Many arrived bearing wedding presents for the bride and groom: silverware, household appliances, lamps, rugs, chairs, jewelry, and even television sets.[13]

Shirley Feld remembers that the wedding concert was the Felds' biggest success to that date. "The sale was fantastic," she says. "And [Rosetta] was excited about that, too. And then she was excited about the wedding. The bridal gown and the whole nine yards. It was a big event." Allen Bloom, only sixteen, recalls taking home $7,500 in cash, more than he could fit in his pockets. Much of his earnings came from the sale of souvenirs: everything from program books and "Abe Lincoln" pennies (coins wrapped in tin foil) to novelty items like lucky key chains, "holy" handkerchiefs, and midget Bibles, which Allen had dutifully rubber-banded together with matching miniature magnifying glasses in the days leading up to the wedding.

The Bibles and holy handkerchiefs were trademarks of Dolly Lewis, the featured "prophetess" of the evening. A singer and evangelist born in Dublin, Georgia, in 1910, "Miss Dolly" was a physically striking woman who always appeared on stage wearing a robe, a symbol of her status as a "seer." According to Abner Jay, who was her driver for nine years, and who briefly managed Rosetta and Marie, Dolly began her professional career in the early 1930s, leading prayer and healing sessions throughout the South.

Rosetta and Marie first met the Prophetess Dolly, also known as The Divine Healer, in the mid-1940s, at one of their Tampa shows. Dolly may have been a "gifted soul," but she was also a shrewd one. Even Marie, who was closest to her, concedes that on more than one occasion Dolly's holy handkerchiefs were blessed by "being hosed down behind stage just before a program."[14] On the other hand, Marie and Rosetta believed in Dolly's talent to foretell. She "would dazzle audiences at revivals by calling people by their full names," Marie remembers. She also provided more practical services. "People would pay what they had to consult with her. She got people out of prison and got pregnant girls out of trouble."

Others were considerably more circumspect about the Prophetess's powers. "She was a prophetess like *I'm* a prophetess," Shirley laughs. "She was telling you the number to play. Oh, I remember those days—Prophetess Dolly Lewis, it was hysterical." "If you said something Dolly didn't like she would speak in tongues," recalls Allen Bloom.

Rosetta's wedding drew thousands of out-of-towners, including Moe Gale and Decca executives, who came bearing a check and an offer of a new multiyear contract. But something about the evening had convinced Irvin Feld to doubt Rosetta's future prospects. In Russell, now calling himself Rosetta's manager, he saw more hindrance than help. Indeed, Irvin and Russell clashed during the week-long "honeymoon tour" of one-nighters that took the entire troupe south after the wedding. On their initial stop, a joint homecoming-marriage celebration concert at the Richmond City Stadium on July 5, Russell violated the terms of Rosetta's contract with the Felds by selling his own concessions. To get him to stop, Irvin finally obtained a restraining order against him. The incident was relatively minor, but it spread tension among the ranks. It also hinted at the ways that Russell, in later years, would indeed help himself to the spoils of Rosetta's stardom.

In addition to various singles, both solo and with Marie, Rosetta issued two Decca extended players (33⅓ rpm) in 1951: *Blessed Assurance: Gospel Hymns Sung By Sister Rosetta Tharpe with The Rosettes and Organ Accompaniment* and *The Wedding Ceremony of Sister Rosetta Tharpe and Russell Morrison* (Russell's name was written with a notable diminishment in typeface). Both consisted of spiritual music, but they were the fruit of contrasting endeavors. *Blessed Assurance* compiled contemporary as well as traditional material, and featured Rosetta singing—but not playing—on songs such as "What a Friend We Have in Jesus," and "Amazing Grace." It had the imprimatur of folklorist Alan Lomax, who contributed album notes that declared, "Sister Rosetta Tharpe is basically a folk-artist, with a hold on a great folk audience."[15] *The Wedding Ceremony* was a novelty item, a recording of the marriage rites in their joyfully irreverent entirety (side A), complemented by selections from the celebratory concert that followed (side B). Far from folksy, it reveled in the pleasures of ostentation and cheeky fun.

Blessed Assurance was an earnest musical endeavor, while the wedding had been a stunt to keep Rosetta in the headlines. In this respect, it succeeded—but at a price. Even as the wedding had celebrated her standing as a gospel attraction, so it compromised some people's sense of her as a legitimate artist. *Ebony* dutifully detailed the extravagance of the affair, in keeping with its habit of covering lavish society events, while at the same time holding its nose. If twenty thousand people came out for the wedding, the article implied, another twenty thousand stayed home from embarrassment or refused to patronize an event in such poor taste. In England, where she had already acquired an audience among jazz aficionados, *Melody Maker* complained that the wedding concert sounded "more like a circus performance than an act of the church." Derrick Stewart-Baxter, opining in the English *Jazz Journal International,* found the wedding to have "the atmosphere of a cheap, phony publicity stunt."[16]

Exhausted and ready to return to normal life, the Rosettes retired after the wedding tour. They had persevered through perilous weather and shows in dangerous places. They had put up politely with the intrusive oversight of Mother Bell. They had learned how to eat, sleep, and practice routines on a bus. They had made records for a major label and appeared on national television. And they had grown in their craft as individual singers and as an ensemble. "It was such a lifetime experience I wouldn't trade anything for it," says Sarah Roots, looking back. "But you couldn't pay me to go do it again, because the first year was fun and new and adventurous, but the second, it was just a job, and it was getting to be monotonous."

A few of the Rosettes followed in their mentor's footsteps. In December 1951, six months after Rosetta's wedding, both Lottie Henry and Sarah Brooks married, Sarah to Rosetta's pianist, Jimmy Roots. Both resettled in Richmond. Rosetta didn't stay there long, however. Now married for a third and final time, she was headed to Nashville and points beyond.

8

SISTER IN OPRYLAND (1952)

*Every now and then someone would come
around like Sister Rosetta Tharpe that really
made an impression on you.*
Gordon Stoker

At the conclusion of her "honeymoon" tour, Rosetta and Russell re-
treated to Barton Avenue. But while Rosetta welcomed the return home,
Russell was restless. "He didn't like Richmond," says Annie Morrison
matter-of-factly. To a self-made man who had found Pittsburgh too
cramped for his teenaged dreams and who had never lived below the
Mason-Dixon Line, Richmond seemed perilously Southern and provin-
cial, a place sorely lacking in the hustle and bustle (especially hustle) on
which Russell thrived.

Russell's antipathy to Richmond irked Marie, who stayed in touch
with Rosetta, although they once again went separate ways. It was
enough that he had insinuated himself so completely into Rosetta's orbit;
that he couldn't even bring himself to disguise his impatience with life in
Richmond seemed arrogant and selfish. Since Rosetta's money paid for
the roof over Russell's head—not to mention the car in the driveway and
the new clothes on his back—she didn't think he had a right to com-

plain. Marie had always felt wary of Russell, and this new development only fed her mistrust.

Rosetta coasted for a time on the wedding concert's adrenaline boost of publicity, spending the money she made from it as quickly as it came in. Like many musicians, especially those who grew up poor, Rosetta gave little thought to the financial details of her career. It was more satisfying to spend her earnings than to attend to the details of investing them. On the road in the South, she frequently opened her pockets to fans who clearly needed the money more than she did. She had William J. Bailey, her attorney and sometime road manager, take care of her legal affairs. To Russell she left the everyday details of collecting fees and paying the bills on time.

In 1952, Rosetta was no longer the nation's most popular gospel soloist; that title clearly belonged to Mahalia. To many listeners, Rosetta had begun to sound countrified and old-fashioned. On the other hand, she could still claim importance and even uniqueness as a gospel guitarist. The image that photographer James Kriegsmann had created around 1938—of a player organically connected to her instrument—had not lost its luster. In the postwar period, Rosetta was the only "hot" guitarist in the gospel world, not merely the only woman guitarist. Moreover, whereas many acoustic players had faltered once electric instruments became common, Rosetta made the switch gracefully. Her expressive singing was in some ways better suited to the electric instrument, with its greater sustain, than to the acoustic guitar, on which she by necessity had a "busier" style. With the electric guitar, "there's a cohesiveness between the way she plays and sings, which wasn't there in her acoustic," notes writer and guitarist Elijah Wald. "She had to deal with huge rooms of shouting parishioners. . . . She and T-Bone [Walker] to me are the two people who really invented an electric guitar that was not simply an imitation of an acoustic."

Both highly ambitious and keenly aware of the fragility of her success, Rosetta made a point of remaining open to changing musical currents. Her harshest critics leveled charges of capriciousness and opportunism at her, failing to notice her versatility and ability to adapt. Yet, despite her resourcefulness, it was unclear how and where Rosetta would carve out a place for herself amid the rapidly changing musical landscape of the 1950s. An astute listener in late 1951 could already hear murmurings of a growing impatience with the musical aesthetics of even five years earlier. Singers like Nat "King" Cole and Bing Crosby still appealed to large and diverse audiences, but more viscerally emotional and personally expressive voices were finding their way onto the hit parade. Some of these spoke in Southern accents, others in Spanish; still others —newly emboldened by their outrage at a nation that would allow black people to fight its wars but would not desegregate its schools, neighborhoods, or workplaces—experimented with assertive new sounds that coalesced into bebop, doo-wop, and mature rhythm and blues. Major labels still had a lock on many of the day's big-name musical talents, but for several years they had been feeling the pinch of the younger, more creative and risk-taking independents. In 1954, one of these small labels, Sun Records, would put out a single called "That's All Right," by an unknown singer named Elvis Presley. Before long, young people all over the United States would be clamoring for this new music and calling it rock and roll.

Country music, too, was changing quickly in the early 1950s. At Castle Studios, Decca's recently established Nashville outpost, producers Paul Cohen (brought down from Cincinnati) and Owen Bradley had begun working with a group of crackerjack young musicians including upright bassist Bobby Moore and guitarist Grady Martin, who had played on Rosetta's recordings of "Silent Night" and "White Christmas." Together, this "A-Team" of studio players were hitting their stride as the force behind an emerging "Nashville sound," smoother and more pop-friendly than the country music of yore. Along with Castle's innovative engineers, known to put a lot of "level" in their recordings, they were helping to transform the city from a Southern outpost to a music hub to rival established centers like New York and Chicago. Already, people were using different language to describe the sounds coming out of places like Nashville. In a sign of the times, *Billboard* had ceased using the word "hillbilly" and adopted the awkward, if modern-sounding, amalgam "country & western" as an official category.

It fell to Cohen and Bradley to figure out how to capitalize on these trends for Decca. By 1951, they had begun experimenting with bringing marquee names south for two- or three-week Nashville stints, in the hope of taking advantage of the national craze for country ditties like "Tennessee Waltz," sales of which were approaching those of "White

Christmas"—something inconceivable just a few years earlier.[1] Even Crosby was experimenting with a "countrypolitan" sound; that March, he would record at Castle Studios with Grady Martin.

Rosetta immediately warmed to Paul Cohen's proposition that she come down to Castle Studios for some sessions at the beginning of 1952, especially when he mentioned his intention of having her record a duet with white singer Red Foley, who helped put Nashville on the map with massive late 1940s hits like "Tennessee Saturday Night" and "Chattanoogie Shoe Shine Boy." Decca had been so certain of Foley's commercial potential that they'd signed him to a lifetime contract in 1941, and he'd spun plenty of gold for the label in the decade since.

Red and Rosetta were not friends, but they had met before, in Los Angeles around 1949, when Rosetta and the Rosettes were doing some West Coast dates. It's possible that they discussed the idea of collaborating then, but more likely, they simply said hello and chatted a bit before parting ways. It was a case of mutual admiration, according to Lottie Henry: Foley liked Rosetta's music, especially the guitar picking that set her apart from other gospel soloists, while Rosetta admired Red's big, lush baritone, the kind of warm voice that made you want to curl up inside it and take a nap. Rosetta especially enjoyed his rendition of "(There'll Be) Peace in the Valley," the Dorsey standard that was a favorite of white singers. In the 1950s, a lot of performers would try their hands at it, and although Elvis scored a million-seller with the song, Red's version is more affecting. His approach to the song's simple opening lines ("Oh well I'm tired and so weary but I must go along / Till the Lord will come and call me away") elevated it from a flimsy affirmation of faith to a profound commentary on the meaning of life lived amid harsh circumstances. The key lay in Red's languid pacing; instead of rushing the words, he sang them unhurriedly. His timing was the perfect musical analogy to the song's message of trusting in God to set the tempo of one's days.

Released the same month as Rosetta's wedding concert recording, Red's "Peace in the Valley" solidified his reputation both as a gospel singer and as a favorite of African Americans audiences. " 'Peace in the Valley' was a wonderful song," recalled Harold Bradley, producer Owen Bradley's brother. "After Red recorded it he'd attract a large black audience when he went out on the road." Such was the regard with which black Nashvillians held Red that when a young black boy died, his family asked the vocalist to sing "Steal Away to Jesus" at the boy's funeral. Red "loved and respected black people," said his son-in-law Bentley Cummins. Growing up among black people, "he got a feel for their music. He was able to project this in his performance."[2]

Lottie Henry and Sarah Brooks were among those black fans listening when Red came out with "Peace in the Valley." In fact, he had been on their radar since the late 1940s, when he became host of the *Prince Albert Show,* the Grand Ole Opry network radio broadcast. As children, they and their friends had listened to music on *Arthur Godfrey Time,* named for its folksy, ukulele-playing host. On Saturday afternoons, they looked forward to the treat of ten-cent movies starring Roy Rogers or the singing cowboy Gene Autry, the latter a particular favorite with Lottie. Their time touring with Rosetta only corroborated what they knew from experience—that Southern audiences went for both types of music.

Sarah's and Lottie's memories reveal a world in which sounds crossed social barriers, even if, as black Americans, they could not. Music was not a source of transcendence, but it could and did create overlaps and alliances that defied common wisdom about race, class, and region. "You have to understand that the South was full of country-and-western sounds—hillbilly music, we called it—and I can't recall a single Saturday night [in the early 1940s] when I didn't listen to the *Grand Ole Opry* on the radio," recalled Georgian Ray Charles.[3] LeRoy Crume, a Missouri-born singer-guitarist with gospel groups, including the Christland Singers, the Soul Stirrers, and the Staple Singers, remembers growing up in Chicago and tuning in to WJJD, the nation's first "big-city" country station, to hear Red Foley, Tex Ritter, and Lefty Frizell. When journalist Ben Grevatt interviewed Clara Ward about her favorite singers in 1959, he reported in *Billboard* that she "repeatedly referred to the great country singer, Red Foley," and his recordings of "Just a Closer Walk with Thee" and "Peace in the Valley." "These are great records and great songs," Ward told him. "And we do both of them often."[4]

Although associated with New York, the site of her nightclub and recording debuts, Rosetta had what Sarah calls a "country way"—nothing she can identify specifically, but just something you could hear in her music. Gordon Stoker of the Jordanaires attributes this to her approach to guitar. "She had a lot of guitar beat," he says, "a guitar slap-beat that a lot of country songs have." Tony Heilbut, the producer and writer who worked with Rosetta late in her career, notes that Rosetta parted ways with other Sanctified singers in her approach to meter, which on songs like "Rock, Daniel" is "much more akin to hillbilly than to the loping, graceful rhythms of gospel."

Cultural critic Greil Marcus has called Rosetta "the black church in the Grand Ole Opry," and indeed, even before she came down to Nashville to record, she had racked up considerable experience at the Ryman Auditorium, the Opry's legendary home.[5] In 1946, she brought the house down for two nights running as part of a bill with the Fairfield Four, the enormously popular Nashville-based quartet that got regular airtime on radio station WLAC. Seven thousand people came out to see Rosetta in Nashville on Thanksgiving Day, 1949, and that same year she and the Rosettes, still newcomers to the touring life, appeared on the venerated *Opry* program itself.

Like the Pentecostal Church, the Ryman Auditorium, known as the "mother church of country music," originated as an interracial institution. At midcentury, however, its heterogeneity had diminished; if anything, the field of country music was growing more segregated, the music considered more and more the exclusive bailiwick of white performers. As the 1950s wore on, it became rarer and rarer to find African American recording artists like Sister O. M. Terrell, Rosetta's contemporary in the Sanctified Church, who released several gospel-flavored "hillbilly" sides for Columbia in 1953. By 1962, the year Ray Charles—billed early in his career as "The Only Colored Singing Cowboy"—released *Modern Sounds in Country and Western Music*, such sounds were no longer associated with black musicians, largely because of marketing categories that relegated them to rhythm and blues. As O. B. McClinton, a Mississippi-born Baptist preacher's son, observed, "You can take a black guy to Nashville from right out of the cotton fields with bib overalls and two watermelons in his back pockets, and they will call him r&b. You can take a white guy in a pinstripe suit who has never seen a cotton field, take him to Nashville right out of a subway in Manhattan, and they will call him country."[6]

A duet between Rosetta, the flamboyant gospel guitarist, and Red Foley, the suave white prince of country, thus cut across the grain in 1952, even if, musically speaking, it was anything but farfetched. According to Gordon Stoker, Paul Cohen probably saw it as a way of cashing in on the combined audiences of two of Decca's top moneymakers in their respective fields. "I assure you, if Rosetta weren't selling some records at the time, Cohen would never have paired her with Red," he says.

Duets were at the peak of their popularity in the early 1950s. But what Cohen may not have realized is that, in pairing Rosetta and Red, he was helping to make musical history. In the course of commercial popular recording, had two well-known stars of different races—people who, in Tennessee, were legally prohibited from marrying—ever appeared as a duo? When Foley and Kitty Wells, country music's two biggest stars at the time, paired up in 1953 for the duet "One by One," listeners could imagine the two as a couple. Unlike Foley and Wells, Roy Rogers and Dale Evans (married in real life), or later, the African American rhythm-and-blues duo Mickey and Sylvia, Red and Rosetta could not claim the intimacy of lovers, although their voices would intertwine in song.

Despite what made Red and Rosetta's collaboration remarkable, Bobby Moore, who was in the studio with them that January day, can barely remember the session, let alone recall it as a watershed. The mood, he says, was laid back and friendly, as it always was, not solemn with any awareness of history in the making. Walking into Castle, Rosetta would have found a studio like any other: a small room with a sound board where the engineers did their mixing, and a larger room littered with a messy jumble of microphone stands, loudspeakers, and other assorted equipment. If it was like the sessions that Gordon Stoker later witnessed as a member of the Jordanaires, then Rosetta and the young A-Team musicians—Bobby and Grady Martin, as well as guitarist Jack Shook and drummer Farris Coursey—probably were having a good time while they ran through a few practice numbers under Cohen's or Bradley's watchful eye. Rosetta could be counted on to play the cutup in the studio. "She was so cute; she had such cute sayings," Stoker remembers. "She had the studio laughing. I mean, engineers laughing, everybody laughing that was around her. She had a good attitude about everything, and a good spirit."

Good-naturedly competitive when it came to her playing, Rosetta might have made musical mischief by challenging fellow guitarists Grady and Jack to a little friendly rivalry, playing their fancy riffs right back at them. Word had it she only needed to hear new things once or twice before she committed them to memory. Or, being the only woman in the room that day, she might have teased the young men, calling them her "white babies," as she had Gordon and the other Jordanaires when they toured briefly together in Nashville a few years earlier. "Everything that we did with her was with a smile," Bobby Moore remembers, comparing Rosetta with Dolly Parton, another vivacious female singer-guitarist with whom he later recorded.

The smile Moore remembers may also have been protective; as gospel musician Alfred Miller points out, flirting, as Rosetta used it, was not merely a way of getting along with the men, but a means of elevating herself above the fray of racism. Not for nothing had Rosetta instructed the members of the Rosettes to "keep a smile on your face and your big mouth shut"; she herself had learned, no doubt from hard experience, that a smile was one way to ward off what was euphemistically called "trouble." Rosetta disliked confrontation even more than she disliked dealing with other people's assumptions about her, and smiling was one strategy—a particularly effective one, it turns out—for disengaging from potentially hurtful situations.

In the morning session before Foley arrived, Rosetta, Jimmy Roots, and the Castle musicians laid down the masters of three songs, including "Tell Him You Saw Me," a revamped arrangement of the Thomas Dorsey song "If You See My Savior." Along with the Millie Kirkham Singers, Rosetta and the A-Team rendered Dorsey's ultimately hopeful narrative—about a person watching a friend die and pondering his own time-bound humanity—brooding and atmospheric, like a cowboy dirge or a blues about cosmic homelessness. Bypassing the verse, which in Dorsey's original contains a starchy description of the friend approaching death, she and the band launched right into the more emotionally immediate refrain, with its hypnotic repetitions and striking second-person address. Rosetta's performance had an uneasy solemnity, evoking the spiritual on which Dorsey's song was based.

By the time Red got to Castle for the afternoon session, the mood in the room was good, recalls Bobby Moore. The weeks leading up to the session had been difficult ones for Red; that previous November, his wife of more than a decade, Eva Overstake (better known professionally as Judy Martin), had committed suicide. There was no somberness, however, in "Have a Little Talk with Jesus," a slight, spirited number by the African American preacher-composer Cleavant Derricks, which Red and Rosetta recorded. As material, "Have a Little Talk" was a wise choice, inoffensive enough to pass the muster of those who might question the propriety of a Foley-Tharpe collaboration. Indeed, with both voices addressing themselves to God, the song deflected attention away from the relationship between the singers except as partners in prayer. In the early 1950s, it would have been difficult to come up with something less controversial than a white man and a black woman promoting Christian faith—not political protest—as a solution to everyday troubles. You don't have to carry your burdens around with you, Derricks's song insists: "*Just a little talk with Jesus makes it right.*"

The recording was pleasant, but it failed to generate spiritual heat. "She had a deep voice, he had a deep voice, but the two of them together just wasn't the greatest match," says Gordon Stoker, a little regretfully, as though he still wishes it could have worked out. Listening to the record, he notes that the difficulty of the pairing lay in Red's and Rosetta's different approaches to timbre and phrasing. Whereas Red had sweetness and depth in abundance, his voice sounded glossy and practiced next to Rosetta's, which had greater emotional immediacy. They approached rhythm differently, too. Hovering behind the beat, Rosetta sounded at times as if she was rushing to catch up to Foley, whose feet were planted more firmly atop it.

Paul Cohen must have shared Stoker's view of "Have a Little Talk with Jesus," judging by Decca's failure to market the single. Ultimately, the label slapped it on the back of an undistinguished Red Foley and the Sunshine Boys cover of Rosetta's arrangement of "Strange Things Happening Every Day" that had been languishing in the vaults for more than a year. The song never turned up on an album by either musician. Bobby Moore, who after the 1952 session teamed up with Foley on the popular television show *Ozark Mountain Jubilee,* cannot recall a single instance during that period when Red mentioned Rosetta. After 1952, Red Foley and Rosetta never recorded or performed together again.

Yet even if it is not remembered, "Have a Little Talk with Jesus" is memorable. "It's a significant record because of who was doing it," says Ron Wynn, a Nashville-based country music writer. If Red had joined Kitty Wells in the studio that day, "Have a Little Talk with Jesus" would not have told the same story. By pairing Rosetta and Red, however, the record captured a unique moment in time and space. For that fleeting moment, the tangled relationships of black and white, of country and gospel, came clearly into focus, illuminating their complex webs of artistic influence and the centrality of Rosetta in Nashville, the home of country music. On "Have a Little Talk," Red and Rosetta—and the histories they embodied—"talked" briefly with each other. Their record went on to be shelved on the B-side of history, but it still told a vivid story.

9

DON'T LEAVE ME HERE (1953–1957)

*I heard people talking about it, you know, "Rosetta's singing
blues," and well, she always had that bluesy-type guitar ...
[and] even when you're singing about the Lord you're singing
about love. A man sings blues, he's singing about the love of
a woman, or 'I had a woman did me wrong' and all that kind
of stuff. Telling a story. But, well, a lot of people see it different.*
LeRoy Crume

None of the sides Rosetta recorded at Castle Studios in January 1952 ever
came to anything. She refused, however, to be discouraged. At Paul Cohen's urging, she returned to Nashville in March and again in December, recording another five solo sides and four new duets with Marie. Of
these, "I Just Couldn't Be Contented," featuring the Southwind Singers,
a quartet who occasionally made appearances at her live shows, recalled
Rosetta's nimble work with the Dependable Boys, and "Let's Go On,"
with Marie, garnered a solid review in *Cash Box*. But the songs lacked the
commercial legs of Rosetta's records of the late 1940s. It seemed as though
nothing—not a pairing with Red Foley, a reunion session with Marie, or
a collaboration with a male quartet—could restore Rosetta to her former
stardom.

In her grand shows with Marie, according to onetime Dixie Hummingbird member Barney Parks, "people would almost break in" to see Rosetta. Within a year or so of the wedding, she was doing shows in out-of-the-way churches and auditoriums where the people were long on love but short on money. The people of Seaford, Delaware, were so thrilled to have her at Frederick Douglass High School in August 1952 that they burst into applause and wouldn't stop clapping, prompting Rosetta to laugh and throw kisses at everyone, recalls William Robinson, then a star-struck ten-year-old. So many people had to be turned away from the high school that Rosetta offered to return the next evening to do a freewill offering at the Seaford Church of God. At that event, the grateful crowd overflowed into the church dining hall.

Without the means to draw attention to herself—whether through a new collaborator or a hit record—Rosetta all but disappeared from the popular and trade presses, important conduits of her national fame. The quality of her bookings waned, and she found herself playing smaller venues, or programs on which she served as the supporting act for bigger names. Even when Rosetta sold out a big venue, as she and Marie did in a 1953 reunion concert at the Booker T. Washington Auditorium in New Orleans, a city the two had last visited in 1948, her appearance evoked fond memories of the good old days, not visions of the future. The black teenagers tuning in to New Orleans's bustling r&b scene might have been forgiven for thinking of Sister Rosetta Tharpe as "old people's music"— the sort of thing their mothers or aunts hummed along to while making Sunday dinner, but certainly nothing that spoke to them.

Rosetta's struggles to develop new material after her Nashville sessions coincided with new initiatives at Decca to reach out to the rapidly expanding rhythm-and-blues market. In July 1953, the label brought producer Bobby Shad over from Mercury to head up its r&b division. Shad's mission was simple: to beef up rhythm-and-blues production, not only by hiring new talent, but also by capitalizing on the talent of already signed Decca artists. With a mandate from the label, Shad thus began working with a diverse roster of musicians, including stalwarts like Rosetta and Louis Jordan, as well as newcomers Little Esther, formerly of the Johnny Otis Revue, and Arthur Prysock, whose "I Didn't Sleep a Wink Last Night" was an r&b hit for Decca in 1952. By late summer, there was evidence that Shad's work was paying off. In August 1953, Decca released seven rhythm-and-blues songs; in September, Shad upped that number to ten.

Rosetta's studio work reflected the label's increasingly urgent need to attract young consumers. In New York sessions that summer and fall, she recorded the masters for nine new songs, including several with pointed rhythm-and-blues appeal. On "Crying in the Chapel," she covered the country-gospel ballad that was a crossover hit in the summer of 1953 for the Orioles, a popular "bird" group (others included the Ravens and the Flamingos) led by gospel-trained lead tenor Sonny Til. "There's Peace in Korea," released as the B-side of "Crying in the Chapel," was another departure for Rosetta: a topical song recorded on the very day President Dwight Eisenhower signed the armistice marking the official end of the war.[1]

She also did more traditional gospel fare, including a soulful and heartfelt reprise of Dorsey's "Hide Me in Thy Bosom," which Decca released under the title "Feed Me Jesus." The recording even features a short spoken-word introduction: "This is a song I want all my many friends to pray along with me," Rosetta says. "It is a song that's praying to God." Unlike the song marketed under the title "Rock Me"—which she recorded in her 1938 debut and again in 1941 in a big-band arrangement with Lucky Millinder—"Feed Me Jesus" is a slow-paced showcase of Rosetta's ability to dig deep into a lyric. (Through overdubbing, she even answers her own call.) When she sings the words "rock me in the cradle," there is no room for secular misinterpretation: the address is quite clearly to God, a plea for protection and succor.

Given that at her next studio session, four months later in November 1953, she would record straight-out, no-denying-it rhythm and blues, "Feed Me Jesus" was an interesting choice. "I think Rosetta's career is bookended by the song 'Rock Me,'" says gospel scholar and producer Tony Heilbut, comparing Rosetta's different versions of the Dorsey song she once was accused of stealing. Perhaps her suggestion that the audience "pray along with me" contained a bit of foreshadowing?

Indeed, it's difficult to surmise why Rosetta decided to delve into material she had publicly sworn off since the days of "I Want a Tall Skinny Papa." She may well have been convinced, by Bob Shad and others, that the only way to breathe new life into her career was to pitch herself to a younger public, or she may have hoped, against the odds, that a new generation of listeners would embrace her if only she met them halfway. Perhaps she still had hopes of capturing the audience that eluded her when she and Red put out "Have a Little Talk with Jesus."

Or perhaps Rosetta—said by Marie and Mother Bell to possess a gift of insight as well as music—intuited the synthesis of gospel and rhythm and blues that Ray Charles would achieve with the early 1955 release of "I Got a Woman." Based chord-for-chord on the hymn "Jesus Loves Me," Charles' song, which went to number two on the r&b chart, demonstrated that gospel could be transformed into popular music with the simplest turn of a lyric. It also set Charles on the path to being a very wealthy man. With Ray and other church-rooted artists blazing a trail onto the charts, the allure of secular success was stronger than ever. "People were always probing her, prodding her: Sing some blues," recalls Alfred Miller. "They told her that she would get filthy rich from it."

Ira Tucker Jr. recalls that "there was a definite effort to go after" Rosetta to go the way of her friend Ray, but that she refused. "I asked her, I remember asking her, 'Why don't you do this?' She said, no—she called me Brother—she said, 'No, Brother, I'm a little bit too old for that.' . . . She said, 'Maybe one or two minutes you're out there, but then you're gone.' That's exactly what she said, one or two minutes you're out there, then you're gone. And she never went over. She never changed her mind neither. Even though she did some other things, she was just like never really considered anything other than a gospel act, you know."

Rosetta's 1954 release "Don't Leave Me Here to Cry," backed with "What Have I Done," was one of these "other things." Both were fairly standard fare, secular blues ballads that required Rosetta to play the role of the forsaken femme, a far cry from the snazzy and self-assured "hot" gospeller. In "What Have I Done," she asks Cupid, the god of romance, rather than Jesus, the divine emblem of Christian *caritas,* to explain why her lover has left her. Not since the secular second verse of her 1938 recording of "The Lonesome Road," with its similar lament about lost love, had Rosetta so opened herself to expressing loneliness and heartache untouched by divine consolation. The wretched and self-abnegating sentiments of "Don't Leave Me Here to Cry" were even more uncharacteristic for Rosetta, who usually sang about faith, not despair, and certainly not about misery caused by a lover.

Rosetta was far less convincing singing pitifully about romance than she was roaring the glory of God. Wacky and off-center, "Don't Leave Me Here" zigzags between self-conscious pathos and almost vaudevillian comedy, landing somewhere in the realm of satire. In the vein of Ruth Brown's "Mama, He Treats Your Daughter Mean," another song that cries heartache but conveys cheeky resolve, "Don't Leave Me Here" presents Rosetta's voice as big and powerful, not what you might expect from someone awash in romantic desolation. Then, at the instrumental bridge —that part of her gospel songs where she typically launches into an ecstatic guitar solo—seriousness gives way to levity and misery dissolves into satire. With a crocodile tear in her voice, Rosetta makes a U-turn from Desolation Street, testifying about buying her lover a Cadillac, clothing, and three diamond rings, begging him to stay for the goods if not for her. Delivering her lines with gleeful overstatement, she invites listeners to identify with, and perhaps even laugh at, a character (Rosetta herself?) who *knows* better but can't or doesn't want to do anything about it.

Unlike "Have a Little Talk With Jesus," released on Decca's "popular" series but then allowed to wither on the vine, "Don't Leave Me Here to Cry" and "What Have I Done" were widely promoted. The record got big billing in the trade press, appearing that spring in a full-page *Billboard* advertisement that included notices of recent releases by Marie, Ella Fitzgerald, and Louis Armstrong, among others. "Look to Decca for Great Rhythm & Blues & Jazz," the ad decreed, grasping in vain for the right "big tent" under which to market such different musicians.

Yet what was even more noteworthy than the label's promotion of Rosetta as a rhythm-and-blues artist was its flagrant juxtaposition of sacred and secular work. Listing her most recent gospel record, "Feed Me Jesus" backed with "Smile It Through," directly underneath her rhythm-and-blues debut, Decca made it all but impossible *not* to notice that Rosetta was delving into both realms at the same time. Crossing over was bad enough, but this was rubbing salt into the wound. How could the audience trust Rosetta's sincerity as a spiritual entertainer if they couldn't determine which side Rosetta was on?

In a 1960 interview, gospel and classically trained singer Roy Hamilton, who had several r&b hits around the same time that Rosetta released "Don't Leave Me Here to Cry," recalled his own musical struggles, putting the perilousness of Rosetta's move into perspective. "When I had the chance to sing pops for money, I had a long talk with my minister," he said. "If you make the jump to pop, there is no turning back. You have to understand the spiritual audience. They feel that the singers they like are somebody special—clean and untarnished by the world. If such a person, virtually idolized by the people, makes the jump and fails, he can

Billboard, April 24, 1954, advertising both Rosetta's and Marie's r&b and gospel releases simultaneously. Courtesy of Universal Music Enterprises.

never go back to the spiritual audience and get the same acceptance. He is no longer clean and untarnished."[2]

For the people Hamilton had in mind, gospel and blues *were* different, and the distinction was moral rather than musical. A conventional ballad, "Don't Leave Me Here to Cry" was rhythmically tame and instrumentally bland, and yet it deviated from gospel in banishing God to the margins of its concerns. Although the singer assures her lover that God will bless him if he stays with her, beyond this small and rather coerced consideration of a divine presence, there's no sense that the lovers inhabit a world determined by that presence. From a Pentecostal Christian viewpoint, on the other hand, faith is the salve that would heal the sorrow at the center of "Don't Leave Me Here to Cry"; indeed, such sorrow required the "little talk with Jesus" that Rosetta and Red Foley had so enthusiastically sung about.

Despite the money Decca invested in floating it to a broad public, "Don't Leave Me Here to Cry" sank without a trace. Not only had Rosetta alienated her gospel fans, but the young rhythm-and-blues audience she had hoped to attract with it simply did not materialize. As a result, she found herself mired in the greatest identity crisis of her career. While she was trying to satisfy producers at Decca, it seemed, the gospel field had passed her by. In December 1953, the African American picture magazine *Our World* published a long piece about the "new rage" in spiritual singing, a twenty-eight-year-old Philadelphian who had become a prosperous star while turning down offers of "as much as $10,000 to switch from gospel songs to the blues."[3] The "diminutive" new gospel VIP was Clara Ward of the Ward Singers, who had come to prominence in 1950 with the magisterial "Surely God Is Able." Given how African American news outlets revered her, she seemed like the second coming of Mahalia Jackson, but as a singer, Clara did not seriously challenge Mahalia's towering status. For one thing, she would never equal Mahalia in finding favor with the masses of white Americans, as Mahalia did in the '50s, especially after the debut of *The Mahalia Jackson Show* in 1954. Yet Clara had crowd-pleasing charm that distinguished her from other talented women gospel musicians. Slim and light-skinned, considered prettier and daintier than "Mother" Mahalia or the Ward Singers' own magnificent Marion Williams, she was a gospel princess well matched to an era and a culture that valued petiteness and refinement as womanly ideals— even making size a measure of class and taste. As Jackie Kennedy would be lauded for bringing stylish elegance to the White House six years later, so Clara Ward was acclaimed as gospel's glamorous First Lady, musically gifted but also reassuringly, conventionally feminine.

"Don't Leave Me Here to Cry" were words that, in 1954, Rosetta might as well have been singing to her fans. Where was this absent lover? After the disappointing results of her one and only r&b single, Rosetta must have known that it was not in the cards for her to make millions as a secular artist. Looking back, not many people think Rosetta made a wise decision, although Walter Godfrey, Marie's road manager when she sang r&b in the early 1960s, believes Rosetta could have made it in rhythm and blues had she really wanted to. "I think Rosetta's fans were more devastated that Rosetta would [sing rhythm and blues] than Marie's. She was always the better known of the two. I do believe that had Rosetta gone forward—I don't think she was too old—but if her heart was in it, she would have been successful. She always had that flair."

The flair, but not the heart. Godfrey's point was hammered home that same year when Chess Records' artists Little Walter and the Jukes released "My Babe," a rewrite of "This Train"—Rosetta's hit of 1939—with lyrics and arrangement by resident Chess polymath Willie Dixon. As pioneering black radio personality James "Early" Byrd notes, Dixon took "This Train" and gave it secular lyrics, transforming the traditional lines about the procession of the saints to heaven into a story about a woman who won't stand for her man's cheating. In a different world, perhaps a world in which she had wanted it more, "My Babe" could have been Rosetta's; after all, her "This Train" had swing and energy to spare. But was America ready for a powerful, electric-guitar-playing black woman gospel musician leading the charge toward the rock-and-roll future?

Although it must have been dispiriting, if not outright depressing, for Rosetta to hit such walls, she toured the new material—including unreleased secular songs—in concert with Marie. In 1954 and 1955, the two frequently traveled together, doing nontraditional shows that mixed gospel with rhythm and blues. Occasionally they were joined by Sister Wynona Carr, an up-and-coming gospel singer on the Specialty label whose early career, down to her professional name, had been modeled after Rosetta's—much to Carr's frustration. "Gee whiz, why do I have to have a Sister Carr handle," she wrote in a letter to Art Rupe, Specialty's owner, who had insisted on affixing the "Sister" prefix to her name, to milk the similarity between the sounds of Carr's first recordings and Rosetta's work with the Sam Price trio. "I hate it. Mahalia doesn't have one. That sounds like I'm 90 years old. Must I have it?"[4]

Ironically, this was a time when Rosetta was receiving some of the best and most comprehensive reviews of her career—not from gospel fans, but from jazz critics. Her recent moves away from straight gospel were, it turned out, highly appreciated by people uninterested in the religious meaning of her material. When she and Marie did a run in February 1955 at the Village Vanguard, the downtown New York jazz institution known at the time as an interracial gathering spot for left-wing intellectuals, a *Variety* reporter rhapsodized about their performance. "The team concertizes with 'Shadrach' and 'Daniel in the Lion's Den' and then renders unto Caesar a series of racy blues," he wrote. "Indeed this duo could fit into virtually any vocal situation. Their primitives have a universal appeal. They can convey a message from pulpits and they can be successful in saloons. Of course, their rhythm and blues are very unclerical indeed, but they do epitomize the wide range of feelings that the American Negro experiences, all of it told in melodic and rhythmic terms that make them top entertainment even for sophisticates."[5]

To be sure, there was plenty of stereotyping in such praise, particularly in the sociological nugget about the "wide range of feelings" of "the American Negro." Yet the review also recognized Rosetta's talent and universality, without the usual anxiety about her gospel credibility. Jazz critic Nat Hentoff voiced similar feelings about Rosetta and Marie's performance in a 1955 encore presentation of John Hammond's From Spirituals to Swing concert. The two women "build each number toward a swinging, emotional climax that eventually draws everyone in the room into the act with them, clapping, beating their feet, nodding or just plain moved out of their 'sophisticated' complacency," he wrote in *Down Beat*, echoing not only the *Variety* review, but coverage of From Spirituals to Swing itself. "The duo sings breaks like jazz instrumentalists; they move with a rock-steady, pulsating rhythm that is the beat behind rhythm and blues, and the visual effect of these two unaffected women, singing with enormous warmth and pleasure, is enough to make one wish that more singers of whatever style would invade life with similar dedication."[6]

Not since the early days of her Broadway stardom, when white swing connoisseurs offered up loud hosannas for her authenticity, had Rosetta received such high-wattage recognition. Yet the price of this recognition —as Ralph Ellison might have noted—was paradoxically a sort of invisibility. It was not just the attribution of Rosetta and Marie's "unaffected" performance to natural enthusiasm rather than to painstaking professionalism; there was also the annoyance of having to be discovered all over again. When, later in his write-up, Hentoff estimated that Rosetta's shows at the Vanguard ended a fifteen-year absence from nightclubs, he omitted from his calculations the most productive years of her career, which included hundreds of appearances at clubs and theaters. Hentoff wasn't ignorant of Rosetta's productivity during this period; he merely meant—and took for granted that his reader understood—that ever since her days at Café Society, she had not appeared regularly at venues like the Vanguard.

Jazz critics such as Hentoff appreciated Rosetta for what she was not: namely, a teenager. In 1955, she would turn forty years old—only five years past the midpoint of the Biblical lifespan of threescore and ten, and still robust as ever as an entertainer, but a veritable relic in an industry increasingly focused on young audiences. As a concept and a postwar demographic reality, the teenager drove the record business of the mid-1950s. As imagined by marketing departments, she or he had needs and desires separate from those of adults, and suffered from angst brought about by romantic desire, social anxiety, or—if she was a girl—a blemished reputation. So ubiquitous was this figure that a two-month period spanning late 1955 and early 1956 saw the release of no fewer than five songs featuring some form of the word "teenager" in their titles: "Teen-Age Prayer," "Teen-Age Heart," "Teen-Ager," "Teen-Age Meeting," and "Nina, Queen of the Teeners." Shortly thereafter, the Columbia film *Rock Around the Clock* went into production, launching the genre of the high-school teen flick. One magazine's pronouncement made the point succinctly: "Teeners Wielding New Influence on Singles Record Market."[7]

Two other teenagers were in the news in 1955, but for very different reasons. Before he was lynched on a visit to see relatives in Mississippi, allegedly for whistling at a white woman, Emmett Till was like other fourteen-year-old black boys from Chicago enjoying the summer off from school. As Till's classmate Richard Heard recalled, "That was a good time because where we grew up [on the South Side], a lot of guys listened to the Moonglows, the Coasters, the Flamingos and the Spaniels.... We'd try to imitate them in our little singing groups. It was a lot of fun."[8] The murder made international headlines when Till's mother, Mamie Till, a member of Rosetta and Katie Bell's church at Fortieth and State Streets, decided to have an open-casket funeral. Thousands of people lined up outside Fortieth Street—by then called Roberts Temple, after its founder —to bear witness to Emmett's mutilated body, images of which fed growing African American impatience with the pace of postwar civil rights change.

The other teenager in the news was Elvis Presley, widely rumored to have remarked, "The Lord messed up on me in two ways. He didn't make me black and he didn't make me a bass singer." The summer before Till's murder, when he was nineteen, Presley released "That's All Right," the single that launched his career. Through subsequent records and television appearances, the greasy-haired, hip-swiveling white boy with a "black" sound and a sassy, sexy charm inalterably shifted the terrain of American popular culture. Among other things, Elvis took the signifiers of black American sound and style, including gospel, and reinterpreted them for a mainstream youth audience that he, but not his black models, could access. The Elvis effect was two-sided: black music and style suddenly gained new popularity, but the conduit of these new sounds and styles did not have to be black.

Alice Walker's "Nineteen Fifty-Five," a 1970s-era short story that fictionalizes Elvis's rise to fame, explores these issues from the perspective of Gracie Mae Still, a middle-aged African American woman from rural Mississippi. In Walker's story, Traynor, a young Elvis figure, becomes an overnight sensation when he releases a recording of a song originally written and performed by Gracie Mae. Yet the attention, fame, and money Traynor receives leave him feeling empty and befuddled; why, he wonders, has he been crowned "The Emperor of Rock and Roll" while Gracie Mae is "Nobody from Notasulga," a forgotten singer who never rose above regional celebrity? Walker patterns the characters in "Nineteen Fifty-Five" on Elvis and Big Mama Thornton, the big-voiced singer who first popularized the Leiber and Stoller song "Hound Dog," scoring a major hit with it on the r&b chart before Elvis made it a pop sensation. But "Nineteen Fifty-Five" also characterizes Rosetta, who ironically found herself overshadowed in the mid-1950s by the very force of the rock-and-roll music she had helped to unleash upon the world.[9]

In February 1956, when "Heartbreak Hotel" was in high rotation on major radio stations throughout the nation, Rosetta arrived at West Fifty-second Street for her last Decca sessions. She had been out of the studio since 1954, the year her contract with the label expired. Joining her in New York were her old Richmond pals, the Harmonizing Four, and a house band that included noted blues-jazz guitarist Everett Barksdale on guitar. Although her vocal range was not what it had been in October 1938, when she cut her first Decca recordings, the day found her in good voice, and together with the other singers and musicians she produced four tracks, including "Don't You Weep, O Mary, Don't You Weep" and "I've Done Wrong," a light, lively jubilee song that narrates the well-known Bible story of the prodigal son. Working with a rhythmic background provided by the Harmonizing Four, Rosetta sing-raps, like an improvisational "whooping" preacher delivering an instructive Sunday sermon, about the son who disobeys his father but eventually tires of his dissolute ways. When she calls out the penitential title phrase, her mood is jubilant, a celebration of second (or third or fourth) chances. The bright conviction in her voice makes it easy to imagine her there in the studio, gospel's prodigal daughter, the rebellious one who strays from the fold but who returns again and again to the musical traditions that sustain her.

Returning to gospel was apparently Rosetta's objective. Early in 1956, some time before Decca issued "I've Done Wrong," she released a press statement announcing her future plans. "The husky-voiced vocalist, who once combined night club singing with her gospel career, recently abandoned café circuits to devote all her time to religious music," *Jet* magazine told its readers that March, in an article that simultaneously announced Rosetta's forthcoming appearance on CBS's *Stage Show*.[10] Rosetta's decision meant that once again, and for the last time, she and Marie would part professional ways. While Rosetta had recommitted herself to gospel—at least publicly—Marie had signed a contract with Baton Records, an independent label, hoping to "concentrate on pop and rhythm and blues material." While she never was to Baton what Ruth Brown was to Atlantic, Marie toured in the late 1950s and 1960s, sometimes as a solo act, often on huge r&b shows featuring multiple acts. When her music failed to find an audience, she took a day job at Blue Shield, working first as a telephone operator and later as a manager. It was the first time in years that she had a nine-to-five job.

It was around the time of Rosetta's re-return to gospel that Creadell Copeland last saw her perform. Copeland, a founding member of the

Chicago-based gospel quartet the Highway QCs—the group that Sam Cooke sang with before he joined the Soul Stirrers—was in Philadelphia with the QCs for a program, when he found out that Rosetta was singing just across the Delaware River in Camden, New Jersey.

> I just remembered her from her records, and I had somebody from the Philadelphia area to carry me and the group over there so we could see her. I wanted to see her. And we did, we went there, she was working alone, and it was a small church setting. And there wasn't very many people there.... [And] I was sort of hurt, because she seemed like she was very sad, seemed as if she was not enjoying being in those circumstances. And I do remember her records were very popular.... So at that point I really didn't know how to feel about it, but I didn't enjoy looking at her in that situation.... I remember her records and I know they were too good ... for her to be playing a room like that.

Copeland was further surprised to find that Rosetta didn't seem to know who the Highway QCs were. He wondered what this meant, whether it was a sign of fatigue, isolation, or estrangement from the gospel world.

Different people offer quite different pictures of Rosetta in these years. For Copeland, she seemed a sad figure, musically and personally diminished. In contrast, Bertha Robinson, wife of the late gospel singer Cleophus Robinson, remembers Rosetta as still "number one," even though she lacked "backing"—all of the secondary and tertiary structures of management and support that go into the making and sustaining of a great artist. "Oh she had an audience wherever she went," Robinson says, referring to the shows her husband booked at venues like the Kiel Auditorium in downtown St. Louis. But she believes Rosetta never had the proper industry backing. "I don't think that Rosetta had that opportunity [that Mahalia had]. Had she had that opportunity she would have been equally as great."

In the mind of Annie Morrison, then operating an elevator at the Carlyle Hotel at Fifteenth and Poplar Streets in Philadelphia, Rosetta was just another celebrity. She was one of the stars you could see in those days at either of the two downtown establishments—the Carlyle and the Chesterfield, at Broad and Oxford Streets—that catered to black patrons.

As a hotel worker, Annie was privy to the behind-the-scenes goings-on in the black entertainment world, and saw firsthand how some people, even religious people, could be led astray. By 1957, the year Russell first started flirting with her, she harbored no illusions that gospel musicians —Rosetta included—were any more disciplined than their secular-music peers.

A few musicians remember being approached around this time by Rosetta, apparently on the lookout for a male collaborator to reenergize her act. To singer-guitarist Kip Anderson, then still under the tutelage of singer Madame Edna Gallmon Cooke, she pitched the idea of pairing up to be "the Mickey and Sylvia of gospel." She made an almost identical appeal to South Carolina–based musician Drink Small. "She wanted a partnership. She said we could be another Les Paul and Mary Ford," he remembers. Yet neither musician joined up with Rosetta, Anderson because he was young, Small because he considered Rosetta "a nice-looking lady who talked a lot of trash." Although he admired her music, Small was wary of partnering with a woman like Rosetta—someone who threatened to "make a sweet man out of me."

Small's impressions do more than recall the Sugar Mama figure Rosetta evokes in her campy delivery of "Don't Leave Me Here to Cry." They also hint at the difficulties that often arose when women musicians attempted to exercise professional authority over men. In the recording studio, a man might take orders from another man, but coming from a woman those same directives could seem officious and overbearing, a reversal of the "natural" order of things. Men going back to Sammy Price in the 1940s chafed at Rosetta's "bossiness." Although he says it with some hesitation, LeRoy Crume, whom Rosetta recruited in the late 1950s to play rhythm guitar, admits to feeling put off, both in his specific experience with Rosetta and on principle, by the idea of a female superior. "Well, now, I know I'm talking to a woman now, but you know, women when they're in the power seat, you know, it kind of... it might be a little bit too bossy and you know, dominating, and I can't deal with that." Among other things, he says, Rosetta could be a maddening combination of demanding and indecisive. In the middle of a song—on stage, even—she would turn around and yell at him to turn the volume up or down. "Seems like she couldn't make up her mind what she wanted." Rosetta wanted Crume, a versatile singer and instrumentalist, to join her on

tour, but he declined. As much as he admired her, he couldn't see working with Rosetta; besides, with Sam Cooke on his team, he had his own
career to attend to.

In the spring of 1957, Rosetta received shocking news: the bank had re-
possessed her house on Barton Avenue because she had failed to keep
up with the mortgage payments. On April 25, after the expiration of the
legally mandated waiting period, during which notice of the forfeiture of
the lien ran in the Richmond *Times-Dispatch,* 2306 Barton was sold at
auction for $9,050, the amount that was owed to the bank. The loss of
what she had cherished as home came hard to Rosetta, Marie remembers.
It was especially devastating because Russell had let the bills go unpaid
—"accidentally on purpose," according to one of Rosetta's friends. It's
possible, however, that Rosetta had run short of money. Alfred Miller,
for one, worried that Russell was spending her into the ground. "Russell loved money," he says. "He loved big rings on his finger. He loved to
smoke the best cigars and to wear the best shoes, two three hundred dollars. Of course, with all the money she was making—and it didn't cost
him anything—so he dressed the best, and she performed. And he managed everything. He took over." As Ira Tucker Jr. sees it, even if Russell
spent her money, Rosetta "made Russell pay." "She might be out there on
the stage, burning it up, right, but she would burn Russell up when she
wasn't on the stage. 'Cause she made him *work.* When she was in the diva
role, Russell was the gopher.... It was, 'Russell'...and he'd [say], 'OK,
Sister.'"

If Rosetta blamed Russell for the loss, why did she stay with him after 2306 Barton was sold out from under her? She could have fired a blun-
dering or underhanded manager, but she could not fire a husband; she
could only divorce him, and perhaps that was not an option she wanted
to pursue. So after April 1957 she picked herself up and moved on. She
sold the bus, and she and Russell took up semipermanent residence at the
Carlyle, the hotel where Annie Morrison worked. The hotel wasn't home,
but Rosetta had plenty of friends in Philadelphia, including Ira Tucker,
Marion Williams, and Willa Ward. And after years of touring, as she
liked to brag, she could perform miracles with a hot plate.

With Russell's help, meanwhile, she was also cooking up plans. Back
in March 1939, in her first major interview as Broadway's hot new

"swinger of spirituals," a twenty-three-year-old Rosetta Vashti Tharpe had boldly announced her intention to tour in Europe. "It'd be silly of me to go until I'm well enough known to demand the right sort of price," she told the reporter, pioneering black newspaperwoman Marvel Cooke, demonstrating that she, too, was a cultured person.[11] Of course, Rosetta was not thinking merely in terms of dollars; she was also articulating a dream held by black American women ever since Josephine Baker had achieved superstardom in Paris in the 1920s. Notwithstanding the fact that "La Baker's" success was predicated on her persona as an exotic primitive, her career exemplified the relative opportunities available to African American entertainers in Europe, where racial segregation was less pervasive than in the United States, and where there was notable enthusiasm, especially after the war, for black musicians. Although Rosetta enjoyed an audience in Britain from the early 1940s, tensions between British and American musicians' unions made it impossible for her to follow the path taken by Baker and singer-dancer Florence Mills for nearly two decades.

That changed, however, in November 1957. "After a very successful concert tour of this country's leading churches and auditoriums, Sister Rosetta Tharpe will leave on November 19 for an extended tour of England and Scotland," an item in *Billboard* announced. The announcement included a curious postscript: "Due to the popularity of Sister Tharpe, a line of ladies' hosiery has been named after her."[12] No other evidence survives of a Rosetta Tharpe hosiery line, a concept that was likely dreamed up to compete with Mahalia Jackson's semisuccessful ventures into canned goods and fried-chicken franchises. But the part about a U.K. tour was true. Not long before the British Invasion of 1960s rock and roll, Britain was about to experience its very own Rosetta Invasion.

BRIDGE

"THE MEN WOULD STAND BACK"

If you get carried away in your work you really
don't know if you are a woman or a man.
Mary Lou Williams, in a 1957 interview with Marian McPartland

Rosetta played the guitar like she owned it. Even in moments of performance when she was "in the possession" of the Holy Ghost spirit,
she possessed the instrument with electrifying physicality.[1] To watch her
play was to be aware of how fully she threw herself—quite literally—into
making her music, how she used her body to coax different sounds out of
the guitar, even as she swayed to the rhythms she produced. She loved
showing off with hot-dog moves. On an episode of *TV Gospel Time,*
which she hosted in the 1960s, she sang "Down by the Riverside" while
strutting like a peacock in a circle, as if she was out for a walk and her guitar was along for the ride. When she played, she dug in, not only with her
fingertips but with her arms, shoulders, and even her neck. The woman
with the showbiz smile sometimes grimaced like a weightlifter; at other
times, she closed her eyes and nodded her head gently back and forth, as
though savoring the taste of something delicious. She gazed upward, she
made eye contact with the audience, she focused inward, concentrating
all of her intellectual and emotional force on the music. But she never,
ever looked down at the strings.

Virtually all of these characteristics of Rosetta's guitar playing are associated with masculinity, which is why her fans sometimes said she could play "like a man." The phrase was offered as a compliment, and yet it spoke less to Rosetta's agility with a guitar than to the speaker's preconceptions about the embodiment of guitar virtuosity. In reality, and like every great player, Rosetta played like herself, forging her own style through the power of her imagination, careful observation, and unceasing practice. "With her it was a gift, it was an individual thing," says Marie Knight, who recalls many an evening when Rosetta would keep her up at night with her playing. "She didn't copy off of no one."

Men even played like *her*. Few of Rosetta's male peers, in gospel or any other field, would have cared to admit the fact, however, especially in an age when masculinity and guitar skills were inextricably linked. As late as 1969, a historian of the guitar could note the instrument's female shape and associate facility in playing it, particularly in rock and roll, with a man's "playing" of a woman's body. One scholar has even dubbed the electric guitar a "technophallus," in recognition of the way male players have used it to link technical proficiency with sexual prowess.[2]

This is an old story—the guitar as symbol of male potency, an instrument of masturbatory male heroics and masculine glory. But what, then, of a woman like Rosetta, who was as much a master of her instrument as any man?

Ella Mitchell, a founding member of New York's Original Gospel All-Stars, recalls:

> I remember at the Apollo Theater when she would perform she would pick the guitar of course and sing.... [The male gospel groups] thought they had the greatest guitar players in the world. And she would say, Come up here, baby. C'mon honey! In front of the whole audience! C'mon, can you do this? And she'd go: *do dodo do dum dumdum dum du du do.* And then as she was doing it, he would try doing it, he'd go: *didididididumdi.* She'd say, Uh-uh, baby, you gotta do it like this: *downdowndowndown.* Oh she would tear it up! Oo-oow! And that's how she would battle against the other guitar players. It was like a battle. Listen, the whole audience went crazy. It wasn't just no ladies. They would holler, Go on Rosetta, play them down!... The audience would clap and scream. Yes, it was something!

That Rosetta beat out men in guitar battles at the Apollo did not nec-essarily mean that men or women in her audience ascribed masculin-ity to her; indeed, it was precisely her femininity that posed the greatest threat to the male guitarists' identity as properly masculine men. "You had to get on [stage]," explains Mitchell, referring to the men who bat-tled Rosetta, "or otherwise you was a sissy."

"The fellows would look at her, and I don't know whether there was envy or what, but sometimes she would play rings around them," recalls Inez Andrews, who also appeared with Rosetta on gospel programs at the Apollo. "She didn't care who they were. And we used to stand up and watch her from the sideline, at that time we were doing a lot of travel-ing with the Soul Stirrers and the Caravans.... And Sam Cooke used to tease all of the guitar players, and say, Man, I wouldn't let a woman out-play me!"

Having a woman outplay a man could upset the "natural" order of things: both the pecking order of gender, in which men are supposed to be stronger and more competent than women, and the stability of alpha-male sexuality, in which real men never lose face in front of other men. "She was the only lady that I know that would pick a guitar, and the men would stand back," says Inez Andrews. Even today, men "don't give her no credit because she was competition. You *know* a man's not gonna sit up and say a woman can beat him doing nothing! He's not gonna do that, oh no. Well, you see men have egos...they don't want to be deflated." Former Rosette Sarah Roots is also blunt. "When people said [that she played like a man]," she says, "I think they meant that she could play good because they thought, oh, women couldn't do anything."

The irony, or perhaps the tragedy, of such thinking is that Rosetta never thought of herself as a "woman" guitarist. Indeed, she and others in the gospel world had plenty of models of female guitar players, par-ticularly in the realm of Sanctified religion. Like pianist Mary Lou Wil-liams, another female instrumentalist sometimes said to play "like a man," Rosetta cared about playing well, not about playing well for a woman. As Williams told fellow musician Marian McPartland in a 1957 *Down Beat* interview, "You've got to *play*, that's all. They don't think of you as a woman if you can really play."[3]

On the other hand—and here she differs from Williams and other women in the world of modern jazz, who were more surrounded by male players of their own instruments—Rosetta was often willing to call attention to her novelty value as a female gospel guitarist. Sometimes this became part of her routine, especially later, when she played before audiences likely to view her in the context of rock and roll. "You never saw a woman play a guitar like this before," Ralph Gleason, jazz critic for the *San Francisco Chronicle,* recalls her announcing to a crowd at the Hungry i nightclub in 1964. According to Gleason, she said this "smiling, her hair pulled high on her head and her strong arm grasping an electric guitar. She slid her hand up and down the neck. 'I play it wrong, but I play it!' she said."[4]

Paradoxically, Rosetta's "aw shucks" modesty about playing wrong asserted how *right* she could play. At the same time, in the quintessentially phallic gesture of stroking the guitar neck, she let her listeners know that she was a force to be reckoned with, not a guitarist to be treated with patronizing good-for-a-girl approval. No less self-assured a rhythm-and-blues singer than Etta James, who later made a career of playing the bad girl, was blown away the first times she saw Rosetta.

> Even though I was just a child, I knew immediately that this woman was playing a different kind of music. It was gospel, but the way she put it across, in her bluesy-jazzy style, was a real "revelation." And she looked like something else, too. I saw her once when she was the perfect picture of a church-going lady. But the next time she came to town, she was a lot more glamorous, with lots of lipstick and all. It was only later that I realized she played guitar kind of like T-Bone Walker, in a real "bad" groove.[5]

Rosetta was different, she was revelatory, she was *bad,* embodying for James the nascent possibility that an African American woman might disrupt the groove of musical genre and gender expectation alike. Having rebelled, as a girl, against the restraint of the popular ballads so beloved by her mother, an ardent fan of Billie Holiday, James notes with particular interest Rosetta's sacrilegious approach to religious music (her "bluesy-jazzy style"). Yet she seems equally taken with the mutability of Rosetta's display of sexuality: churchy and plain one day, glamorous and done up the next. For James, Rosetta's fearless flaunting of different styles of black femininity did not render her any less an artist; in fact, it only confirmed her authority as a musician.

As James implies, the spectacle of a black woman wielding so much power as a guitarist could produce an unbalancing vertigo in a culture in which no woman was supposed to play the instrument commandingly. If playing the electric guitar well has been likened to bending it to one's will, then Rosetta conveyed the image of a black woman—a Sanctified *church*woman, no less—decisively and threateningly "on top." Her self-presentation as a glamorous and often bawdy large-and-in-charge black woman was culturally and socially noteworthy, especially in the sexually conservative 1950s, when anxieties about women's roles prevailed.

"I never seen a woman play," says Isaac Hayes, recalling the first time he heard one of Rosetta's recordings, when he was seven or eight years old. "Never heard of a woman playing guitar. That impressed me, but I wasn't mature enough to differentiate, but I just noticed it was a woman playing. I didn't know that as a whole, women weren't recognized as musicians playing guitars, but I knew that I'd never heard of that, so that's why I respected her. Maybe that's why she stuck."

"Mostly back in those days, [women] just sang, and she, you know, she brought a whole new thing to women that said, Hey, I can do that, too," says Carla Thomas, like Hayes a veteran of the great r&b label Stax Records. She was a child when her father, Rufus Thomas, and other Memphis soul musicians were listening to Rosetta's records. "That's one thing I remember—that stood out to me. That she was actually a musician as well." For Inez Andrews, Rosetta set an example of bravery as well as virtuosity. "You don't catch a woman who will stand up and just play a guitar, just play a guitar in a spiritual, or singing spirituals, like Rosetta did. You find it in the rock and roll, you find it in the jazz, but not the gospel. And there is none like her, and none since her. You don't have anybody here who can even imitate her or even try."

10

REBIRTH AND REVIVAL (1957–1964)

They Call Her 'Holy Roller': Rosetta Flies in to Rock
London Daily Mirror, November 22, 1957

LONDON, November 24, 1957: Backstage at the Chiswick Empire Theatre, Rosetta was brimming with emotion. There she sat, as one observer
put it, "with her head in her hands on the verge of tears, completely over-
whelmed by the tremendous reception she had earned at her first London concert." Although largely unfamiliar with gospel, the sellout crowd
of almost 1,900 that had turned out to see the evening's main attraction,
the Chris Barber Band, had warmed easily to Rosetta's performance. The
audience had laughed at her jokes, clapped along to hits such as "Didn't
It Rain," and called for more when she and the band fired off a New Orleans–flavored "When the Saints Go Marching In." By the time she took
her final bows, to thunderous applause and whistles, the annoyances of a
malfunctioning amplifier that had rendered her electric guitar "a shambles of slurring sound" were all but forgotten. The music press showered
her with favorable headlines. "Sister Rosetta Makes a Flying Start," declared *Melody Maker,* Britain's premier music magazine.[1] For the rest of
her debut European tour, cheering audiences and glowing reviews would
follow Rosetta, first across the Channel to France, then on to Monte
Carlo, Germany, Denmark, Sweden, and Switzerland.

After the imbroglio caused by her Decca venture into rhythm and blues just three years earlier, Rosetta delighted in her overseas triumph. The enthusiasm of audiences thousands of miles away from home—in places she had never been, among people who did not worship as she worshiped or eat what she ate or even speak her language—rejuvenated her spirits and rekindled her confidence in herself as a performer who still had it. The saints were right: God would lift you up; He wouldn't leave you lost and alone, as long as you had faith in and tried to live by His holy word.

Rosetta's rebirth as a star of the European blues revival began in late 1957, when Chris Barber, leader of Britain's most popular traditional jazz band, invited her on a three-week, twenty-city British tour, for which she was reputedly to be paid £10,000, or roughly $28,500.[2] Counting a brief trip to Canada with the Cab Calloway Revue back in the 1940s, it was Rosetta's second international appearance, but her first as a star in her own right. She spent the weeks before the trip in her apartment back in Philadelphia, engrossed in planning. "It's one of the most exciting things that has ever happened to me. I guess I'll act like a typical tourist when I arrive in England. There's so much I want to see and do," she told *Melody Maker* a few days before her departure. "From what I hear from other people who have played for British audiences, it's not just the sights that I'll enjoy. You know, there is nothing like a friendly warm audience. It makes you feel that what you are doing and saying is reaching inside people."[3]

Rosetta's optimism—which, like many of her press pronouncements, has the feeling of being simultaneously canned and heartfelt—indicated that she had lost none of her youthful enthusiasm for conquering Europe. "I hear vicars in this country might feel a bit stuffy about my kind of religion just because I make a good living at it," she joked to one reporter. "Why, I'll play anywhere for free—St. Paul's, Buckingham Palace, or Westminster Cathedral."[4] She was only half jesting—about playing for free, that is.

Rosetta had heard from musician friends about the allure of touring abroad: not merely warm audiences, but good treatment—which black performers couldn't get in the United States in 1957—and a mainstream press that showered visiting Americans with attention. Back in Washington in 1951, neither of the city's white newspapers noted Rosetta's wedding concert, although it was a leading item on the national black wire service. In London, in contrast, from the moment her plane touched down, Rosetta was greeted as visiting musical royalty. Reporters flocked to her hotel room, eager to have a word with the American "Holy Roller." What they found was a buxom "Negro" woman, elegantly dressed, smiling cordially, with a Les Paul electric guitar and an amplifier mixed in with her luggage.

It was touch-and-go at first. "I think she must have called a press conference," recalls Ottilie Patterson, vocalist with the Chris Barber Band.

> [The reporters] were all assembled in her bedroom, and they of course they had no idea what Sister Rosetta Tharpe *meant*. They thought she was a missionary, out to convert people and all that, and they thought she was a female Billy Graham, an evangelizing one. And they were asking her all these obscure questions . . . and I could see she was nervous and she wasn't really equipped for conversation on that level, you could say that. And the more she would lighten up the more they hardened; these press guys were *hard* on her, you know? And she was getting herself into knots and whatever they asked her she would sort of say, Well it's a gift, you know God gave me this gift. And I said, Sister, play "When I Move to the Sky." And she plugged it in, and there wasn't a dry eye when she finished. And they stopped asking her the hard questions, and they were moved, they were really moved. Once she opened her mouth, if you heard her at all, you had to be completely knocked over by her.

By the end of that first impromptu hotel room concert, pageboys had crowded at the open door to watch "Sister Tharpe" sing her spirituals with a rock-and-roll beat. "I'm just getting hep," she wisecracked, smiling her sweetest "Jesus loves me" smile.[5]

Interest in Rosetta in Britain was part and parcel of a larger trend—the postwar blues revival, which saw the emergence of a white public who "sought a heightened reality in the realm of black [American] song."[6] British blues and jazz fans not only listened to records, but formed their own bands and spent time studying the music, compiling discographies, and starting blues and jazz journals. Seventy-eights by Jelly Roll Morton and obscure but revered blues musicians were hunted down and treated like newfound treasures rather than yesterday's sounds. Occasionally, an expert such as Englishman Paul Oliver would go on an extended field trip through the Southern United States, searching for musicians whose careers, like their youths, had long since withered. (Some of these, like Joshua "Peg Leg" Howell and Booker T. Washington "Bukka" White, had already been rediscovered by white Americans such as Sam Charters and Ann Danberg.) Many of the old blues musicians had not played professionally in decades and had enjoyed only moderate success at their peaks, but the British revivalists gave them a platform for performing and touring, paving the way in turn for record reissues and blues festivals.

British and European fans saw themselves as key players in the struggle to keep African American blues and early jazz vital. "The British jazz revival movement took the initiative and helped to build up jazz-consciousness all over Europe," observed Chris Barber in May 1961. Visiting Americans "are infinitely more honoured here than in their own country.... The incredible truth is that we now have to undertake the Herculean task of teaching the American public what jazz is."[7]

"What always amazed us in England," recalls former Blues Incorporated bassist Andy Hoogenboom, "was that like these fantastic musicians that appeared—not just [Rosetta], but people like Little Richard and, you know, Bill Broonzy, it was only years later that we realized these people were being totally neglected in America. You know, and they were coming over to Britain and blowing us all away. This was fantastic for us. It really was." Hoogenboom and his friends paid close attention to what they saw and heard. "Keith [Richards] was a fanatic," he recalls, "and Brian Jones was a *total* fanatic!"

The first African American blues musician to tour Europe in the postwar years was Huddie Ledbetter, the singer-guitarist "discovered" by folklorist Alan Lomax at the Louisiana State Penitentiary in the 1930s and touted for his physically imposing presence and rough-hewn authenticity; as Leadbelly, he was well known for the stunt of performing in prison stripes. He visited Paris in 1949, and then died shortly thereafter, penniless, in New York's Bellevue Hospital. But by then, the legend of Leadbelly in Europe had been ignited, his records eagerly consumed well into the 1950s and beyond. "Leadbelly was very important," recalls Martin Bernal, a scholar of ancient history who listened to Leadbelly 78s as a secondary-school student in Devonshire, England, in the early years of the blues revival. "I mean, he was 'glamorous' because he was from a jail and that made him attractive in that way, but his virtuoso, you know, twelve-string guitar-playing was just fantastic, his voice had a very nice timbre, and he had good tunes.... And it was moving to be involved in black suffering—obviously at some distance—and that, by the early '60s, was extremely widespread. I mean in the '50s we were a very small group."

Although his concerts drew disappointing crowds, Ledbetter's visit to France laid the groundwork for subsequent overseas appearances by the likes of Josh White, Lonnie Johnson, and, most famously, Big Bill Broonzy, who quickly became an idol of the blues revival. "For me the idea of hearing an American Negro singing the blues was almost unbearably exciting," recalled George Melly, flamboyant vocalist with the Mick Mulligan Band, who saw Broonzy in 1951. "This was the first live blues music I'd ever heard in my life, the music I loved, and love above any other, sung by a great artist."[8] "I saw Broonzy, who was amazing," says Andy Hoogenboom. "God, he was good. 'Cause all we'd ever heard were crackly old records that sounded as though they were recorded under the bed."

Broonzy's visits, which ended with his death a little less than six years later, inspired quite a few British jazz musicians to look into bringing other American performers to the U.K., where they could be heard and, perhaps more importantly, *seen*. Such, at least, was the desire of Chris Barber. Only two years after starting the Chris Barber Band with several college mates in 1954, Barber had acquired enough clout as a jazz celebrity in England to begin to think about sponsoring Americans on his own dime. When the chance came to realize his ambition to learn jazz "at close range, by example," Rosetta topped his wish list. "We knew that in fact the vocal African American music was the source of the beautiful inflections and emotional intensity of all the jazz, so it seemed perfect if we could work with some of the great performers of that vocal music," he recalls, explaining why he and the band were drawn to Rosetta. "And Sister had made some of our all-time favorite records, which we longed for the chance to add our voices (or even trombones) to. We had no particular hope of being good enough, but we had to try.... We just wanted to be near her while she was singing and playing [and] as much part in it as we might."

"To hear her in the flesh!" recalls Ottilie Patterson, who says Rosetta's voice sounded fuller and rounder—a little more like Marie

Knight's—in person than it had on record, where it came across as a little thin. "It was quite astounding.... The first time we heard her, there wasn't a person in the band who hadn't wiped their eyes for tears."

Although they stood in awe of African American performers, British and European fans often tended to perceive them through what W. E. B. Du Bois called the "veil" of race, looking upon black music as an index of black suffering as well as innocence. Coming of age in the shadows of the wartime air raids and the revelation of Nazi horrors, and amid the identity-shattering upheavals of the loss of Empire, such young people turned to African American "roots" music, rather than the self-consciously modern sounds of bebop, in part because in those postwar years, it was still possible to gaze across the Atlantic in search of something sustaining. American cities, after all, had not been flattened by the terrible Luftwaffe raids. And yet while their interest was well intentioned, the revivalists tended to hear blues as the musical expression of misery rather than of perseverance, cultural memory, and healing.

"We were part of that generation that saw blacks as oppressed," recalled John Broven, an Englishman who later cofounded *Juke Blues* magazine. "So there was that kind of moralistic approach to it. We felt that by supporting the blues, we were supporting the civil rights movement. There was that romantic side to it." British journalist Val Wilmer, who spent time with Rosetta and Russell on several occasions during their visits to England, groans at the memory of how she "disgraced herself" in a 1960 interview by asking Rosetta "whether she felt Black people were better at music because of their 'natural sense of rhythm.'"[9] "I used to feel guilty about earning my living singing the music that was born out of suffering, other black people's suffering," says Ottilie Patterson, who grew up in postwar Northern Ireland feeling self-conscious about her "foreign-sounding" first name and Latvian mother, carelessly referred to by the local children as "that Russian lady." "It seemed wrong for me to get so much happiness—and when I say happiness I mean musical happiness—in singing songs that were created by people who had lived it first hand."

Sometimes this led to comical cultural miscommunications. When he debuted in England in 1958—for a ten-date tour with the Chris Barber Band—Muddy Waters, whose very name evoked the Delta, upended audiences' expectations by playing electric rather than acoustic guitar, anticipating the ill-received electrified second half of Bob Dylan's legendary concert at the Royal Albert Hall with members of The Band in 1966. But Waters had not been intending to play the bad boy; unlike Bob Dylan, he had no need to instruct anyone to "Play it fucking loud!" just to get in people's faces. Mostly, he was confused by the seeming desire of English audiences to preserve blues in amber, as though it were not a living music. "Now I know that the people in England like soft guitar and old blues," he told *Melody Maker*. "Next time I come I'll learn some old songs first."[10]

Calcified notions of the unspoiled earthiness of blues joined readily with stereotypes of the natural religiosity of African Americans, who in Hollywood films could often be seen offering up "Hallelujah!" and "Amen!" As in the reviews of Rosetta at the Cotton Club and Carnegie Hall in the 1930s, gospel as an expression of "the black soul" became a common trope in the British and European press. "If the coloured race are uninhibited in their secular music, how much more do they let themselves go in the ecstasy of religious fervour," observed one critic in the (English-language) *Zurich New Jazz Club* newsletter. "There's none of the white man's pretty prettiness in the Negro's approach to religion."[11] Swiss jazz fans weren't alone in perceiving gospel as an unfiltered outpouring of African Americans' naïve exuberance or utter wretchedness. "Most of her performances, both vocally and on guitar, have a magnificent passion and folk quality unspoiled by her appearances before sophisticated audiences," remarked the eminent British jazz critic Leonard Feather, in his program notes for Rosetta's second English tour, in March and April 1958. This was remarkably close to Alan Lomax's idealized 1947 portrait, in which Rosetta appeared as a Popular Front heroine à la Woody Guthrie or Josh White. "Her voice rings out like the stroke of a steel blade on an anvil—it is a prophet's voice ringing out hard and clear against the sins of this old world."

No one would have been more surprised by the comparison than Rosetta, who tended to favor prophets like Dolly Lewis and knew plenty about "the sins of this old world"—as well as the new one. Europeans who made her acquaintance in the 1950s and '60s recall a generous, vivacious woman, alternately pious and bawdy, who occasionally had a drink, often flirted, and generally enjoyed being the life of a party. They recall a forty-two-year-old traveling with her quiet husband who, like most American tourists, enjoyed seeing the sights and shopping in between gigs.

Because of overseas ignorance of gospel music and black Pentecostalism, Rosetta was frequently peppered with questions about her beliefs and her background. After the first disastrous interview in London, she learned how to respond with the deft touch of an improvising jazz musician. A typical interview might go as follows:

Do you really believe the words you are singing?
Yes, absolutely.

What kind of Negro Christians play music like yours?
Well, I am from the Sanctified church. Some people call us "Holy Rollers."

Are all Negroes so enthusiastic about their religion?
In the Church of God in Christ, yes, but there are different styles. Some people make the songs sound very solemn, and they don't put as much rhythm in them.

Where did you learn to sing and play guitar, and why do you play so loud?
I am what you call an autodidact. My musical ability was a gift from God. I also learned from my mother. I play loud because I want to express my happiness in the Lord!

Isn't it strange to worship God with a guitar?
Not in my church. We like to worship Him with all the instruments. Gospel music should be noisy!

Is it true the American Negro "swings" better than anyone else?
Yes, I suppose Negroes are generally better.

Who are your favorite singers?
I like so many: Mahalia Jackson, Brother John Sellers, the Reverend Samuel Kelsey, the Dixie Hummingbirds, the Harmonettes, Cleophus Robinson, and of course my mother, Katie Bell Nubin! In pop, I like Frank Sinatra, Ella Fitzgerald, and Nat Cole.

What do you think of the people in our country?
Lovely! Everybody has been so kind! I hope I can return soon![12]

Once she became comfortable with the press, Rosetta flattered and cajoled, exaggerating one moment and holding back the next; occasionally she told outright falsehoods, such as shaving five years off her age, when the fancy struck. To a reporter who asked whether the mezuzah she wore as a necklace "conflicted with" her religion, she replied that her great-great-grandfather had been a Jew (a possibility, but not one she had ever spoken about before). At one point, she even claimed that the church honorific "Sister" had been bestowed upon her by "some Jewish ladies" in Florida.

When Chris Barber had initially announced that he wanted to bring Rosetta on tour with him, his booking agents expressed skepticism. They politely reminded him that the Barber band was popular enough without an added attraction; they had already sold out their late 1957 British tour without benefit of Rosetta's name. "We thought it was a good thing," Chris recalls, "but the promoters said, 'What do you want to bring [American musicians] in for? You're going to ruin the show and people won't come and see you.' And we said, 'Of course they'll come and see us.' 'Well, you pay them with your own money then, the house is full anyway for you, I'm not going to pay you any more money for whoever you're going to bring in.'"[13]

It was not the first time promoters were wildly off the mark in their predictions. Indeed, instead of ruining the shows for the Barber band, Rosetta rendered them bigger hits. She debuted on a Friday evening at Birmingham's Town Hall, a venue that held about two thousand people. Chris had given Rosetta billing on the souvenir programs as "America's Sensational Gospel Singing Favourite," and that evening, she proved she was worthy of the title. The temperature in the hall rose palpably when she made her entrance after the Barber band, which typically played eclectic sets consisting of Dixieland jazz, obscure material from the 1920s, and popular tunes such as Ellington's "Black and Tan Fantasy." From her experience playing auditoriums and stadiums throughout the States, Rosetta knew exactly how to hold a large audience's attention. Tuning her guitar to an open C, she ended numbers by raking her fingertips over the strings and then, with the amplified sound still ringing out, raising her arms in a U-shape and tilting her head and eyes upward. It was a deliciously ambiguous posture, at once evoking religious supplication and the expectation of applause, the giving and the receiving of glory.

Whatever it was, prayerful or playful, the audience loved it, just as they loved it when Rosetta displayed her mastery of gospel vocal and guitar technique. In a single song, she sermonized and rapped, growling one moment and executing an elaborate glissando the next. On a sped-up arrangement of "Up Above My Head," she urged on trumpeter Pat Halcox and clarinetist Monty Sunshine as they took solo flights. On "This Train," she accompanied herself, playing with the dynamics of her electric guitar to heighten the drama of her performance.

Rosetta took an interest from the first in singing and playing with the Barber band—including vocalist Ottilie Patterson. "I wasn't put down to do anything with her," Ottilie remembers. "She had done a rehearsal with the band in the afternoon, but not with me. Then in the interval [intermission], she had heard me from side stage, and she came belting into my dressing room, and she said, You're on with me in the second half. And I said, No I'm not! And she said, Yes you are. And all you have to remember is that when I say 'You wanna be,' immediately you answer 'I wanna be.'" The song, as Ottilie quickly came to realize, was "When the Saints Go Marching In," and when the time to sing it came— just after they and the band had run through "Old Time Religion"—she knew exactly what to do and how to do it, because Rosetta, a practiced duettist, created the perfect space for her counterpoint. The crowd was so thrilled to see Rosetta and its own homegrown jazz stars in one glorious improvisation that it wouldn't leave the hall until the band played several encores—not additional songs, that is, but repetitions of what they had already played.

They were backstage, basking in the rapturous reception the crowd had given them, when Rosetta turned to Ottilie and announced, "You ain't nothing but a white nigger." "And she smashed her hand over her mouth," Ottilie recalled, "and her eyes grew big with fear and terror at what she'd said! She got her wires crossed, because I mean I couldn't have said it to her, and she thought she was insulting me, and I burst out laughing and said, You've just given me the best compliment I've ever had. . . . Oh, we got on like a house on fire!" It was especially gratifying for Ottilie, the lone woman in a band of men, to have a female traveling companion.

Performing with the white Barber band was quite unlike anything Rosetta had previously done. Ottilie wasn't Marie, Chris wasn't Count Basie, Birmingham and Leeds weren't Atlanta or Greenville, and playing at London's Chiswick Empire bore little resemblance to playing at New York's Apollo. Indeed, her concerts before British and European audiences probably had more in common with her U.S. appearances at Café Society or Town Hall, where she played before liberal white American audiences. At the gigs Rosetta had been doing at black churches in the late 1950s, it would have been a sure sign of disaster if no one shouted back and or "fell out," physically succumbing to the spirit of the music; abroad, in those same years, she would become accustomed to attentive, but less demonstrative, audiences. In Europe, they didn't give the same credence to the words she sang or to the spiritual feeling she brought to a performance. They had to be encouraged to clap, and then helped to find the backbeat! Some didn't even appreciate that gospel meant religious singing.

British gospel shows in the late 1950s lacked the glorious pageantry of American programs, which were commonly see-and-be-seen events. Ira Tucker Jr. remembers Easter Monday programs at the Met in Philadelphia, where the show would start at seven in the evening and continue until two in the morning. The women would parade with their men on their arms. "When I was a teenager, I'll never forget, I used to go to the shows with my friends, and we used to watch them walk in, you know, and it would *all* be about getting the attention of everybody, you know, it was like, everybody would walk in with their *man,* and their man was all *dapped out,* you know? It was great." The women that night would work to outdo each other to see who would walk home with the coveted hundred-dollar prize for the best hat. Once, Ira saw a woman with a real bird in a cage on her head.

Rosetta incorporated the whimsical spirit of such spectacle in the glittering gowns and accessories she wore for her shows in Britain and on the Continent. "Not too many [African American] artists came over then, so I can't say that many people knew what kind of music she was playing, what were the roots of her style, but she was very well liked and completely at ease," remembers Jean-Pierre Leloir, a French photographer who took pictures of Rosetta in the late 1950s, including several memorable portraits of Rosetta wearing her own rhinestone-studded guitar earrings.

As Elijah Wald points out, Rosetta made goodwill gestures toward her audiences, especially in France, where she would politely offer a "Merci beaucoup" in response to applause, or even acknowledge the kindness of "mes amis français."

Those initial shows in Britain and on the Continent in late 1957 and early 1958 revitalized Rosetta. Artistically speaking, they buoyed her belief in

Rosetta photographed in France, late 1957.
Photograph by Jean-Pierre Leloir.

herself, fulfilling her hope "that what you are doing and saying is reaching inside people."[14] Practically speaking, they put some needed cash in her pockets. But Europe was refreshing in other, unquantifiable ways. Clyde Wright, the Charlotte, North Carolina–born singer and longtime second tenor with the Golden Gate Quartet—a group that has made France its home base since the 1970s—knows how Rosetta must have felt to have people from another continent cheering her on, despite their cultural and racial differences. "Music is an international language, and what touches you, touches these people, and they don't have to understand the words," he says. "Like Louis Armstrong says, 'A cat is a cat.' I don't care where you see them.... a cat is a cat, and people are people."

In Britain and continental Europe, Rosetta was a cat. Writing of her three-week stint in Paris in early 1958, the influential French critic Madeleine Gautier noted that Rosetta "has a splendid voice, very black, which sounds like a trumpet." The audience in Paris "could hardly resist her dynamism," wrote Jacques Demêtre, a critic who had earlier visited the States on a research tour. "In certain pieces, she launches into sensational [guitar] solos, full of glissandos and vibrating notes, which I will not soon forget."[15]

Wherever they traveled during that first tour, Rosetta and Russell—for, although Chris Barber didn't expect him, in fact explicitly hadn't invited him, this was one tour Russell was not going to miss—went about their daily lives with an ease unknown to African Americans in the United States in the 1950s. They were paid promptly (in cash), welcomed at hotels, enjoyed restaurant meals without incident, and had no trouble hailing the distinctively boxy London taxis. Like a lot of African American musicians, Rosetta found in Europe a welcome haven—if not from racism, then from the very particular and insidious insults of American Jim Crow. "We were handled in a prestigious way, the best hotels, the best food, an excellent bus," recalled Len Kunstadt, who accompanied singer Victoria Spivey on a European blues festival tour in the mid-1960s. "The blues was performed in the same halls that Mozart, Beethoven and Brahms were performed in." And yet the Americans, unaccustomed to such good treatment, sometimes responded with an understandable wariness to the hospitality extended them by white people, no matter whether they spoke with fancy accents. "A lot of the artists were bewildered by it," said Kunstadt. "A lot of them were suspicious of what was going on."[16]

"For a lot of these artists, sometimes unsung in the United States, Europe came across as an El Dorado," recalls Willy Leiser, organizer of the Montreux Jazz Festival. "As soon as they arrived in a city, or in the theater where they were supposed to play, they found themselves idolized. You never knew who was more surprised: the public, or the musicians or singers they fetishized. Certain were given gifts, others were forced to submit to the ritual of interviews and photo-sessions, they were invited to people's homes, where they were surprised by collections of rare records, most of which were unavailable in Europe. It was often the world upside down!"

Europe embraced black Americans in a way their own country did not. "I think the same for us is the same as for Rosetta," says Clyde Wright, who debuted with the Golden Gates in Paris in 1954. "It's prejudiced over here, but it's a different type. It's not the same thing that existed in America... it doesn't hurt as much as back in the States, because you can walk in any restaurant in France and, you know, and you sit down, even at the time. And when I did come to Europe, I felt more free."

The freedom he felt, as Clyde Wright makes clear, was relative. The French in the '50s were "aware of the way blacks were being treated in America," he says, and yet racism was endemic, less toward "American blacks" than toward "real African people," especially Algerians. His experience mirrors that of many of the African American intellectuals who had migrated to Paris beginning in the late 1940s, including the writers Richard Wright and James Baldwin. As these expatriates came to realize—some, like Wright, reluctantly—the French were perfectly capable of granting honorary white status to African Americans, while treating North Africans with manifest contempt. The same year that Rosetta crossed the Atlantic for her first concerts abroad, Baldwin had grown disaffected enough, over conditions of Algerians in the French capital, that he took flight in the opposite direction, committing the better part of the rest of his career to fighting for the burgeoning civil rights movement in the United States.[17]

A gulf of experience and social class separated the community of black American intellectuals in Paris from most of the musicians who came to play there in the 1950s and '60s as part of the blues revival. The paths of a Richard Wright and a Rosetta Tharpe likely never crossed in Paris, because, like other black intellectuals abroad, Wright gravitated more toward the "sophisticated" bebop of Dizzy Gillespie, played in smoky Parisian nightclubs on the Left Bank, the 1950s French equivalent of Café Society.

And yet their status as icons of Negro vernacular culture did not inoculate the musicians at the center of the blues revival, especially in Britain, against racism of a seemingly homegrown variety. In 1956, a bartender at a Leeds pub refused to serve Big Bill Broonzy, then at the zenith of his fame among British blues connoisseurs. When Broonzy asked why, he was told matter-of-factly, "We don't serve Blackies."[18]

Broonzy had been visiting the pub with Bob Barclay, the half-Scottish, half–West Indian leader of the popular Yorkshire Jazz Band and owner of Studio 20, a Leeds club. "Of course," wrote Pearl Bailey in her memoirs, "the English don't have too high an opinion of how we're handling our problems, but they have one of the greatest of all race problems, I think, with their West Indian people, the people from their is-lands. In 1948 I saw people who looked like dogs lying in the street. They had ship's ropes around their waists to hold their pants up." One area of particular interest to American musicians was the multiracial district known as the Bay, or sometimes Tiger Bay, in Cardiff, the capital of Wales. Isolated by its physical location near the docks, the Bay was a place where people from India, the Middle and Far East, Africa, and the Carib-bean lived and intermarried with the Welsh and English. It was known for its racial freedom and vibrant music scene, notes Val Wilmer. Neil M. C. Sinclair, a black Welshman, remembers that on one of Rosetta's visits—probably her 1957 tour with the Barber band, which included two dates in Wales—Rosetta, "having been aware of the Tiger Bay legend she had to see us for herself. I remember she threw a handful of coins into the air and we kids darted about trying to collect them."[19]

Rosetta and the Barber band gave one of the best performances of that initial 1957 tour on December 9 in Manchester, a city whose audiences were reputed to be among England's best. Good press in the capital had elevated expectations, and Rosetta rose fully to the occasion, especially with her heart-stopping rendition of "Peace in the Valley." Introduc-ing it, she adopted a serious tone, paying homage to the man she had recorded with five years earlier. "And now I'd like to play for you a little song that I loved so very dearly," Rosetta enunciated, in a voice that fell somewhere between the singsong supplication of a preacher and the pol-ished sincerity of an expert saleswoman. "Red Foley, he loved it and he made this song, and I made it after him.... And I'd like for you to sit quietly and receive it because it's wonderful." She then proceeded to give the sort of performance that encouraged the opposite of quiet reception. At the outset, she stuck closely to Dorsey's version, but by the time she ar-rived at the third repetition of the chorus, she launched into a glorious series of improvisational flights. Consciously using her voice as an in-strument, she reshuffled words, editing some phrases and expanding others, while strategically interpolating "ohs" and "ahs" where the feel-ing demanded it. It was as though she were taking Dorsey's text, making it into a jigsaw puzzle, and then dismantling that puzzle to reassemble it in a new and highly idiosyncratic way. When she finished, the crowd, moved and exhausted, applauded for more than a minute.

Backstage, the musicians were pretty spent, too. Each night, they played for several hours; by the time the tour ended, they would have played twenty nights out of twenty-four, all while traveling the length and breadth of the country together. The only one who didn't seem over-whelmed by it all was Russell, Ottilie says. "Oh, he didn't exert himself too much," she chuckles, recalling Rosetta's nattily dressed husband. "The band used to laugh because after we'd finish, we would finish the gig and there was a lot of excitement and we would all come offstage perspiring and sweating and Russell would see us backstage and say 'Yeah, it's been a long hard day.' It became quite a byword in the band. 'It's been a long hard day. Yeah, Chris, it's been a long hard day! Long hard day, Monty!'"

The English music press unanimously concluded that Rosetta out-played her hosts in late 1957. The Barber band, as Val Wilmer puts it, was "very clunky-clunk," while Rosetta rose to "another league, aesthetically speaking." Moreover, her performance made painfully clear the distance between the musical idiom of the jazz traditionalists—characterized, in George Melly's disparaging words, by "the pianoless rhythm section, the relentless four-to-the-bar banjo, the loud but soggy thump of the bass drum"—and Rosetta's more emotionally charged style.[20] Looking back, Chris Barber defends the band's work with her, however, suggesting that such criticisms were motivated in part by the very romanticizing ten-dencies that characterized the blues revival. "Our aim and desire for the band was to be a part of the living music, not to be either some sort of 'Antique Forgers' or imitators of somebody else's music," he says. "Some English jazz critics—self-appointed, of course—complained bitterly at us for 'spoiling her wonderful music with our poor imitation stuff,' and although we were sure we could do it properly, and so was Sister, we fol-lowed their wishes part of the time, against our better judgment, for fear that they were perhaps right. They weren't."

As for Rosetta, she was far too busy enjoying herself to criticize her hosts, if indeed she felt the need. Mahalia Jackson had made it to England six years earlier—in fact, she appeared at the Royal Albert Hall on a 1951 bill featuring Broonzy, further proof that when American gospel musi-cians went abroad, many of the usual taboos were temporarily lifted. Yet even if Rosetta wasn't the first gospel soloist to tour Europe, her 1957 tour made her a preeminent heroine of the blues revival and its leading gospel protagonist. Abroad, not a few gospel lovers even considered Rosetta Ma-halia's superior.

Notwithstanding this interest in gospel, Rosetta's British fans knew and loved her music the way they knew and loved jazz: because it was up-lifting in a nonreligious way. "Most people on the jazz scene then—or at least those around the musicians, were devoutly secular," notes Val Wilmer. "Thus many jazz fanciers were embarrassed by expressions of belief." In a review of Rosetta on her second British tour, in spring of 1958, *Melody Maker*'s Bob Dawbarn conceded such discomfort. "Religion in popular song, with its phoney sentiment and doubtful theology, invari-ably makes me squirm," he wrote. "Why, then, can I listen to gospel sing-ers with unqualified pleasure? On renewing acquaintance with the art of Sister Rosetta Tharpe at the Royal Festival Hall on Sunday, I feel the answer is a mixture of authenticity and sincerity. The philosophy may sound strange to European ears, but Sister Rosetta so obviously believes in what she is doing that one accepts it without question."[21]

Others approached the question of Rosetta's religious sincerity with less earnestness. When he first met her, George Melly feared that Rosetta would be "ostentatiously pious" and thus, by definition, not to his liking. Yet when he toured with Rosetta in spring 1958, he found a kindred spirit. "In fact," he later remembered, "it was a rave. It's true that Sister Rosetta, who could, as we discovered at a private session, belt out a marvelous blues, would never do so in public, but that was about her only strict rule. One of her numbers was called 'God Don't Like It,' and the words were aimed at the most pleasurable human activities. It became clear to us within the first two days that if she believed in what she was singing, she must realize that she was causing the Almighty almost non-stop dis-pleasure, but that there was no sign it bothered her at all. On stage her performance was splendid, although we all found her introductions a bit strong. The sentimental piety of these was, however, in part relieved by the outrageous way she managed to plug her recordings in the same breath as the love of Jesus."[22]

Rosetta could be a hoot offstage as well. During her 1957 tour with Chris Barber, Rosetta arranged for photographer Terry Cryer, a member of the band's traveling entourage, to marry his girlfriend—in a modest ceremony that recalled her own Griffith Stadium extravaganza only in its use of musicians as the wedding party. As gifts, Chris presented the cou-ple with a reception after the band's Bradford concert, and Rosetta footed the bill for them to stay two nights in an elegant hotel. Photos of the wed-ding ceremony made the paper, and Cryer's association with the ebul-lient Sister Tharpe made him, for a day or two at least, a minor celebrity.

On another occasion, Rosetta and the Barber band were appearing at Grimsby's Central Hall, a venue that doubled as a main meeting place of the local Methodists, who were dubious about religious songs played with an electric guitar. "The whole auditorium was rocking to Sister Rosetta's music," recalls Les Triggs, former secretary of the South Bank Jazz Club. "The overwhelming reaction from the audience and the demand for encores was so great that I recall Ottilie Patterson...being a little peeved as she had difficulty getting on the stage to perform. Harry Lannigan, the minister in charge at the hall, had held reservations about 'hot gospel' being performed in a Methodist church, but he was so knocked out by Sister Rosetta's performance that after the concert he gifted her one of his favorite Bibles."

In 1958, Rosetta toured Scandinavia with the British Diz Disley band, featuring a young Ginger Baker, the drummer who would go on to fame as a member of Cream and Blind Faith. The first time they met at rehearsal, he recalled, "She said, Hey honey, I love your hair color. What dye do you use? Her hair was bright red. When I told her it was natural she said, You'll have to drop your pants to prove it!" On another occasion, Rosetta displayed her tenacity when she accidentally fell off the platform at the Copenhagen rail station, after a long trip from Stockholm "in a compartment with some Danish military happily drinking." As "a little girl stepped forward to present her with a bouquet of flowers," Rosetta "stepped off the train and disappeared," Baker remembers. "All that was visible was her head and shoulders." But even then, Rosetta "didn't stop smiling," although she had two "huge grazes on her shins." "I was her favorite," Baker says, "and she used to give me huge smiles on stage, especially during her show stopper 'Didn't It Rain.' I loved her."

With success all over the Continent, Rosetta was quick to inhabit the role of gospel star. Everything about her exuded fabulousness: from her stuffed-to-bursting wardrobe bags to her wigs—variously described as blonde, auburn, or "flaming orange"—to the scent of her Arpège perfume. But what young blues aficionados mostly noticed was Rosetta's guitar playing. "I had no idea who she was, I mean just this great player suddenly appeared and we went, Wow listen to that! She was stunning," recalled Andy Hoogenboom, who saw her at the Humphrey Lyttelton Club, a London hangout for blues aficionados.

Not only were we not used to playing blistering guitar, but we weren't used to a woman playing blistering guitar. . . . She was ripping the wallpaper off, you know. What you have to understand is we were only just starting to play electric guitars, you know, we were still playing jazz and skiffle and that kind of stuff, and to suddenly hear this kind of booming blues music, you'd think, Wow, I must do some of that!

What struck really strongly was how, I mean, I didn't even know the word "visceral" then, but it *was*. It came at you from a completely different direction. Very much like when I first heard Elvis Presley. I was 14 years old and suddenly, there's Elvis, you know, and it was like a light coming on, you know, it was the whole country, everybody of my age was listening to that music all at the same time, you know, and it was a very powerful experience. And I think when you came across, I dunno, people like Little Richard, the first time I saw Little Richard it blew my socks off. What do they say—the hairs on the back of your neck stand up at moments like that? That happens, you know, and she [Rosetta] had the same effect. One minute we were just clowning around being in a club together and suddenly there was this great playing going on. Not that the Chris Barber band weren't good, but this was markedly different and it had a real "American" feel to it as well, which [was] a very important thing.

What blew the socks off Hoogenboom and other young Brits leading the blues revival was Rosetta's innovative use of the electric guitar as a solo instrument with its own distinctive power of speech. Most of the songs Rosetta played for her English audiences—whether "Down by the Riverside" or "Didn't It Rain"—had a similar structure, beginning with a verse and maybe a chorus, climaxing in an electric guitar bridge, and then ending with more singing. It was a bit like a Pentecostal preacher's routine of warming the congregation up, bringing it to a frenzy of shouting and dancing, and then bringing it down to earth again, sweating and exhausted and satisfied. But Rosetta had managed to render the preacher's routine in her staged performances, introducing European listeners to a kind of secular rapture. While performing what were, strictly speaking, gospel songs, she displayed the nascent possibilities of contemporary lead rock-and-roll guitar: playing loudly, drawing out notes, playing for maximum visual impact, making the guitar "talk." For a whole generation of English blues rockers coming of age in the 1960s, like their

Southern white counterparts a decade earlier, Rosetta's playing constituted an important model of the electric guitar as *the* lead rock instrument extraordinaire.

At home in the late 1950s, the storm clouds of displeasure at Rosetta's
venture into the pop realm dissipated as quickly as they had gathered,
largely because of her stardom abroad. Beginning as early as 1958, major African American news outlets around the country—in Pittsburgh,
Philadelphia, Baltimore, Washington, Chicago, Memphis, and Norfolk,
Virginia—began touting Rosetta's popularity in Europe, establishing her
as an internationally renowned artist in whom American Negroes could
take pride. Rosetta's international fame fit squarely within what Elijah
Wald calls the "aspirational ethic" of the bourgeois black press; if she had
played to full houses in chic cities like Paris, London, and Monte Carlo,
the reasoning went, then she might be forgiven her tastelessness of years
past. But the appeal of an international reputation also cut across class
lines within black communities. For many church audiences who invited
Rosetta to perform in the late 1950s, it was enough to know that she had
gone overseas to preach and to sing her gospel songs.

Rosetta's visibility in the British blues revival also caught the attention of the primarily white folk-music audiences rallying around black
roots music as the U.S. folk revival was gaining steam. Like the blues revival in Europe, the folk revival was driven by serious-minded, educated
young people with disposable income and countercultural aspirations.
In the late 1950s, in response to what they viewed as the commercial
abomination of rock and roll, the folkies were discovering spirituals,
blues, work songs, and prison songs, including the work of Brother John
Sellers and Josh White—the last ironically considered "inauthentic" by
English jazz fans. To the young Americans, these constituted an authentic, indigenous American music, not the pandering dross played on commercial radio, especially the soulless stuff that made teenage girls scream.

In such an environment, Rosetta quickly discovered the value of the
folk credentials Alan Lomax had bestowed upon her in his notes to her
Blessed Assurance album a decade earlier. If "folk" was the rage among a
record-buying public of earnest young people, then "folk" she would be.
In 1958, she was one of the acts on opening night at a new Los Angeles
nightclub, the Avant Garde. By the following October, she appeared with

fellow blues revival favorites Brownie McGhee and Sonny Terry—the latter an alumnus of From Spirituals to Swing—at New York's Town Hall, on a bill featuring white South African balladeers Marais and Miranda and white folk singer Ed McCurdy. The sons and daughters of those most likely in her audience that night would later patronize places like Gerde's Folk City to see Lightnin' Hopkins and John Lee Hooker.

Thanks to her success abroad, Rosetta had the luxury of focusing on domestic appearances and of setting her affairs straight in Philadelphia in 1959. She did some dates with the Chris Barber Band when they came to the United States on two separate occasions that year, their reputation boosted by the unexpected popularity, in the spring of 1956, of "Rock Island Line," an old Leadbelly song remade by ex-Barber-band banjoist Lonnie Donegan. Despite what they knew they might encounter, Chris and Ottilie were nevertheless appalled by segregation. In Alabama, they wandered by mistake into a Ku Klux Klan town, and in New Orleans, home of the music they loved, they found that the Jazz Society "was all white guys" (in Ottilie's words) and that the municipal auditorium prohibited them from appearing onstage with black musicians. By a strange twist of fate, that same year, Rosetta opened at the Dixie Manor, Kansas City's first white club to allow African American patrons and performers. It was indeed the world upside down.

Perhaps Rosetta's most memorable concert of 1959 was a cruise with steel guitarist Willie Eason. On July 27, she and Eason, an old friend, plus a multiracial crowd of several hundred spectators, boarded a cruise ship docked at Philadelphia's Chestnut Street Wharf for an event billed as "The Biggest Battle of Songs and Guitars Ever to Be Held!" As Willie's wife, Jeannette Eason, recalls, however, "They didn't have a contest between each other, they just played" until everyone was exhausted. By the end of the evening, after several go-rounds of "Ninety-nine and a Half Won't Do," says Jeannette, "Willie's sitting in the chair"—as he'd have to be, to play an instrument that rested on his lap—"but she's down on her knees in front of him playing this guitar.... Everybody, they were just happy, they said both of them was the same. One wasn't no better than the other one.... But the funniest part about it," Jeannette continues, is that "the boat never sailed." Upon discovering that the motor didn't work, the boat's owner came up with a clever solution. "Well, they rocked the boat, and when people come off, everybody was saying, Oh my God, what a smooth ride! Said you couldn't even tell you were moving!... So, they had a fantastic program there that night, I mean, everybody... on that boat."

In late January 1960, Rosetta traveled to New York for an appearance at the Apollo Theater hosted by WWRL deejays Fred Barr and Doc Wheeler; among the featured guests on the bill were the era's leading acts, including the Caravans and James Cleveland. So impressive was that show that Barr and Wheeler had Rosetta back as the headliner in May, on a bill featuring Cleveland (then riding high on the popularity of his hit "For the Love of God"), the Gospel Wonders, and the Consolers, among others. Tony Heilbut, who was in the audience at the Apollo, remembers Rosetta stealing the show both nights he saw it. By then, he recalled, "her voice had lowered an octave, and she chanted more than she sang." But "it made no difference. One night she came out in tailored street clothes, in worldly contrast to the billowy robes of the Caravans. She romped through 'This Train,' hitting fancy riffs, holding her guitar notes while making silly faces as if to say, Well, my, my, think of that. In her own words, she 'cut the fool.'" When she sang "Peace in the Valley," he added, "she had truck drivers rolling in the aisles. Rosetta cut some steps herself, after judiciously removing her guitar." On another number, she performed with Ma Bell, who got the audience to holler back at her when she sang "Ain't No Room in the Hotel."[23]

A number of younger artists recall Rosetta's mentorship of them backstage at the Apollo gospel "caravans," shows featuring several acts. "She was so comforting," recalls Ella Mitchell, who started out with Professor Charles Taylor and then joined James Cleveland. "Sometimes before I get ready to go I get so nervous and she would say, Oh don't be nervous honey. She says, You know what, get in the corner, and take the *Lord* out on that stage with you. Yes she would. And she taught me that! And I do it right today." "Rosetta's voice had in my opinion never changed," recalls Sullivan Pugh, singer-guitarist with the husband-and-wife duo the Consolers. "It was an honor to work with someone who had toured overseas."

After her "comeback" years of 1957–1959, Rosetta found herself busier than ever in 1960, with engagements that had her crisscrossing the Atlantic literally from month to month. On March 30, 1960, she returned to England for her third tour—her second with the Chris Barber Band—

where she attracted noticeably younger crowds than she had only a couple of years earlier. English teenagers had begun to catch on. "People in this country were ready for something exciting and dynamic and rooted and soulful," says Val Wilmer, then still a teenager herself. "Elvis was revolutionary and exciting, but this"—meaning Rosetta—"was more authentic." In fact, Rosetta made it clear to Wilmer that gospel was at the root of all the modern sounds that were so popular among young people. "Blues is just the theatrical name for gospel," she told her in April 1960, "and true gospel should be slow, like we start off with 'Amazin' Grace.'... Then you clap your hands a little and that's 'jubilee' or 'revival'... and then you get a little happier and that's jazz... and then you make it like rock 'n' roll."[24]

11

RIDING THE GOSPEL TRAIN (1960–1970)

I'm in the control room, separated by a glass that goes into the studio,
and she was sweating from working so hard at her performance, and
there was one moment, you know, the glare of the glass, the light,
you know it just looked like she was covered in rhinestones.
Singer Toni Wine

In 1961, her finances restored by her overseas tours, Rosetta again bought herself a home, in Yorktown, a federally financed North Philadelphia housing development specifically targeted at middle-class blacks. The house at 1102 Master Street that she and Russell (and Mother Morrison —Katie Bell was now in her own apartment) moved into was modest, but the fact that they were the original occupants made it special. Rosetta could look out her front window at a quiet, clean street as she cooked in a brand-new kitchen featuring a matchless stove, and she could entertain herself or guests by playing the small upright white piano in the living room. She and Russell furnished it nicely, says Roxie Moore, with Italian furniture, matching draperies, and a "great big round bed" in the bedroom. Some time in the mid-1960s, the picture of domestic comfort at 1102 Master was perfected by the addition of Chubby, Rosetta's white poodle, whom she spoiled by feeding him table food and occasionally even taking him on tour with her. According to Donell Atkins, Rosetta's half-brother, who visited from time to time, Chubby would bark at anyone except Rosetta. Annie Morrison, with sly wit, counts Chubby as among the many friends of Rosetta who had no love for her husband.

Rosetta and Russell saw a good deal of Ira Tucker and his family in the early '60s, at least on those occasions when neither she nor the Dixie Hummingbirds were away on tour. She and Tucker loved nothing better than a day of fishing. When the weather was fine, they would rent a party boat to take them out for the day down in Cape May, New Jersey, or Kent Narrows in Maryland. "Yeah, she loved to fish, that's the one thing she really loved, is fishing," recalls the gospel singer Frances Steadman, a friend who also enjoyed going out with Rosetta.

Word had it that the singer of "Two Little Fishes" could outfish just about anyone, including Tucker, who considered himself pretty proficient. "Oh, she could *fish*," Ira Junior says, recalling the way Rosetta would psych out even her most accomplished fishing buddies. "She'd fish and talk. You know, she'd be talking to you, talking all fast, and just catching 'em while she's talking to you. And then laughing at you at the same time." Just as she liked showing up men on guitar, being better on a "male" instrument than women were supposed to be, so she liked showing them up with a fishing rod and reel. "And my old man can fish, now!" exclaims Ira Junior. "He's been known as a top fisherman, but Rosetta could put him to task."

If there are two kinds of people in the world, those who enjoy fishing and those who can't imagine a day worse spent then out on a boat, immobile, in the middle of a body of water, then Russell was the second kind. He liked staying ashore where he could protect his foreign investments—the suits and hats he had purchased in Paris. "Russell liked to *eat* what fish Rosetta caught, sure, but he couldn't mess his hands up," Ira Junior says. "Russell was like, No, baby, we'll buy them." He chuckles. "That's the kind of guy he was. I loved him for that, though. I mean, he never allowed himself to get ruffled by anything. I mean even when his hair was turning grey and he had dyed it so much that he couldn't dye it no more, and the grey was coming through, and he was saying, You know, I think, maybe I'll need to go bald. I loved that. It was like, he could make up—he had a way of reinventing things."

When she wasn't fishing, Rosetta spent her downtime in those early years on Master Street with her girlfriends, including singers Marion Williams and Kitty Parham, Ward Singers alumnae who, along with

Frances Steadman, had recently fled Gertrude Ward's penny-pinching dominion to form their own Philadelphia-based group, the Stars of Faith. "At that time, everybody was singing, trying to make a dollar," recalls Steadman—now Frances Steadman Turner—so it was a while before she discovered that she and Rosetta had become neighbors. When they finally did connect, it was through a chance meeting. "I saw her husband one day," Frances recalls, "and I said, Whatcha doin' in Philadelphia? and [Russell] said, Well, I live right around the corner! I said, Is Rosetta home? He said, Yeah, she's home right now. So that started a little close friendship, you know."

Once she settled into the neighborhood, Rosetta also joined Bright Hope Baptist, the Yorktown church that Frances attended. Because the pastor, Reverend William H. Gray Jr., was not merely a local leader but a former college president and an early comrade of Martin Luther King Jr., the church attracted a fair share of prominent and politically active congregants. Rosetta might have joined out of an awareness of herself as a public figure in North Philadelphia, says Ira Tucker Jr. Or, as Roxie Moore speculates, her switch to a Baptist church might have been a sign that the saints had finally worn her down after all those years. Some people in the Sanctified Church would turn their backs on a member for one little sin; even after twenty years of spotless living, that single transgression would never be forgiven.

Although she was not the national superstar she had been in past decades, Rosetta's career was relatively prosperous in the early '60s. She might have taken a bit of satisfaction in noticing that, more and more, gospel music seemed to be playing catch-up with her. Even some of the most stubbornly traditional performers had shifted course as gospel drew a greater share of the white commercial audience. Clara Ward took to playing club gigs, first with Thelonius Monk at the Village Vanguard, later in the sinner's paradise of Las Vegas. "I was against it for years," Ward explained to *Jet* magazine when word of her downtown jazz gigs got out. "I was brought up to believe night clubs were bad, wrong, immoral. I don't see it that way now. I have long wanted to reach a larger public and I think I am doing it this way. I might help some of the club patrons spiritually, who knows?"[1] Her reasoning echoed Rosetta's on "We the People" twenty years earlier.

As the nightclub barrier continued to fall, so the early 1960s saw a rise in gospel's visibility: through the continuing success of Ray Charles, hitting big at ABC-Paramount; the ongoing interest of folk revivalists; and the success of Langston Hughes's play *Black Nativity*, which debuted on Broadway in late 1961. Against the backdrop of such developments, Rosetta channeled her considerable energy during this period into recording. Although they are generally not associated with her finest work, the late 1950s and early 1960s were the most prolific years of Rosetta's career, measured in terms of sheer output. In the span of about thirty-six months between 1959 and 1962, she released a total of five long-playing albums: *The Gospel Truth* (Mercury), *Spirituals in Rhythm* (Omega), *Sister Rosetta Tharpe* (MGM), *Sister on Tour* (Verve), and *The Gospel Truth* (Verve). Together, they included an astonishing fifty-six songs, demonstrating her masterly command of the gospel repertoire, as well as the vitality of her singing and playing in a variety of musical contexts.

Sister on Tour and *The Gospel Truth*, the two albums on Verve, Norman Granz's highly respected jazz label, were the most noteworthy. The first paired Rosetta with top-notch producer Teacho Wiltshire, the second with a young producer named Creed Taylor, who would later become famous for launching the global bossa nova craze with "The Girl from Ipanema." "I didn't pick any of the songs. Didn't ask her anything," Taylor recalls of their sessions. "We just talked, got acquainted with each other, and she came in and recorded.... I didn't *produce* her, per se. I *allowed* her, I guess you might say, to sing her great stuff and I recorded it."

The Gospel Truth was recorded at Webster Hall, a place with "a huge ceiling, like three or four stories high," Taylor recalls. Rosetta got up on one side of the room, the side with a stage on it, where he thought she'd be more comfortable performing. "And we all had a ball recording it. She was dynamic, I just remember her guitar filling that whole large area with such great blues stuff, wow, gospel blues—whatever you want to call it.... She was a blues shouter just like Esther [Phillips].... If you didn't understand it, it'd be actually frightening. What's all the excitement about, you know?"

Ella Mitchell, a member of the All-Stars, remembers how Rosetta took control of the *Gospel Truth* session, even as they recorded the album on the fly. "We came to the studio that day and recorded that day and finished it that day," she says. "We took 'em one at a time." At one point, the All-Stars and Rosetta were rehearsing "I Looked Down the Line," when Rosetta said, "C'mon whatcha gonna do behind that?" "And I said we just should sing 'Wondered, wondered,'" Mitchell recalls, singing.

"And she said, That's it, that's it right there! Don't go no further. And then she'd holler in the air [to the engineers] 'Y'all got that? Y'all got that? These girls was bad, y'all got that? These girls was bad.' C'mon let's show em up one more time.... She made sure that you understood exactly what she wanted, like she said, and the moment she explained it and showed you, then she'd make a joke of it, in other words she would make it fun. And that's the key, she would make it fun."

Rosetta wasn't the only one pursuing multiple musical projects in the early 1960s. Mother Bell was busy, too. For one thing, she had her usual work of saving souls to attend to. Ira Tucker Jr., then a teenager, remembers helping Miss Katie tote her guitar and her amplifier to Speedy's bar at Fifteenth and Columbia Avenue in Philadelphia to play until she won a new soul for Jesus. "She wouldn't quit until she did," she recalls. "No, she was there for real. She wasn't there to play, she was there to do damage. I mean, she set up in front of a *bar*. That's what I liked about Miss Katie, she set up in front of a bar!...And she would hit 'em from, like, twelve o'clock until it got dark."

"My mother, Katie Bell Nubin, sang in the local church choir and gave me a thoroughly religious education from the musical and all other points of view," Rosetta told an English journalist in 1957, on the eve of her first European tour, "but it was she who encouraged me more than anyone to regard jazz and the blues as healthy music rather than a sinful pastime as some preachers would have us believe."[2] Rosetta may have been rewriting history a bit, and yet on New Year's Day, 1960, Katie Bell, then in her midseventies, would make good on such beliefs, recording her first and only LP in collaboration with their old New York friend Dizzy Gillespie. The pairing of the gospel matron and the spiffy bebop innovator was surely anomalous—jazz critic Martin Williams tactfully referred to their "appropriate but unusual alliance"[3]—but the album, a collection of traditional and contemporary material set to arrangements that evoke the connectedness of gospel and blues, worked out surprisingly well, if only because the younger musicians respectfully let Miss Katie do her thing.

"We just followed her," recalls bassist Art Davis, "because Dizzy had respect for her and didn't want to tell her what to do and just let her go.... She sounded, and then Dizzy took some solos, some jazz solos, on her, and we did some background while she played and sang, and then let us do our instrumentals." Junior Mance, then a relative newcomer to Gillespie's band, recalls that, before the *Soul, Soul Searching* session, he knew nothing about Katie Bell Nubin—not even that she was the mother of Rosetta Tharpe, the gospel singer whose records his mother used to play around the house when he was a boy. But he was impressed by what she could do: "She had a strong conviction in the voice. She just came right out and sang."

On August 29, 1963, Marion Williams celebrated her birthday with a party at her Philadelphia home. The day before, Martin Luther King Jr. had led the March on Washington for Jobs and Freedom. No one at the party had attended the march, but everyone had watched it on television, along with the rest of the nation, recalls Tony Heilbut. They discussed King's famous speech, but in particular, the crowd of gospel singers talked about Mahalia Jackson's performance of "I've Been 'Buked and I've Been Scorned." Jackson's alliance with King and the movement was well known, but it was another thing to see her on TV, boldly singing the song King himself had requested.

Rosetta never had Mahalia's political cachet or her connection to the civil rights movement. Earlier that summer, she had appeared at the Newport Folk Festival, but she remained at best marginal to the folk scene, whose core audiences preferred the music of pioneering freedom singers like Odetta, a proud black woman who wore her hair in a "natural"—unlike Rosetta, who wore her hair in a mortifyingly out-of-date pressed and dyed style. At Newport, moreover, where the acoustic guitar was considered authentic, Rosetta's new solid-body white Gibson SG custom electric instrument, said to have set her back $750, lost its significance as a symbol of her modernity and polish.

In England, on the other hand, Rosetta's music was attracting a new cohort of fans. As early as 1957, Rosetta had told London's *Daily Mirror,* "All this new stuff they call rock 'n' roll, why, I've been playing that for years now."[4] Now, toting a glossy instrument with impressive-looking stainless steel hardware, she was making good on that claim. If there was anyone to contradict her, it was not Marie. "Rock and roll actually started from the church, because it's [about] time, and music is time," she says. "If there is no time and no beat, there is no sound. Ninety percent of rock-and-roll artists came out of the church, their foundation is the church.... All the way back as far as you can go back, rock-and-roll

Russell Morrison points to a sign advertising a show by
"The World Famous Sister Rosetta Tharpe" at the Chinese
Rhythm and Blues Club, Bristol, England, November 1964.
From the collection of Mrs. Annie Morrison.

artists started in the church." In England, Rosetta's instrument announced her status as "rock." "I was there at the beginning," it said, "and
I'm still here. Just watch what I can do."

For the floppy-haired English youth who enthusiastically greeted
Rosetta at her solo gig at Bristol's Chinese Rhythm and Blues Club in November 1964—a day after Martha and the Vandellas arrived in London to
promote their single "Dancing in the Street"—the attraction was precisely those aspects of her persona and her music that had befuddled the
revivalists only a few years earlier. No longer was the loudness of her guitar something to be painfully endured; now it was a celebration of musical energy, its ability to take listeners "higher." The metaphor of elevation
came directly from the church, where prayer and faith had the power to
lift you up, but by 1964, getting "higher" also referred to the increasingly
widespread practice of using drugs to experience something akin to religious ecstasy.

Virtually all of Britain's young Turks of rhythm and blues honed
their craft by studying the musical licks and tricks of the group of African American "roots" musicians who toured Europe in the 1960s. The
Spencer Davis Group, the Yardbirds (featuring eighteen-year-old Eric
Clapton), the Animals—all of these groups based their earliest music on

12-bar blues, and many scored their first hits covering songs either by their heroes of the blues revival or by contemporary rock and rollers. Sometimes the material they covered was preposterously remote (Mick Jagger, for example, singing about driving down the New Jersey Turnpike at dawn, in a remake of Chuck Berry's "You Can't Catch Me"), but as expressions of feeling, such songs also made a strange and profoundly compelling sense to an English lad from Kent. Once bitten by the blues bug, moreover, most found there was no turning back. Even the Beatles, known for having an accessible pop sound that contrasted with the "blacker" sounds of the rhythm-and-blues purists, bore traces of the revival in their music. Listen to the opening bars of "Love Me Do," and you can hear the revivalists being channeled in John Lennon's youthful attempts at blues harmonica.

No other American woman was as central to the transatlantic flow of sound that we know today as the British Invasion as Sister Rosetta Tharpe. A woman among men and a gospel musician among secular blues players, she was still somewhat sidelined as an anomaly. Paradoxically, however, the very qualities that had always rendered Rosetta an outsider—her flamboyance, her over-the-top style, her association with the guitar, her need to differentiate herself from other Pentecostals through unconventional choices and outrageous behavior—rendered her irresistibly compelling to the British blues-rockers of the 1960s. "We had heard the original rock 'n' roll—Buddy Holly, Elvis and Gene Vincent, Little Richard, the Everly Brothers and Chuck Berry," said Moody Blues drummer Graeme Edge in 1992. "We put all of that together, and at the same time, discovered another 30 years of American experience on record—Sonny Terry and Brownie McGee [sic], Sister Rosetta Tharpe and all of those people. Then we repackaged it and sold it back in a very free approach."[5]

Young British rhythm-and-blues fans acquired regular access to their American musical heroes through music festivals that toured Western Europe. The most famous of these were the annual American Folk Blues festivals, initiated in 1962 by a pair of German promoter-aficionados intent on educating a curious public about black American music. In preferring aging male guitarists and harmonica players to younger players, pianists, and women, the festivals cemented the quintessential image of the blues musician as a hard-bitten male troubadour. And yet they also provided an important outlet for a variety of sounds—

including New Orleans jazz, Chicago electric blues, and country blues—at a time when such music wasn't getting much of a hearing in the United States.

In the spring of 1964, Rosetta toured Britain as part of the American Folk, Blues, and Gospel Caravan organized by George Wein, the American promoter behind the Newport folk and jazz festivals. The lineup included Sonny Terry and Brownie McGhee, Chess Records house pianist Otis Spann, the ever-popular Muddy Waters, New Orleans pianist Cousin Joe, and the country gospel musician "Blind" Gary Davis; although not featured performers, drummer Little Willie Smith and bassist Ransom Knowling rounded out the roster. Mississippi John Hurt, a hero of the 1963 Folk Festival, was originally scheduled to appear, but had to withdraw at the eleventh hour because of illness; so, too, did Lightnin' Hopkins, rumored to have an aversion to airplanes.[6]

To manage the package, Wein hired Joe Boyd, a recent white Harvard graduate. Boyd had a bit of promoting experience under his belt, but nothing to prepare him for the challenges of a packed two-week tour of Britain with artists who—far from a fulfilling the myth of a blues community rooted in the "black soul"—not infrequently found it hard to get along. Brownie and Sonny, despite having been a team for years, disliked each other in the manner of an old married couple bitterly resigned to mutual dependency. And then there was Rosetta, who arrived in England with Russell—an exception to the "no managers" rule—and a chip on her shoulder. "I think when she arrived, she felt like she was a glamorous show-business star and that she was kind of slumming it with these funky blues guys who didn't dress as sharp as she did, and some of them were pretty country, as far as she was concerned," recalls Boyd. In particular, Rosetta was cool to the Reverend Gary—a surprise to Boyd, who assumed they would have lots in common. Eventually, after listening to Rosetta's stories "about Katie Bell, about growing up in Arkansas, and about working the little churches in the rural Pentecostal circuit," Boyd came to suspect that the roots of Rosetta's dislike were deep. "She depicted [her childhood] as very hard," he recalls, "and that was sort of how I interpreted her aversion to Gary—as being the kind of thing she escaped."

The American Folk, Blues, and Gospel Caravan debuted on April 29 in Bristol, before a large auditorium overflowing with excited teenagers. "Here were these guys who could barely fill a 150-seat coffeehouse in

America, and there the hall, with nearly 2,000 seats, was packed," recalls Boyd. "I think at first everybody was kind of amazed that it was full and that there were kids queuing up for autographs." That's when Rosetta's defensiveness melted away, he says. "It was a combination of being impressed with how big the tour was from the kind of audience point of view and also being really impressed with the musicianship of everybody else on the tour."

One of the fans at the Caravan's Sheffield show was Phil Watson, a teenager who had discovered Rosetta's music a couple of years earlier, although he tended to prefer the rawer sounds of Muddy Waters, Lightnin' Hopkins, and Blind Willie McTell. He came away from the Caravan impressed by Rosetta's glittery sophistication, however. "Her showmanship and 'front' was in such contrast to the rest of the cast, except maybe Sonny and Brownie who, by 1964, had developed a polished act," he recalls. "She was immaculately dressed and her hair—wig?—was beautiful. Her guitar playing was a revelation, and the electric guitar highly polished and she used it as a mirror to flash lights around the audience. She had a very nice stage patter and was clearly a very polished and sophisticated stage performer, unlike many of the others on the tour."

John Broven, then a young blues enthusiast who craved the electric Chicago blues of Muddy Waters's records on the Chess label, remembers his initial disappointment at the Caravan show he caught in London at the New Victoria Theatre. "I was looking forward most of all to seeing Muddy Waters and his pianist Otis Spann perform," he recalls, but "incredibly they proved to be rather perfunctory, even with the backing of Ransom Knowling on upright bass and Little Willie Smith on drums.... Muddy was presented in a plodding folk blues format; this was how the Europeans wanted their blues—or it was thought.... The show did not spark until an exuberant Sister Rosetta Tharpe came on stage. A gospel act rocking? It was a total surprise. And a lady with an electric guitar, too!"

A couple of nights before the last Caravan performance, the musicians filmed a truncated version of the show for English television. Dubbed *The Blues and Gospel Train*, it was set at a defunct suburban Manchester railroad station turned into "Chorltonville," a half-Hollywood, half-Disneyland fantasy of a Deep South rural rail depot. On one side of the tracks stood bleachers to hold about five hundred young fans; on the other side were hokey props, including a bale of hay (for Sonny Terry to sit on as he played), a rocking chair, two goats tethered to a rail, a "Wanted" poster advertising "$2,250 Reward for the Recapture of Robbers Connected with the Train Robbery," and a sign advertising "Green Mountain Vegetable Ointment... It Cures Any Ailment."

Had the special been filmed "the first couple of days of the tour," Boyd speculates, Rosetta "would have freaked out." After all, she had played run-down auditoriums, small churches, and theaters on the chitlin' circuit, but never a train depot; back in the States, she didn't even *travel* by train. But coming toward the end of the run, she and the other performers were in good spirits, despite a cloudburst just as the "Blues and Gospel Train"—a refurbished British Railways car decked out with a cowcatcher and a "Hallelujah" plaque—rumbled into the station. Brownie and Sonny opened the show, followed by Cousin Joe, who did "Chicken à la Blues" on a baby grand piano decorated with a cage of live chickens. By the time Cousin Joe introduced Rosetta, who was to close the first set, the rain was audible. "Ladies and Gentleman," he announced, "at this time I take great pleasure in bringing to you one of the *greatest,* one of the *world's greatest,* gospel singers and guitar virtuosos, the inimitable Sister Rosetta Tharpe!"

It was a genuinely generous introduction, and Rosetta acknowledged it by taking Cousin Joe's arm, held out in gentlemanly fashion, as she descended from a horse-drawn surrey driven onto the Chorltonville platform by a man in livery. "Oh, the sweet horsey, oh the sweet horsey," she cooed, trying to make the descent on high heels. In a sign that she had mastered the basics of British humor, she cracked a joke about the weather. "This is the wonderfulest time in my life," she pronounced, as the rain poured down. Then she strapped on her white electric guitar and gamely played "Didn't It Rain," making use of the instrument's considerable vibrato and attacking the solo bridge tastefully, without extraneous moves. As Cousin Joe looked on from the comfort of the rocking chair, she moved next into "Trouble in Mind," taking the luxury of two guitar solos—one in which she ripped it up with a devilish laugh, another in which she made the instrument talk in a fanciful tone, while she stepped about the platform with delicate grace. "Pretty good for a woman, ain't it?" she called out to the crowd, but no one dared to respond, understanding that it was pretty good for a man, too.

The television special concluded with Rosetta returning to the platform to lead the entire cast in a version of "He's Got the Whole World in His Hands." By that point, damp and exhausted, the Caravan players seemed genuinely at ease. Cousin Joe rocked contentedly in the chair, and Muddy Waters looked positively beatific. Plus, Rosetta had finally made her peace with Gary Davis. "By the end," recalled Joe Boyd in an interview with Robert Gordon, "Rosetta had done a 180-degree turn on Gary and decided he was the deepest man she had ever met." Two nights later, during their last British show, Boyd continued, "she told me, 'When he does "Precious Lord," get me a microphone off stage.' He starts into this incredible version and Rosetta is on her knees backstage moaning right straight out of Arkansas, like she sang with her mother. Gary heard the voice and said, 'Sing it, Rosetta.' It was just incredible."[7]

Had George Wein and Joe Boyd had their wishes, the American Folk, Blues, and Gospel Caravan would have had a future on American college and university campuses. But although the English had loved it and the French had gone into raptures over a special May 12 Paris concert, the organizations that controlled the U.S. campus circuits weren't buying into it. The following winter, Boyd says, he attended a conference of performing arts presenters, but "I couldn't get anybody interested, I mean in 1964, *nobody* was interested in this stuff in America." The American Folk, Blues, and Gospel Caravan had only one American stop: at Hunter College on Sixty-ninth Street in New York City.

Around that same time, Rosetta and her white Gibson SG made two appearances as guest host on *TV Gospel Time,* a short-lived Sunday-morning variety show that aired on NBC beginning in late 1962.[8] The brainchild of a Chicago-based producer, Harold A. Schwartz, *TV Gospel Time* created opportunities for nonprofessional gospel musicians to appear on television alongside national stars, and it pioneered the practice of bringing the production crew and featured guests on location, so that large choirs around the country could appear without facing daunting travel expenses. "Practically all the gospel stars at that time appeared on that show," recalls Georgia Louis, who began working for *TV Gospel Time* soon after someone noticed her singing in a Stamford, Connecticut, paper-novelty factory where she was making Christmas bells. Louis, Marie Knight, Mahalia Jackson, Ernestine Washington, James Cleveland,

and Jesse Farley, an original member of the Soul Stirrers, all filled the host slot of *TV Gospel Time* in its prime.

TV Gospel Time was the nation's first series to use "all-Negro" talent exclusively, from singers and musicians to models and announcers. Yet some black middle-class viewers complained that a gospel show merely reinforced old stereotypes about black people as naturally religious. "The reaction of most college-bred Negroes in New York and Washington," reported *Sepia*, "was one of dismay that a company"—in this case, the white-owned Feen-a-Mint, one of the show's sponsors—"should select gospel music as a vehicle to show Negroes. To the white firm it seemed like the best idea since it is the Negroes' aboriginal music and America's only real folk music. But Negroes were not buying it in the North. However, the show, still on the air, has gone on to attract many listeners, many of whom are turning out to be white."[9]

Such comments reflected the different cultural-political stakes of the image of gospel music in the mid-1960s in the United States and Europe. The overseas audience for gospel was considerable; *Black Nativity* had done fine on Broadway, but in its traveling European tour it was an all-out smash. In Europe, as well, gospel played to the liberal sympathies of jazz and blues fans. But in the context of U.S. civil rights, sensitivity about images of robe-attired, obedient, church-going "Negroes," who put their faith in God rather than the ballot box, discomfited some viewers, including those who still recalled the mixed message sent by even well-intentioned representations of gospel, such as the 1936 film *The Green Pastures*.

Rosetta was pleased, however, to be asked to host not one but two episodes of *TV Gospel Time*. The first featured soloist Delois Barrett, the St. Timothy's Gospel Chorus, and the Five Blind Boys of Alabama; the second, singer J. Roberts Bradley, the Imperials, and the Mount Olivet Institutional Baptist Church Choir. On the episode with the Blind Boys, Rosetta performed "Down by the Riverside" as her finale, taking the stage in a full-length flowered gown and blond hair, doing a "walk-about" move that dated from her late-1940s shows with the Dixie Humming-birds. "You know the guy that goes down?" asks Ira Tucker. "Yeah, Chuck Berry got a lot of that stuff from her. . . . See, she would turn this way where you couldn't see," he says, motioning with his body. "She wore dresses, and she would turn this way where, you know, she'd be safe, you

Rosetta and her friend Madame Ernestine Washington join
Mahalia Jackson for an interview on a gospel radio program hosted
by Thurman Ruth on station WOV in New York, in the mid-1960s.
Mahalia was the only one scheduled to appear; Rosetta and Ernestine
stopped by to say hello. Photograph by Lloyd W. Yearwood.

know. She wouldn't turn where you could see in.... Oh yeah, she turned
sideways to do that duck thing. But she didn't go down quite as low as
Chuck."

"She would make that guitar ring! I never saw a woman play guitar
like that before or since," recalls J. Roberts Bradley, a classically trained
singer who remembers that once, as publicity for an upcoming Memphis
show, Rosetta had herself driven around town, playing and singing, on
the back of a pickup truck. Georgia Louis recalls an instance, however,
when even Rosetta's considerable gutsiness couldn't spare her embarrassment. During the filming of one episode, she says, Rosetta kept flubbing
the plug for Feen-a-Mint. For one reason or another, she kept cheerfully
urging the people at home to try "the little brown pill"—not "the little
white pill"—as the recommended remedy for constipation. Rosetta had

to repeat the pitch three or four times before she got it right. The queen of gospel guitar pushing laxatives on Sunday morning television, and messing the words up! Georgia Louis still chuckles at that one.

Rosetta made her living through the end of the 1960s doing programs at home, as well as touring the European and American festival circuit, which remained strong even as the British blues revival began to ebb. In addition to appearing at the Newport Jazz Festival in 1964, on a program that reunited her with Count Basie, she performed at the First Annual Copenhagen Jazz Festival (1964); the Folk Blues and Gospel Song Festival, sponsored by the Hot Club de France (1966); the 1967 Newport Folk Festival, where she played piano while Katie Bell sang until she practically had to be pulled off the stage; and the 1970 American Folk Blues Festival. In each venue, she remained supremely confident; of Newport in 1967, she told Tony Heilbut, "I showed those children how you can play anything in gospel: blues, jazz, country and hillbilly."[10] While she was abroad, she did solo tours of anywhere from two days to two weeks— in France, Germany, Scandinavia, Spain, Denmark, the Netherlands, and Great Britain. After a several-years' absence from the studio following her two Verve recordings, she also released three albums: *Live in Paris, 1964; Live at the Hot Club de France* (recorded in 1966); and *Famous Negro Spirituals and Gospel Songs* (recorded in late November 1966, but probably not released until late 1967 or 1968). The latter, the sole studio album she made abroad, found her working with Willy Leiser and a Swiss quartet, the White Gospel Four, a group that had learned to sing by copying what it heard on records by Mahalia Jackson and the Golden Gates. Hughes Panassié, Rosetta's friend and the influential president of the French Hot Club, dubbed the Four the "weak point" of the LP, and yet nothing could shake his faith in Rosetta's talents: "More than ever after having listened to this record," he wrote in April 1968, "I think that Rosetta Tharpe is one of the greatest, most moving artists of our time."[11]

At the time, Mother Bell, then in her mideighties, was living in the house on Master Street, where she passed her time tending the small garden out front and playing her mandolin or the piano. "She lived for singing and Jesus," wrote Tony Heilbut; "if you asked her about speaking in tongues, she'd tell you 'Lord, yes. The Holy Ghost, that's my company-keeper.' "[12] One day, however, she called Rosetta aside and told her she was feeling cold, and that she heard music "like Count Basie's playing in the next room." Rosetta reassured her, "Oh, you poor thing, that's just the angels getting you ready." Soon after, Rosetta's premonition came true: Mother Bell had her stroke.[13]

Two weeks later, Louise Tucker and Roxie Moore, Rosetta's closest Philadelphia friends, came to visit Mother Bell at St. Luke's Hospital, where she lay dying. "We were standing by her bedside," remembers Roxie:

> Louise had one hand on one side of the bed and I had the other hand on the other side of the bed. And we were talking with her even though she was like in a coma, but she would blink her eyes and we would ask her, you know, to do something, or to squeeze our hand if she understood what we were saying. And she would do both. And we stood there and we promised her not to worry, that we would take care of Sister for her and that we would be just like Rosetta's sisters, and that she didn't have to worry—she could go on home to be with the Lord, you know, rather than lay there and suffer. And I think it was just that night or the next day that she passed.

Few relatives attended the funeral at the William H. Brown Funeral Home on Girard Avenue; Mother Bell, apparently, had outlived most of her contemporaries. However, two church dignitaries showed up to pay their respects: Bishop O. T. Jones, senior bishop of the Philadelphia Church of God in Christ, and Bishop O. M. Kelly of New York. Ernestine Washington made the trip down from Brooklyn, and the three women —Ernestine, Louise, and Roxie—sat together with Rosetta and Russell during the service. The Reverend Robert Cherry of Washington, D.C., preached the sermon, Roxie read the eulogy, and both Ernestine and Marion Williams sang, Marion doing Mother Bell's song "Ninety-nine and a Half Won't Do," until, as Rosetta later recalled, "the folks hollered and carried on like we had revival."[14] After the ceremony, Mother Bell was laid to rest in Merion Memorial Park in the Main Line Philadelphia suburb of Darby. Roxie Moore made sure to send a photograph and an obituary to the *Philadelphia Tribune*, so that Mother Bell's passing would be properly noted.[15] It was, in a banner headline that ran above the masthead on page one.

Katie Bell had been by Rosetta's side—as mother, collaborator, protector, friend—for so many years that the loss, for all that she anticipated it, must have cut especially deep. Tony Heilbut, who saw Rosetta regularly in the months and years following the funeral, remembers that, despite her temperamental buoyancy, Rosetta seemed noticeably down. At Mother Bell's interment, as she watched the coffin being lowered into the ground, she had wept and told him, "Don't let them put her in that cold, cold place." As Roxie remembers it, Rosetta took her mother's death as well as might be expected. "We were there with her, we talked to her, and we hugged her and we comforted her, and Ernestine...to have Ernestine there [at the funeral] was a big help," she says. She and Louise never broke the deathbed promise they made to Katie Bell: they made sure they saw a lot of Rosetta that first year, especially Roxie, who for unrelated reasons spent part of 1968 living with Rosetta and Russell in the house on Master Street.

Rosetta cut back on her touring in the wake of Katie Bell's passing. She also did less overseas traveling. "She was still going to places like Washington, you know, and nearby places and churches," says Roxie. "She wasn't doing the big things." Those "nearby" places sometimes extended as far south as Florida and the Carolinas, in the small towns where Russell knew that the Rosetta of "Beams of Heaven" had never been forgotten. But for the most part, that part of her that loved performing had dimmed.

Condolences came in from Rosetta's family, as well as from friends in Britain and Europe. Occasionally she even received a visitor from abroad. Willy Leiser shared Christmas dinner with Russell and Rosetta in December 1968, Rosetta's first holiday without her mother. Leiser can still remember the spread Rosetta prepared: fried chicken, Virginia ham, greens, rice, sweet corn, salad, biscuits, and cornbread. After dinner, she sat at the piano and sang "Precious Lord'" in honor of her mother. On another occasion around that time, when Willy joined Russell, Rosetta, and their chauffeur for one of her appearances in Norfolk, they went to have a meal at a motel restaurant and were refused lunch service, although it was nearing 11:50 a.m. Not wishing to put up a fight, Rosetta and Willy ordered pancakes, only to see a parade of fish and chicken come out of the kitchen for the other "breakfast" customers. The final straw was when the white waitress who was serving them came out with one plate of pancakes, which she placed, with obvious intention, before Willy. "So, I pushed my plate toward Rosetta and said in my broken En-

glish that in *my* country, we served ladies first," he remembers announcing. "My plate finally came, but I had to wait to be served until she had
finished serving everyone."

In the late 1960s, the label at the forefront of the gospel field was Savoy
Records. Under the careful direction of producers Lawrence Roberts,
a black Baptist pastor, and Fred Mendelsohn—like label founder Herman Lubinsky, a Jew from Newark—Savoy put out many of the greatest
gospel records of the 1950s and '60s, including work by Dorothy Love
Coates, Clara Ward, the Caravans, and James Cleveland. Rosetta teamed
up with Lubinsky and Mendelsohn in late 1968 and in quick succession
released two LPs, *Precious Memories* and *Singing in My Soul.* Both consisted of new recordings, featuring Rosetta and a stripped-down rhythm
section (organ, drums, piano, guitar), and yet both looked backwards, as
though in implied tribute to Katie Bell. The nostalgically named *Precious
Memories,* which earned Rosetta her only Grammy nomination, for Best
Gospel Soul Performance, gathered together some of her most popular
material: "Savior Don't Pass Me By," "No Room in the Church for Liars,"
"Precious Lord," "This Train," and "Peace in the Valley." *Singing in My
Soul* took a similar tack, resurrecting old songs and giving new treat-
ments to others; as Tony Heilbut noted, Rosetta paid homage to Katie
Bell with the solemnly beautiful "When the Gate Swings Open." In his al-
bum notes, Heilbut portrayed Rosetta as ahead of her time merely for
having stayed so consistent to her musical vision, however the wind
blew. "Today when every pop singer is returning to his roots," he wrote,
"Rosetta Tharpe's music is truly where it's at."[16]

Rosetta was the featured female act at the 1970 American Folk, Blues
and Gospel Festival, which began on October 26 in Germany. The pace
was brutal: Copenhagen, Berlin, and Paris on three consecutive nights in
the second week of November; Vienna, Frankfurt, and Bristol, England,
on consecutive nights later in the month. With all the traveling, there
was little time for sleep, let alone taking in the sights. It was around this
time, recalls Rosetta's French friend Dimitri Vicheney, that she began
complaining about not feeling well. Rosetta and Vicheney had first met
in Paris in 1957, when Vicheney, who wrote for the French jazz press under the pen name Jacques Demêtre, took to picking her up and driving
her to her concert appearances to save her the bother of a taxi. "She was
very interested, not only by the neighborhood where her hotel was, next

to Montmartre, but she also wanted to see the stores." She was *pleine de vie*, he says, "simultaneously vivacious, energetic, gay, and full of feminine charm. In short, a very strong personality, who didn't 'play the star.'" In time, Rosetta, who had a bit of a crush on Vicheney, began complaining to him about her relationship with Russell; at one point, she even mock-proposed marriage. (Embarrassed but also flattered, he dutifully turned her down.) "Do you believe in God?" he remembers her asking while they were getting to know each other. "Not too much. In fact, not at all," he conceded. "No matter," she responded reassuringly, "I'm not a fanatical believer."

When he reunited with her for the Festival show in Paris on November 9, Vicheney immediately noticed a decline in Rosetta's health. "She was already—how can I say it—sick, and all of the sudden. She kept saying, 'I don't feel my hands.' I don't remember if it was her right hand or her left hand, but she had been visibly shaken by a bout of paralysis. My wife and I left that evening a bit anxious and it was later that we realized that we had been present at the first signs of the illness from which she would die in 1973. After that time, I never saw her again."

Rosetta made it through the festival schedule as far as November 12, when she fell seriously ill in Switzerland and was taken to Geneva Hospital, where, by doctors' orders, she was to rest up to get well enough to take an airplane home. Almost two weeks into her stay, when she was feeling a bit better, she gave a private concert for the doctors and nurses. One doctor even taped it. But Willy Leiser wasn't altogether reassured by these displays of good humor. As it turns out, Rosetta had confided to him almost exactly what she had confided to Dimitri Vicheney: "She told me that she felt numb in her arms, and I understood that it might be serious."

12

I LOOKED DOWN THE LINE (1970–1973)

*She was so strong in her convictions. She didn't let nobody
change her around. She just believed that what she was
doing was what God had given her.*
Ruth Brown

Diabetes, for all its deadliness, is a quiet disease. By the time people manifest even one of its relatively benign symptoms—an odd bruise that doesn't heal, numbness of the hands or feet, bouts of disorientation that resemble drunkenness—the illness usually already has set in, sometimes seriously so. Often diabetics are surprised to learn that they have been living with the disease for years, while feeling relatively healthy.

Like a lot of African American women of her generation—women who grew up poor and spent the entirety of their lives working—Rosetta never knew she had diabetes until she had what was almost certainly a stroke in Switzerland. And like a lot of women in her position—women who grew up in the Sanctified Church, where the healing power of prayer is a central tenet of faith—Rosetta didn't put much stock in the medical profession, never managing to find the time to see a physician regularly. Why should she have cared for doctors, when no white hospital would have admitted Katie Atkins back in Arkansas in 1915? Even when she began to put on extra weight in the 1960s, she didn't worry too much about it, as long as she felt relatively good and could continue performing.

Rosetta's friends, generally less chary about doctors, found themselves frustrated in their attempts to get her to seek medical care when she returned to Philadelphia after her stroke. Tony Heilbut remembers Rosetta telling him that they all should be drinking grapefruit juice as a cure for diabetes, perhaps because she imagined the acidity of the bitter liquid would counterbalance the "sweetness" in her blood. Rosetta's sister-friends, meanwhile, did everything but literally drag her to a physician, that winter of 1970–1971. "Rosetta, she had this diabetes, and I started going to her doctor for a while, and her doctor would tell me to please bring Rosetta in because she had something that was going to kill her if it wasn't treated," Roxie Moore remembers. "But I would call Sister and say, Sister, have you been to the doctor? And she would say no, and I would try to persuade her to go. [The office] was right across the street from her."

"Rosetta's sickness is what stopped her from the road," says Ira Tucker, confirming Roxie's memory of events. "When Rosetta came from Europe, she had sugar so bad that my wife and Roxie tried, begged her, 'cause our doctor was her doctor, and he said, Louise, if you see Rosetta, *please* tell her to come. We told her but she didn't do it." Even Marie, telephoning in from New York, tried to persuade her old friend and partner to get medical aid, but like all the others, her pleas were ignored.

Rosetta assured everyone she was fine, and just to prove it, she acted her usual joke-cracking, ebullient self, inviting the Philadelphia crowd over to dinners where she would treat everyone to meals of the highly seasoned Southern soul food she favored. Then one evening, Roxie remembers—it was not long after Rosetta had returned from Switzerland —"Louise and I went over to the house … and she had this little dark spot on her foot. And she said, 'Look, Sisters,' she said, 'This spot is sore.' And I said, 'Well, Sister, you *have* to go and check that.' "

The "spot" in all likelihood was an ulcerous area caused by problems in circulation and exacerbated by a weakened immune system. But even with her foot bothering her, Rosetta resisted seeking medical attention for another several weeks. By that point, gangrene had set in, and when she finally checked into Temple University Hospital, the doctors saw no other course of action but to amputate the leg.[1]

This was a dreadful blow, even to a woman with as much energy and resilience as Rosetta. Not only did the amputation leave her depressed and weakened, but it threatened her ability to step around while she sang and played. "That leg, when she lost that leg, she lost a lot of passion," remembers Ira Tucker Jr. "Because she was used to being up on that stage and moving around, and she couldn't do that. But she kept that energy up in terms of friendships and these people coming by, you'd never know there was anything wrong with her. But she had the real, real bad sugar."

As soon as Rosetta was well enough after the surgery, however, Russell had her booked onto the church circuit again. There were programs at distinguished COGIC institutions, such as Washington Temple in Brooklyn, as well as out-of-the-way places in small towns throughout the South. Perhaps Russell saw it as a way of protecting Rosetta, keeping her busy doing what she knew and loved best so as to stave off her depression and worrying. But most of Rosetta's friends saw Russell as looking after his own needs, without regard for Rosetta's health. Many believed she should have been resting, rather than running from place to place. But there must also have been tremendous pressure, since, as Rosetta and Russell both knew, without the money she made performing, they had little to live on.

Even before Rosetta's leg was amputated, Russell had been sensitive to people prying into his private business. One time, when Roxie was in the middle of one of her "Sister, get yourself to a doctor!" lectures, Russell picked up the phone mid-conversation and told her, "You take care of Roxie, I'll take of Rosetta." "And when he said that to me, then I didn't know what to think, you know," Roxie recalls. "So, I stopped bugging her. . . . I don't know," she adds, "Russell, at that time, he was so protective of her. You know, I didn't quite understand it. But when a woman has a husband, there's only so much you can do."

Ira Tucker took more liberties in speaking his mind to Russell. "Rosetta was working actually when she was sick," he recalls. "I used to tell Russell, Russell, that's your wife, but man, why don't you *stop* Rosetta from working, now, she's *sick*, man!" Rosetta would defend her husband, telling Tucker, "Brother, I got to make it; I have to make it. Russell say I can make it." And then Tucker would have no choice but to concede: "That's your husband. I can't go over him, you know, I'm just your play brother." Yet it pained Tucker as much as anyone to see Rosetta sweating it out there in little churches, when he knew she was suffering. "She worked, see," he says emphatically. "Don't never let nobody tell you that lie, Rosetta Tharpe worked until she couldn't."

After her operation, Rosetta taught herself to do programs seated, not unlike the way she practiced playing guitar at home or when casually jamming with friends. At other times, when the spirit struck her, she dropped all pretense of worrying about how she looked and hopped around on stage on what friends call "her one good foot." "She was crazy even with the one leg," says Ira Tucker Jr. "She didn't let the disability stop her." In fact, when she was feeling well, Rosetta turned her disability into a dramatic advantage. Gospel had a long tradition of singers flailing their bodies around on stage for the theatrical effect; Ira Tucker himself was famous for the trick of going down on one knee and then being helped up to standing again, in a move that made audiences go wild. The Holy Dance, an important aspect of Sanctified worship, created opportunities for congregants and church leaders alike to give themselves over to displays of self-abandon. In this important sense, Rosetta's physical disability did not compromise her ability to perform authentically. "She used to hop around, she used to sit on the floor, and she would bounce around on the floor as opposed to get up and walk with the cane," Ira Tucker remembers. "She'd rather just bounce around, yeah, that's what she was doing."

Margaret Allison of the Angelic Gospel Singers visited Rosetta after the operation and recalls her friend's determined good spirits as well as her bodily theatrics. "I went to the hospital to see her, and she was an amputee, you know," Allison remembers. "She was laughing and talking with us, you know, because she said she was surprised, she didn't know she was a diabetic... and after that, after she got well, she started back singing again, because she was talking to me, and was telling me I should have seen her hopping around on stage. She was really jolly. She just said to me, she said, Sister, you should have *seen* me hopping around on stage with just one leg!" "Well, thank God you can hop around!" Allison replied.

The spirit of levity didn't assuage Allison's fear that Rosetta was merely putting a happy face on a terribly trying situation. It would have been just like her to make you feel comfortable, Margaret says; Rosetta "was a lot of *fun*," always making it so in her presence "you could feel free to laugh and talk and say whatever you want to say." "Rosetta was jovial," Roxie agrees. "She always had a joke to tell, and she always laughed." On stage and in private, she enjoyed being histrionic, trying out different moves to get attention as much as to see how others responded. "But how she was *doing*," recalls Margaret Allison, "I really don't know." It may have been a moot point in any case, she adds; Rosetta "didn't really have a choice about hopping around because Russell was still depending on her."

"Russell, if it was up to Russell," laughs Ira Tucker Jr., "she'd a worked seven days a week. Russell would've worked [her] seven days a week if he could have. I'm telling you, if he could have got that deal he would have taken it, and he would have stood there on the wings and applauded for her as she came off sweating and tired and fingers bleeding and the whole shot. He would've kissed her on the cheek and walked her to the dressing room and helped her get ready for the next show. That was Russell. No, she worked, she worked *all* of the time."

Even in her illness, Rosetta resisted the stereotype of the tragically ravaged black female entertainer, a living emblem of society's ruthless treatment of both women and African Americans. Unlike Billie Holiday, who did her last gigs looking drawn and exhausted, an emaciated distortion of her healthier, begarlanded self, Rosetta did not generally attract the sort of mock-sympathetic, unseemly fascination with her decline that so plagued Lady Day. Mostly she avoided this through humor—the same weapon she had used against racism in the '40s and '50s. She never tired of joking, "Oh, plug me in, Daddy! Ooo—feels so good!" when she was getting her amplifier in order. That is not to say she did not suffer, however; Tony Heilbut recalls calling her on the phone only to find her weeping with pain, talking about how hard it was to go on. At other times, the suffering was emotional. "You had to be very resilient to have been Rosetta Tharpe and then be doing fifty-dollar freewill offerings," Heilbut says.

In general, Rosetta's fans did not regard her with the unctuous self-interest of the merely voyeuristic; they *wanted* to see her triumph over her adversity. It helped that diabetes lacked the social stigma of illness from drug and alcohol abuse. Her Philadelphia friend Walter Stewart, a prominent deejay, worried, however, that Russell was parading Rosetta around shamefully, like a charity case. On at least a few occasions, he remembers, Rosetta performed with the gospel duo of Yvonne and Yvette MacArthur, Los Angeles–born twins conjoined at the head, giving their programs—the singing "Siamese sisters," the "one-legged, guitar-playing lady"—a decidedly freak-show quality. Russell "would get the money," Stewart remembers. "She was sick. Her words were slurred. It wasn't pleasant for me."

Tony Heilbut, who lived in New York, saw Rosetta frequently in the early 1970s. When his seminal history *The Gospel Sound* appeared in 1971, he took the train down to Philadelphia to read Rosetta the sections he had written about her. Heilbut's memories of these visits of 1971 and '72 are mixed. On the one hand, Rosetta reassured him by playing the role of her old flirtatious, teasing self, confiding in him about sexual fantasies and crushes. One, he remembers, involved Joe Boyd, the young white manager of the 1964 American Folk, Blues, and Gospel Caravan. "I'll get them yet!" Heilbut recalls Rosetta joking, in reference to Boyd's buttocks. In Heilbut's mind, a fifty-five-year-old woman who could get a little silly about wanting to pinch the ass of a man less than half her age still had plenty of life left in her. At other times, however, she confessed to pain and to neediness, acting like the "motherless child" she sang about in the spiritual. "Daddy, Daddy, I'm feeling all cold," she would say, recalling the words she pronounced when they put Mother Bell in her "cold, cold" resting place in the ground.

In the years when Rosetta was touring Europe, and even while she was ill, Marie and Rosetta had managed to keep in touch and even stay close, although the distance, together with the demands of their respective lives, made face-to-face visits rare. In the 1960s, while Rosetta was crisscrossing Europe and influencing many of the major players behind the British Invasion, Marie pursued a moderately successful rhythm-and-blues career, touring with the likes of Brooke Benton, the Drifters, and Clyde McPhatter. After "breaking up" with Rosetta in the 1950s, she had also grown closer to Dolly Lewis, for a time living with Lewis and her husband in Oakland, California, and then later, after Dolly's divorce, living with Dolly in New York. Sometimes Dolly, who was born in 1910, would introduce Marie to strangers as her daughter, says Walter Godfrey, a friend and fellow member of Washington Temple, although it was well known that the two were not related.

In the late 1950s or early 1960s, Dolly founded Gates of Prayer Church, first in a structure on Amsterdam Avenue, later at a location on 145th Street in Harlem. As Floyd Waites, longtime church pianist, explains, "Gates of Prayer was based on the prophecy of Dolly Lewis"—to her congregants a charismatic and "sighted" pastor, capable of performing miracles of healing. Dolly never took credit for her gift, Floyd says, instead insisting that she was a conduit for messages, not their source. Wherever her power came from, Floyd experienced this gift the first time he walked into Gates of Prayer in the mid-1960s, still a relatively recent arrival to New York from Alabama. "I was invited to the church," he recalls. "And I went one Sunday morning, and as soon as I opened the door and walked in, she said, There's a piano player right there. And I looked around to see who she was talking to because no one knew; they knew I sang but they never knew I could play, you know, piano. So she said, Go sit down and play 'cause yeah you can play. And so from that Sunday on I was with her."

Back before Dolly died in 1990, Floyd recalls, "many, many people came through the Gates of Prayer visiting. Not just ordinary people," he emphasizes, "we had people like Esther Phillips, Baby Washington, LaVern Baker...and Professor Alex Bradford." Before she passed away, Baker even became a Gates of Prayer regular. But by far the most memorable guest Waites can remember is Rosetta Tharpe. The announcement that she was to perform at Gates of Prayer in 1971—and sing with her old partner, Marie Knight—was enough to produce an overflow of excitement in their little building, which could hold seventy-five or eighty people comfortably, maybe one hundred in a squeeze. Someone made the wise decision to schedule two services, one in the afternoon and one in the evening, so perhaps two hundred people were there. Some thoughtful church members even had a special chair with a cushion fixed up for Rosetta—ironically, the same woman who years earlier had delighted Gordon Stoker by making "I Can't Sit Down" her theme song.

Yet if Rosetta sat with her guitar—a brown Les Paul guitar, in Floyd's memory, not the flashier white SG—no one else in church sat that Sunday. "Did she *perform!*" Waites exclaims.

> Wow. I was missing a whole lot of notes listening to her and that guitar! She was fabulous. And you know the concert she did, she and Marie performed songs together, and at one point Rosetta did some

of her favorite hymns, just guitar along with the Hammond organ and my piano playing. And then, the highlight of that performance? 'Didn't It Rain' and 'Precious Memories' *rocked that little church....* I'm telling you, it was wall to wall, both performances. And when she pulled back on that guitar [for] 'Didn't It Rain,' her solo? Oh my Lord! It was fantastic! It was just like [the audience] would go off in like a hysteria. You know ... like she had a small amplifier for her guitar and when she would hit off on those solos they would have to, like, kind of tell the people to like calm [down] you know, [so] we could hear that guitar. It was just that great. You know, even with the amputation of her leg, it didn't affect that, her voice *nor* her playing.

Even in the 1970s, Rosetta and Marie had a spiritual connection that to Floyd seemed unbroken. Marie had always talked to Floyd and his wife, Evelyn Waites, about enjoying those years with Rosetta, and she always gave her friend credit for giving her a chance to make it. Marie had love in her heart for Rosetta, he says; if she wasn't talking about her she was thinking of her. He illustrates with a story: At Sunday morning Gates of Prayer services, Reverend Dolly liked to "narrate" a song for Marie to sing. "Precious Memories," she would declaim grandly, as though she were beginning an oration, and Marie would come in on cue. "And sometimes during these different times," Floyd recalls, "[Marie] would get very full, you know she'd be thinking about Sister. You know. Uh-huh. Yeah, she be getting asked, 'You gettin' kind of full now, you think, sister girl?' She'd say, 'Yeah, that Sister [Rosetta] got me.' But it was always a high time, you know."

Rosetta's last major public appearance was on July 26, 1972, at Lincoln Center, where she shared a billing with her friend Marion Williams. The show was part of Soul at the Center, a twelve-day festival of black arts organized by Ellis B. Haizlip, an important behind-the-scenes architect of the black arts movement. Soul at the Center was a landmark in both Haizlip's and Rosetta's careers, albeit for different reasons. For Haizlip, it represented the culmination of a longstanding ambition to bring African American artists to a hallowed hall of New York City high culture. For Rosetta, Soul at the Center represented official public acknowledgment of her status as a living gospel legend. In many ways, Soul at the Center poignantly circled back to John Hammond's From Spirituals to Swing concert thirty-four years earlier. That concert, organized by a sympa-

thetic white supporter of African American artists, introduced Rosetta
to a crowd of progressive whites, for whom she performed a largely unknown music. The 1972 concert, organized by a black man with black
people as an intended audience, showcased gospel as a taken-for-granted
form of black American music, and situated Rosetta as gospel nobility,
rather than a charming novelty.

Nothing emblematized the differences between the two concerts
more succinctly than their respective titles. From Spirituals to Swing was
the creation of a historical moment that believed fervently in "uplift."
From X to Y: the name of the concert itself signified linearity and clarity
in the pursuit of Progress. From Spirituals to Swing said, in effect, that if
black people could survive slavery—and not only survive but produce
the glorious music of the spirituals—then "swing," a relatively modern
invention, heralded the day when they would no longer labor under the
stigma of race.

Soul at the Center put signifying before such symbolic earnestness,
beginning with the indeterminate meaning of the word "center." (As for
"soul," it couldn't be defined, and if, in 1972, you had to ask, clearly you
didn't have it or know where to find it.) Was the "Center" in question
only or primarily Lincoln Center, the arts complex named for the president who had "freed the slaves"? Or was it a "center" of a more general and more abstract kind: the center of the arts, perhaps the center of
America itself? What if, to take the pun a step further, "Soul at the Center" meant that soul itself was central? What if soul—and what if gospel
as the soul of soul—constituted the *soul* of American culture? And what
if blackness itself were not marginal but deep at the core of American-
ness, and thus ineluctably central to the cultural inheritance of every citizen, not just those who were marked by race?

Thanks to performers like Rosetta, in the years since From Spirituals
to Swing, black music *had* moved, culturally speaking, from the margins
to the center. When she took center stage that July evening, she was much
changed from the lithesome, dimpled, brown-skinned girl recently up
from Florida, who performed a music then virtually unknown outside of
certain black churches. In 1972, she still had the dimples and the smile,
but she was a larger woman and a larger presence. Not only had she popularized the music they were celebrating that evening, but directly or
indirectly, her spirit had infused everything from the rock and roll of
Chuck Berry to the rockabilly sounds of Elvis to the groovy, tripped-out

summer of Woodstock only three years earlier. She had demonstrated that a woman of artistic and spiritual conviction could carve out her own path in what Soul Brother Number One James Brown had called "A Man's Man's Man's World." By the time Rosetta took to the stage at Alice Tully Hall, Don Cornelius, 1970s TV's black impresario par excellence, had set the *Soul Train* in motion, taking the old religious metaphor of the gospel train, which Rosetta had sung about for forty years, one step further, its point of arrival no longer the Pearly Gates but outer space.

The extraterrestrial metaphor of a "soul train" fit the moment well. "We're going to leave vibrations at Lincoln Center that will make it impossible for culture to be defined in New York without black people," Haizlip announced to the *New York Times*.[2] Hammond had promised cultural vibrations of a modest sort for a single evening. Haizlip had his sights set on unleashing cultural "vibrations so strong, so mean"—as he put it, in words that bespoke revolution—that they would permeate the atmosphere forever, like a cosmic jazz performance by the mystic and pianist Sun Ra. To fulfill this vision, Haizlip had recruited poets Nikki Giovanni and Jayne Cortez; singer-musicians Taj Mahal, Bobby Womack, Carmen McRae, Esther Phillips, Donny Hathaway, and Nina Simone; jazz musicians Rahsaan Roland Kirk, Cecil Taylor, Betty Carter, and Mongo Santamaria; the all-female rock-soul group LaBelle; and, of course, Rosetta and Marion Williams. From one perspective, Rosetta's vibration was the longest lasting, since she was the link, the only musician who appeared at both Hammond's and Haizlip's events.

Attendance for Rosetta's and Marion's show was disappointingly sparse—less than four hundred—but that didn't diminish the spirit they raised. Rosetta took the stage first, introduced by Joe Bostic, the WLIB deejay and gospel promoter who had booked her into the Apollo in the 1940s. She sang a number of old songs, just as she had in Europe, just before her stroke: "That Old Time Religion," "Down by the Riverside," "Precious Lord," and "Just a Closer Walk with Thee." Slowing down her usual fast tempo, Rosetta stretched the songs out, infusing each with a melancholy air. She had illness and death on her mind, and testified in between numbers about her amputation, her mother's death, and even the death of her mother-in-law, Allene Morrison. She cried and the audience cried. When she tearfully told the audience, "I've got Jesus in my heart. I'm glad to be alive," one man in the crowd "was so moved that he tossed Rosetta a handkerchief so she could dry her eyes."[3]

Tony Heilbut found the concert a bit lachrymose, especially Rosetta's tears about Mother Morrison, who until her dying day, in November 1971, had never tired of reminding her daughter-in-law of her preference for light-skinned women. Yet he still found that "she had all the goods.... She could still do 'Beams of Heaven' and 'Precious Memories' and wreck the church."

It was after Soul at the Center that Heilbut, a gospel producer of some clout, set out to get Rosetta a contract for a new album with Savoy. He arranged a deal whereby Fred Mendelsohn would produce, although he himself would have a hand in the selection of material. Heilbut had done some writing, and had penned a new song, "I've Got a Secret Between Me and My Lord," a 12-bar blues, that he thought might be perfect for Rosetta. She was excited about getting into the studio again, he said, and so they set a date for recording in a Philadelphia studio in the early fall of 1973. In the period leading up to the session, Heilbut occasionally visited the house on Master Street, where he and Rosetta would work out arrangements, almost always on her acoustic guitar, but occasionally on the piano. He told her the record would be best if, rather than fighting the changes in her voice, she made conscious use of them, giving the old songs a "soulful," contemporary flavor.

"Dear Rosetta," he wrote to her from New York, in a letter posted a few weeks before the session:

> *Here's my suggested lineup:*
> ~~*Move On Up a Little Higher*~~ *There's a Great Change*
> *I Looked Down the Line*
> *Hide Me in Thy Bosom (Rock Me)*
> *The Storm Is Passing Over*
> *Motherless Children*
> ~~*Uncloudy Day*~~ *Bring Back Those Happy Days*
> *Mountain Railroad*
> *Just to Behold His Face*
> *I've Got a Secret*
> *Love O Love* ~~*O Wondrous Love*~~ *Divine*
> *I enclose the lyrics to most of these songs. I'm looking forward to the recording session!*
> *Love,*
> *Tony*[4]

Everything seemed fine, and yet there were bad omens. On October 3, 1973, the Wednesday before the session was to take place, Heilbut found out that Herman Lubinsky, the owner of Savoy, needed to postpone it by several days, until October 8. The second bad omen came on that date, a Monday, when Heilbut showed up at the house on Master Street to accompany Rosetta to the studio, only to ring the bell and find no one home. Sensing that something was wrong, he called the studio, where someone said that Russell had called in to say that Rosetta had suffered a massive stroke and been rushed to Temple University Hospital for treatment. Together with Walter Stewart, he drove to the hospital and joined Russell at Rosetta's bedside. Things at the hospital were grim. Rosetta was not in a private or even semiprivate room, as Walter Stewart recalls; to him it felt more like a public ward, certainly not befitting a person of Rosetta's stature. Worse still, Stewart remembers seeing blood on Rosetta's face, and this struck him as an unforgivable affront to a woman who had always been so meticulous about her appearance. All of them, not just Stewart, worried that an African American woman in a diabetic coma was at risk of being treated like another statistic. As Stewart recalls, Heilbut—the only white person at Rosetta's bedside—was practically in hysterics, pleading with the staff to treat Rosetta with the care due to a "great, great artist."

Meanwhile, Stewart kept saying her name: "Rosetta, Rosetta," enunciating the "t" as though from the repetition of such a precise mantra he might pull Rosetta back to consciousness. But she never emerged from her coma. By the time Roxie could get off work to rush to the hospital, Rosetta was already dead. The date of her passing was October 9, 1973—one day after she was to have recorded her new Savoy album. The death certificate, which listed her occupation as "gospel singer," identified the cause of death as cerebral thrombosis due to atherosclerotic cardiovascular disease due to diabetes: in layman's terms, a blood clot in the brain.

Shortly after her death became official, Russell and others set about the dismal task of making calls to out-of-town friends to convey the news. When Marie heard from Dolly that Russell was on the line asking for her, she remembers thinking, "After all these years he wants to talk to me." She was concerned that Russell's neglect of Rosetta in life would extend to lack of proper care for her in death. She told Russell she would be down to Philadelphia as soon as possible to see to the funeral arrangements. "We lived our lives together," she recalled. "We shared with each other while she was alive.... I only wanted[ed] to see her buried as the person that she was."

Rosetta left no will, effectively leaving what material possessions she owned—chiefly the cars and the house on Master Street—to Russell. Louise Tucker, Ira's wife, took some of her gowns. But there was little money for a funeral and interment. Marie says there was an insurance policy from Metropolitan Life that Russell didn't know about until Rosetta died—one that could be used to cover expenses—but if there was, there is no evidence its proceeds were collected.

The viewing took place at Baker & Baker Funeral Home, 2008 N. Broad Street in Philadelphia, on October 15, the day before the funeral. More than 170 people—including neighbors from the Yorktown area, a number of ministers and evangelists from Philadelphia, and friends and family from as far away as South Carolina—signed their names in a condolences book.

The next evening, William Gray III, son of Congressman William Gray, who had recently stepped down from his role as pastor of Bright Hope, led the service. It wasn't modest, as Mother Bell's had been, but neither was it majestic like the funeral of Mahalia Jackson, who had died in January 1972 and whose Chicago memorial was attended by throngs of mourners numbering into the thousands. Marie was there, and Ernestine Washington, and the Tuckers, and Roxie, of course, and Walter Stewart and Tony Heilbut. James Davis from the Hummingbirds attended, as did Paul Owens, a singer at various times with the Hummingbirds, the Swan Silvertones, and the Sensational Nightingales. Scores of Philadelphia neighbors, including Frances Steadman, Margaret Allison, and Marion Williams, came to pay their respects, as did Tommy Johnson of the Harmonizing Four, who made the trip up from Richmond. Only two of the former Rosettes, Barbara and Oreen, were able to attend, so Erma, Lottie, and Sarah, feeling bad about missing the chance to say goodbye to the woman who had been like a mother to them, instead sent a bouquet in the shape of a guitar. A number of relatives from the Atkins side of the family showed up, including Emily Kennedy, Rosetta's older half-sister. Gospel singer Sally Jenkins, who had sung on Rosetta's Mercury album *The Gospel Truth,* came to pay her respects, as did other assorted friends from Brooklyn and Manhattan.

Walter Stewart remembers the attendance as scanty; he thought the city of Philadelphia should have stepped in to do something to honor one of its most accomplished citizens. Mostly, he puts the blame for the "shabby" funeral on Russell. "I don't remember there being a lot of anything. I wouldn't call it a major funeral in any way. I don't think her husband cared about things like that. I think his source of living was gone." Rosetta's half-sister Elteaser Scott remembers it differently. "That church was full," she says. "Most of the whole family was there. They came from Milwaukee to Camden, they were all there, most of them. So she had a big funeral. That church was full." Margaret Allison recalls it as "a nice funeral. See, a lot of people didn't think Rosetta lived here in Philadelphia," she says, explaining why more gospel royalty didn't show up. "I don't know where they thought she was at. Because after she passed, I was talking to some people and they said, 'Where did she live?' 'In Philadelphia.' 'Well, where did she live in Philadelphia?' "

But Allison also speculates that Rosetta, in death, was something of the outsider she had been in life.

> A lot of people didn't know about it, but some of them probably wouldn't have went if they had known. See, a lot of the religious people, they had a thing about her, because when she left gospel and went into the other field, and singing with the band and all that, well they just thought that was awful. And then when she came back, when she tried to come back to the gospel, a lot of people never accepted her. In fact, even on the shows that we were on with her [in the '60s], she would always apologize to the people for her leaving.... She would just talk on stage, she would say like, she would tell like, she was brought up in church and religion and everything, but then she would explain to them how she left the gospel field.

At the service, Marion Williams sang "Precious Lord" and Marie did "Peace in the Valley." Roxie read a statement from The Four Kings Gospel Singers, written on behalf of the citizens of Camden, Arkansas, in honor of their relative, Rosetta Tharpe, and then she read the eulogy she had composed:

> *Almighty God in His infinite wisdom and tender mercy has taken away from our midst, our Beloved Sister, Rosetta Atkins Tharpe Morrison.*

Rosetta was a loving, kind, warm and generous person. She was the first nationally and internationally known Female Gospel Singer and recording Gospel Star.

She started her career at the age of six with her late Mother, Mrs. Katie Atkins Nubin who was an Evangelist in The Church of God in Christ nationwide.

She and her mother toured this nation many times over, and many sinners were converted, saved and sanctified and Baptized with the Blessed Holy Spirit under their ministry.

She was ~~criticized by a few but~~ loved and adored by many. For all who knew her in her youth, know of her dedication to serving the church faithfully and reverently and her devotion to her Mother and to Saints of God.

She started out when the going was rough and when the gospel was not very appealing, because the churches were far less affluent and the only thing to be gained was a hope of Salvation. But she sang in season and out of season. She would sing until you cried and then she would sing until you danced for Joy.

She and the great Songstress, Madame Ernestine Washington, the wife of Bishop Fredrick D. Washington of Brooklyn, N.Y. were childhood friends and the two of them sang for thousands each year at the National convocations of the Church of God in Christ, in Memphis, Tenn., when they were only teenagers. They helped to keep the church alive and the Saints rejoicing.

There is so much about Rosetta's early life, so many good things, that the world at large have never heard about. But those of us who have followed her career know that she was great on the inside.

She was a loving Daughter, a loving wife, a helpful friend and she always testified of God's goodness to her and her undying love for Him. She suffered a lot but she realized that if we suffer with Him we shall also reign with Him. For the way of the Cross leads home.

We are sure that she has found Peace in the Valley. Altho she loved her husband dearly and desired to live because of him, she had to cross over to see her Lord, for all Jordan had to get back last Tuesday morning and let Rosetta cross over to see the man that she Sang about in her Songs!

We'll miss her, but God willing we'll meet her.

Respectfully, (Mrs. Roxie Moore for) Friends and Family.[5]

Afterward, they went back to Master Street, where Russell, according to Marie, was stingy with his wife's mourners, including family members from her father's side. She recalls going to the undertaker's, where she says she fixed and set Rosetta's hair—as she had in the late 1940s when they traveled together—and dressed her friend in a full-length lime gown. The memory, filtered through the tear-stained veil of grief, evokes the tenderness between two women who had shared intimacy as singers and "sisters" for almost thirty years.

Russell had Rosetta's body interred at Northwood Cemetery, six miles north of Yorktown up Broad Street, almost to Cheltenham, in a grave with a concrete base. He had paid about one hundred dollars for the single plot, the depth of which suggested that he might, one day, rest there with her. He never bought a gravestone to mark the site where his wife's body lay.

Indeed, although Marie insists Rosetta was buried with her white SG, rumors circulated after the funeral that Russell had sold the instrument to an unnamed collector for a "trifling sum," on the order of $250. According to Annie Morrison, Russell sold the guitar to a friend in the gospel field who lived in New York. Some people talked behind Russell's back, thinking it wrong to put a price on something so associated with Rosetta, but he may have feared for a future without his wife's earnings. As Annie puts it, "You know Russell wasn't gonna bury no guitar in the ground when he could get some money for it." He also sold her mink coat and, at Annie's urging, Rosetta's Lincoln Continental. "The only thing he would *not* sell was the piano," she recalls. "He never said why."

It was a decrescendo ending for a woman who had lived life in a grande dame manner and who had prided herself on putting on a good show, no matter the circumstances backstage. Ella Mitchell, who sang with Rosetta back in her splendid 1960 appearance at the Apollo, had come down for the funeral from New York. "She always wanted to do things well," Mitchell recalls. "She always wanted to make sure it was very well prepared, and then go ahead and do it, putting the best foot forward at all times. And she did it with ease, like it wasn't no problem, like this is what I was born to do."

EPILOGUE: VIBRATIONS, STRONG AND MEAN

We all respected her for what she could do. She opened
doors for a lot of people, whether given a lot of credit
or not, she did. She made everybody feel important.
Everybody was somebody with her, and everybody was
just as important as she was. I mean, she knew no big I's
and little you's. She just knew people to be people.
Inez Andrews

To pay respects today at the grave of Rosetta Tharpe requires a bit of persistence. Since no stone marks the exact site, a visitor to Northwood Cemetery in Philadelphia needs to inquire at the main office, a cheerless room, where one of the managers will go to a file and pull a sort of index card with information about the location of "Morrison, Rosetta Tharpe." The card provides a number that corresponds to a plot, but the map of the cemetery is unreliable, so a worker will bring around his small truck and drive the visitor down one of the narrow, ribbonlike paths that wend around different sections of the large property. As its name suggests, Northwood is dotted with clumps of deciduous trees, and the green, well-tended grass looks more or less the same from one gentle rise in the ground to another. Arriving at the site for "Morrison, Rosetta Tharpe," what one notices is a nothingness—not an ominous absence, just a patch of grass that bends quietly in the breeze that flows through the miniature cavern created by the granite stones on either side. It is like looking down at a game of hangman with all the letters filled in except for one.

A stone, a marker: these are arbitrary means of memorializing a person, of course. Especially a person like Rosetta, who in life was so unlike a stone—not cold, inert, and silent, but warm, funny, loud, playful, expressive, passionate, bawdy, and constantly in motion. To borrow a phrase from Ellis Haizlip, producer of Soul at the Center, Rosetta was a woman who unleashed cultural "vibrations so strong, so mean"—"mean" as in "oo-ooh, that girl plays a *mean* guitar"—that the vibrations still resonate today. Whenever a rock musician lets loose a glorious guitar solo, we're in the living presence of those strong and mean vibrations of Rosetta Tharpe, who took the gospel blues and, using her guitar as her voice, made the bridge of a song the height of its spiritual and emotional intensity. Whenever a rock or gospel or rhythm-and-blues musician turns the amps up, we're in the living presence of Rosetta, who made a habit of playing as loud as she could, based on the Pentecostal belief that the Lord smiled on those who made a joyful noise.

On the other hand, Rosetta's unmarked grave is symbolic of the fragility of memory, especially our memory of those who, like Rosetta, never fit neatly into the usual boxes. Rosetta "insisted upon a sound and lifestyle of ambiguity," says gospel scholar Horace Boyer. First there was her willingness to share her musical gift anywhere, with anyone, even in the face of disapproval from conservative corners of the Church of God in Christ. Then there was that guitar and the way she played it—like no one else in gospel. And finally there were the ways she pushed the limits, in song and in life: What did it matter if a little blues bubbled over into her gospel song? Who said she couldn't play the fool when the fancy struck? Who cared if she enjoyed a flirtation or a drink now and then?

In a culture that tends to associate artistic greatness with a disdain for convention, such qualities of unruliness should have elevated her to the ranks of creative genius. Yet as much as this romantic version of the artist still dominates thinking about creativity, including musical creativity, it's not part of the dominant image of the gospel musician. In popular culture especially, gospel singers are often portrayed as simple, happy people whose faith renders them ingenuous and unrefined. Occasionally they command an authority associated with their spirituality, but they're seldom depicted as multilayered, let alone conflicted. While we've come to expect blues or jazz musicians to be extraordinary people leading unconventional lives, we don't usually imagine gospel musicians in this way.

Rosetta was what music historian Rosetta Reitz calls an "underneath-it-all" performer—a kind of musical Zelig who turns up everywhere once you scratch the surface. But her fading from popular memory is not merely attributable to the natural passage of time; rather, it's the product of a multitude of small but important acts of forgetting. In 1963, *Sepia* magazine inquired, "Is gospel rock and roll, or is rock and roll gospel? In the white world, people are asking this question, hoping to get a simple answer. The answer is, of course, not simple because there is so much duplication in all music. To the uninitiated, however, the rousing spirit of gospel seems to bring to mind the rousing drive of rock and roll, and since so many rock and roll singers come out of gospel, the connection seems a definite one."[1]

Contrast this with a review of the 1970 American Folk, Blues and Gospel Festival in London, in which Rosetta is described as "so rhythmically exciting that when she accompanies herself on guitar she might be a blacked-up Elvis in drag."[2] Of course, the reviewer has it precisely and perversely backwards, but that doesn't affect the breathtaking power of his misstatement, in a context in which African American women are so relentlessly and profoundly swept under the carpet of history. The same year Rosetta was described as an imitation Elvis, Jimi Hendrix died and Rosetta herself suffered the stroke that led to her eventual decline and death. Thereafter, as rock critic Kandia Crazy Horse has pointed out, the success of the British Invasion would imprint upon most people's imaginations the image of the loud, aggressive rock guitar player as white, young, and male.

Still, the question of how Rosetta disappeared from popular memory so quickly after her death tugs at the sleeves of the imagination—and the conscience—of American music. Where are the legacies of Rosetta Tharpe? Where are the commercially successful black women rockers? Where are the women who have been able to make it as instrumentalists?

A danger behind any project to tell an "untold story" is that it will safely position its subject *in* the past, a collector's item in an aficionado's library, rather than present her as an enduring voice whose influence cannot be fully calculated, if only because it will persist into the future. Musicologist Christopher Small has noted that black performers often get pegged in the role of forebear, as though their contributions were important merely because they led to the contributions of other (usually white) musicians. Small is talking about Chuck Berry and Little Richard, but he could just as easily be referring to Rosetta herself.[3]

Two stories illustrate attempts to counteract this tendency. One comes from Ira Tucker Jr., who in 1998 came up with the idea of naming the Dixie Hummingbirds' seventieth anniversary CD after Rosetta. *Music in the Air*—a CD that earned a Grammy nomination for Best Soul Gospel Album—"was my tribute to Sister Rosetta," Ira Junior says, "even though it was a Hummingbirds project. I told my dad, I said look, man, I really want to call this 'Music in the Air,' because it's connected, you are connected with Rosetta, and 'Up Above My Head, I Hear Music in the Air' was her song. And so he said, no problem, he was all for it."

As for what Rosetta would think about trends in contemporary black women's performance, Ira Junior says, "I'm sure if she were living today, she would be shocked. She would be *shocked!* I mean, because she considered herself to be a rebel. You know, I mean I've always thought of her as one, and I always got the feeling that she did too. She always challenged things. . . . I mean if she was to see beyond, say, today, to [Lil' Kim], I'm sure it will flip her right out of her guitar case. . . . Sister Rosetta Tharpe paved the way for a lot of women, a lot of women. . . . She opened the doors for a lot of them and made it possible for [them] to have a career, you know, outside of the tradition."

The second story comes from the recording of *Shout, Sister, Shout!*, a CD that pays tribute to Rosetta through new versions of her songs, performed primarily by women musicians. On a cold, bright Saturday morning in January 2002, Marie Knight entered a Soho studio to do "Didn't It Rain." Nearly fifty-four years since they had recorded it for Decca, Marie recreated the energy that characterized her collaborations with Rosetta, singing in a voice notably changed and yet qualitatively undiminished by age. Her performance began as a relatively straightforward rendition of the song, on which Rosetta sang soprano and Marie backed her up in an alto register, their voices joyfully swirling around each other. But this time Marie was soloing. Yet as people in the studio gathered to listen to the playback, a remarkable thing happened: Marie, as she listened, began punctuating her own performance with the secondary vocal line she had sung in the original recording, in effect singing the response to her own call. Hearing this, the producer urged her to reenter the studio to record her additional vocal line. She did, and then recorded yet a third track in which she added tambourine. The final product, which combines these three, is a wonderful record of musical history, reviving the voices both of Marie's younger self and of her friend Rosetta Tharpe.

These are the sorts of acts of revival that work against forgetting, reversing the neglect of African American women's contributions to American music. They are both, in their own small way, prayers of remembrance and gratitude. They also suggest that we have a lot of catching up with the past to do. In other words, if the name Sister Rosetta Tharpe is unfamiliar, the reason is perhaps not that Rosetta has been forgotten, but that history failed to *get* her in the first place. Gospel crossover star? Woman guitar sensation? Flamboyant black rocker before rock and roll? All of these formulations work, but only to a certain degree. For the rest, we'll need to invent a new story.

ACKNOWLEDGMENTS

As the saints say, I have come to feel "blessed" in writing this book. My belated discovery of the genius of Sister Rosetta Tharpe around 1998 was the first blessing, followed by the blessing of meeting and talking to so many inspiring people in the course of my research and writing. Although I am an outsider to the gospel world by faith and race, and I grew up in the 1970s—unlike most of the people I interviewed, who grew up during segregation—I have been welcomed at every turn with grace and goodwill. I cannot possibly hope to repay the debts I owe so many people.

For sharing their memories and wisdom, providing insight and instruction, helping me locate people or information, answering my questions, giving me an outlet for the dissemination of my ideas, and/or constituting the community of gospel collectors and aficionados, I thank: Lynn Abbott, Berle Adams, Karen Ahlquist, Chris Albertson, Robert Allen, Margaret Allison, Kip Anderson, Inez Andrews, Donell Atkins, Jenny Bagert, Ginger Baker, Hoover Baker, Lizzie Baker, Alan Balfour, Chris Barber, "Barky" Barksdale, Louie Bellson, Martin Bernal, Jeffrey Blomster, Allen J. Bloom, Brett Bonner, Dave Booth, Joe Boyd, Horace Clarence Boyer, James Boyer, Harold Bradley, J. Robert Bradley, Emily Bram-Bibby, John Broven, Chris Stovall Brown, Ruth Brown, Sharon Brown, Jay Bruder, Joel Buchanon, Tony Burke, Clarke Bustard, Jean Buzelin, James "Early" Byrd, Vira Ann Byrd, Agnes Campbell, Delois Barrett Campbell, Mark Carpentieri, Rosanne Cash, Andy Chard, Reverend Isaac Cohen, Nadine Cohodas, Steve Cole, Derek Coller, Creadell Copeland, LeRoy Crume, Terry Cryer, Steve Cushing, Art Davis, Jim Dickinson, Kenneth Doroshow, Ken Druker, Sherry DuPree, Jeannette Eason, Walter E. Fauntroy, Kenneth Feld, Shirley Feld, Marilyn Ford, David Freeland, Ray Funk, David Gahr, Elder Donald Gay, Odell "Gorgeous" George, Lex Gillespie, Charlie Gillett, Cary Ginell, Naomi Gittings, William Gittings, Walter Godfrey, Jeff Goff, David Gough, Gwendolyn Stinson Gray, Marc Grobman, Peter Guralnick, Geraldine Gay Hambric, Ernest Hayes, Isaac Hayes, Tony Heilbut, Phyllis Hill, Henry Hinkel, Mother May Ethel Holmes, District Elder George T. Holton, Andy Hoogenboom, Musette Hubbard (who passed away in

March 2006), Jeff Hughson, Bruce Ignlauer, Elder David E. Jackson, Jerma Jackson, Greg Johnson, Zeola Cohen Jones, Marcia Jones-Washington, the congregation of Kelsey Temple Church of God in Christ in Washington, D.C., Dred-Scott Keyes, Millie Kirkham, Timothy Kish, David Klowden, Reverend Marie Knight, Stephen Koch, James J. Kriegsmann Jr., Sleepy LaBeef, Willy Leiser, Jean-Pierre Leloir, David Leonard, Nettie Lewis, Kip Lornell, Georgia Louis, Fred MacDonald, Junior Mance, Greil Marcus, Bob Marovich, Charles McGovern, Andy McKaie, Marya McQuirter, Alfred Miller, Ella Mitchell, Bob Moore, Kittra Moore, R. Stevie Moore, Roxie A. Moore, Elder Fred D. Morris Sr., Annie Morrison, Maria Muldaur, Opal Nations, Tracy Nelson, Bruce Nemerov, Per "Slim" Notini, Dawn Oberg, George O'Leary, Barney Parks, Ottilie Patterson, Vincent Pelote, Don Peterson, Eloise Powell, Sullivan Pugh, Ernestine Pyles, Tom Reed, Rosetta Reitz, Del Rey, David Ritz, Alva Doris Roberts, Camille Roberts, the congregation of Roberts Temple Church of God in Christ in Chicago, Don and Mary Robertson, Bertha Robinson, Elder Bill Robinson, Desirée Roots, Sarah Roots, Pastor Benjamin Ross, J. B. Ross, Nick Salvatore, David Sanjek, Kenneth L. Saunders, Bill Sayger, Cheatam Scott, Elteaser Scott, Roy T. Scott, Samuel Scott, Samuel E. Scott, Doug Seroff, Olivia Sheppard, Michelle Shocked, Drink Small, Donald Liston Smith, Eugene Smith, Lottie Smith, Brad Snyder, Peter N. Solomon, Mother Evelyn Spears, Dick Spottswood, Johnetta Steele, Walter Stewart, Gordon Stoker, Howard Tash, Creed Taylor, Carla Thomas, Leslie Triggs, Ira Tucker, Ira Tucker Jr., Frances Steadman Turner, Dimitri Vicheney (Jacques Demêtre), Evelyn Waites, Floyd Waites, Steve Waksman, Elijah Wald, Sharon Joyce Roberts Walker, Pastor Cleven Wardlow Jr., Gayle Dean Wardlow, Willa Ward-Royster, Phil Watson, Eric Weisbard, Hollie I. West, David Whiteis, Val Wilmer, Toni Wine, Charles Wolfe, Clyde Wright, Ron Wynn, Lloyd Yearwood, Zane Zacharoff, and Jerry Zolten.

The following deserve special thanks: Rosetta Reitz, who encouraged me at an early stage; Annie Morrison, who entrusted me with Rosetta's legacy; Tony Heilbut, adviser and telephone operator to the gospel world; the Boyer brothers, Drs. James and Horace Clarence Boyer, for their support and, in the case of Horace Boyer, willingness to read chapters at a late stage; Peter Guralnick, who was, miraculously, a supporter and booster long before I did anything to deserve it (I hope I now have); Marie Knight, who spent long hours talking about the past; Ira Tucker, for his generosity, even when I forgot my tape recorder; Ira Tucker Jr., for his wonderful stories of people he grew up with; Roxie Moore, for sharing her "precious memories" and patiently answering my questions; Lottie Smith and Sarah Roots, Geraldine Gay Hambric and Donald Gay, and Georgia Louis and Pierre Geurtin, for their hospitality and warmth; Val Wilmer, for conversation, ideas, and advice, and (although I never told her this) for being an inspiration as a woman in a field dominated by men; Don Peterson, for allowing me to publish the photos of Rosetta taken by his father, Charles Peterson; David Leonard and Jenny Bagert at Herman Leonard Photography, for allowing me use of the terrific cover image of Rosetta; Cary Ginell at Alfred Publishing and Marcia Webman at Webman Associates, for their help in obtaining print licensing permissions; my European comrades, Alan Balfour, Jean Buzelin, Willy Leiser, Per Notini, and Dimitri Vicheney, who gave of their time and enthusiasm, and are working to keep Rosetta's legacy alive overseas; Elijah Wald, who, though no relation, did me the great favor of reading large chunks of the manuscript with eagle eyes at a crucial moment in its preparation; Charles McGovern, James A. Miller, and David Stowe, colleagues who did the same, and at the eleventh hour; Ruth Brown and Isaac Hayes, inspiring artists.

I have Gayatri Patnaik, my fabulous editor at Beacon Press, to thank for her guidance and attentiveness at every step; she is the kind of editor a writer trusts implicitly, for her judgment, good humor, and smarts; thanks, too, to the entire team at Beacon, especially Tracy Ahlquist, Tom Hallock, Bob Kosturko, Pam MacColl, and Lisa Sacks.

I am "blessed" with friends who combine brilliance with innumerable other fine qualities. All of you read or heard parts of the manuscript, offered your advice, or wrote letters in support of my work. My gratitude to Daphne Brooks, Judith Castleberry, Jill Dolan, Ruth Feldstein, Lisa Gitelman, Farah Jasmine Griffin, Judith Halberstam, Meta DuEwa Jones, Josh Kun, Andrea Levine, George Lipsitz, Maureen Mahon, Melani McAlister, Robert McRuer, Fred Moten, Guthrie Ramsey, Sonnet Retman, Valerie Smith, Sherrie Tucker, and Stacy Wolf. Thanks, too, to Masha Belenky, Carolyn Betensky, Patty Chu, Jeffrey Cohen, Kavita Daiya, Mary Ann Dubner, Chad Heap, Jennifer James, Lisa Lynch, Phyllis Palmer, Rona Peligal, Judith Plotz, Mikaela Seligman, Sarah Werner, and Floyd White, for your various forms of encouragement and support.

Andrea deserves special mention for doing inspired sprinting with me during the final laps.

None of this would have been possible without the support of the George Washington University, especially in the persons of Faye Moskowitz and William Frawley, and in the form of the Columbian Scholars Fellowship initiated under Dean Frawley's tenure. Thank you, too, to Brian Flota, Tim Walsh, Matthew Schnipper, Delaina Price, Emaleigh Doley, and Aliza Schiff for their fine research assistance.

Several institutions have enabled me to take time away from teaching to research and write. Thank you to the Humanities Research Institute at the University of California, Irvine (and to my colleagues Raul Fernández, Michelle Habell-Pallán, Gayatri Gopinath, Herman Beaver, Jocelyne Guilbault, and Anthony Macías); the Cornell University Society for the Humanities (thank you to Mary Pat Brady, Caprice Cadacio, Anne-Lise François, Michael Kim, and Samantha Majic for propping me up during the long Ithaca winter); and, most important, the National Endowment for the Humanities, for a 2005–2006 fellowship through the "We the People" initiative.

My family has been with me every step of the way: my parents, Max and Marlene Wald, who leave copies of my work "lying around" on available flat surfaces in their home; my sister, Heidi Wald, and brother-in-law, Philip Weiser, who have been indefatigable cheerleaders. Scott Barash offered unwavering support, and, in addition to being a sterling editor, he has a downloadable 10-gigabyte hard drive of music knowledge in his brain. He patiently reminded me that writing a biography is "a marathon, not a sprint." He is the joy of my life, and I dedicate this book to him.

APPENDIX

INTERVIEWS

The following interviews were conducted by the author
(letters and e-mail correspondence are indicated).

Berle Adams, May 2, 2004
Chris Albertson, January 30, 2006
Robert Allen, July 20, 2004; August 13, 2004
Margaret Allison, December 30, 2005
Kip Anderson, February 16, 2004
Inez Andrews, February 7, 2006
Ginger Baker, e-mail, March 20, 2006
Alan Balfour, e-mail, September 25, 2003, and September 7, 2004
Chris Barber, September 19, 2003; e-mail December 17, 2005
Martin Bernal, May 4, 2004
Allen Bloom, March 31, 2004
Joe Boyd, January 30, 2006
Horace Clarence Boyer, August 31, 2004; May 4, 2006; April 9, 2006
James Boyer, May 4, 2004; August 13, 2004; letter, May 13, 2004
J. Robert Bradley, February 12, 2004
John Broven, e-mail, February 5, 2006
Ruth Brown, August 23, 2004
Jean Buzelin, December 19, 2005; e-mail, September 3, 2004
James "Early" Byrd, January 9, 2005; February 28, 2006; March 8, 2006
Delois Barrett Campbell, February 5, 2004; June 4, 2005
Rev. Isaac Cohen, May 20, 2004; August 31, 2005
Derek Coller, e-mail, June 29, 2004
Creadell Copeland, November 14, 2005
LeRoy Crume, December 2, 2005
Terry Cryer, August 5, 2003; letter, April 25, 2003
Art Davis, May 2, 2004
Jim Dickinson, December 1, 2005
Sherry Sherrod DuPree, April 8, 2004
Jeannette Eason, January 18, 2006
Walter Fauntroy, October 5, 2005
Shirley Feld, August 5, 2005
Elder Donald Gay, March 28, 2005
William and Naomi Gittings, July 8, 2004
Walter Godfrey, December 1, 2005
Gwendolyn Stinson Gray, June 18, 2004

Peter Guralnick, February 16, 2004; March 9, 2004; March 31, 2004; December 16, 2004; October 6, 2005; letter, November 23, 2003; letter, December 28, 2005

Geraldine Gay Hambric, March 28, 2005

Ernest Hayes, December 30, 2005; January 9, 2006

Isaac Hayes, April 4, 2005

Anthony Heilbut, August 12, 2002; February 17, 2004; June 16, 2004; November 11, 2004; February 13, 2005; April 21, 2006; e-mail, February 19, 2006

Elder George T. Holton, January 7, 2003

May Ethel Homes, August 13, 2005

Andy Hoogenboom, February 8, 2006

Musette Hubbard, April 12, 2004

Sam Jefferson, August 5, 2005

Zeola Cohen Jones, April 24, 2006

Dred-Scott Keyes, November 13, 2005

Millie Kirkham, March 10, 2004; October 7, 2005

Marie Knight, October 18, 2002; October 23, 2002; July 1, 2004; September 2, 2004

Sleepy LaBeef, March 10, 2004

Willy Leiser, September 29, 2004

Jean-Pierre Leloir, September 13, 2005

Georgia Louis, February 11, 2004; July 13, 2004

Junior Mance, January 2, 2005

Alfred Miller, November 13, 2005

Ella Mitchell, February 14, 2006

Bob Moore, February 4, 2004

Kittra Moore, February 4, 2004; e-mail, May 23, 2004

Roxie Moore, March 8, 2004; April 9, 2004; January 10, 2004

Annie Morrison, May 19, 2004; July 7, 2004

Opal Nations, February 9, 2004

Barney Parks, April 8, 2004

Ottilie Patterson, January 6, 2006

Rev. Franklin G. Pryor, August 8, 2005

Sullivan Pugh, July 20, 2004

Tom Reed, May 4, 2004

Rosetta Reitz, October 9, 2002

Alva Roberts, June 7, 2004

Camille Roberts, April 14, 2004; June 7, 2004

Bertha Robinson, September 13, 2005

Elder Bill Robinson, letter, March 12, 2004

Sarah Roots, March 24, 2004; June 28, 2005

Kenneth L. Saunders, May 13, 2004

Cheatam Scott, April 3, 2004

Elteaser Scott, July 27, 2005

Roy T. Scott, July 27, 2005

Sam Scott, January 26, 2004; April 3, 2004

Doug Seroff, March 10, 2004; letter, October 8, 2005
Drink Small, February 19, 2004
Donald Liston Smith, March 15, 2004
Lonnie Liston Smith Jr., March 3, 2004
Lottie Smith, March 24, 2004; June 28, 2005
Evelyn Spears, October 5, 2005
Walter Stewart, June 25, 2004
Gordon Stoker, March 5, 2004; March 10, 2004
Creed Taylor, January 25, 2006
Carla Thomas, April 13, 2004
Leslie Triggs, e-mail, June 28, 2004
Ira Tucker, October 3, 2003
Ira Tucker Jr., May 22, 2003
Frances Steadman Turner, December 18, 2005; December 29, 2005
Dimitri Vicheney, January 5, 2006; letter, January 17, 2006
Floyd Waites and Evelyn Waites, February 13, 2006
Elijah Wald, February 23, 2006; e-mail, February 20, 2006
Gayle Dean Wardlow, February 26, 2004
Willa Ward-Royster, December 29, 2005
Hollie I. West, February 7, 2006
Valerie Wilmer, October 30, 2003; April 7, 2004; letter,
    November 12, 2003; letter, February 1, 2006; letter, February 26, 2006
Toni Wine, January 26, 2005
Charles Wolfe, March 18, 2004
Norman Wood, August 2, 2005
Clyde Wright, December 19, 2005
Lloyd Yearwood, March 3, 2004; June 29, 2004
Zane Zacharoff, September 9, 2005

SELECTED DISCOGRAPHY

Almost all of Rosetta Tharpe's recordings from 1938 to 1953, and many from later years, are currently available on compact disc.

The French label Frémeaux & Associates and the English label Document Records have been at the forefront of Rosetta Tharpe reissues. The most thorough collection of her work to date is *The Complete Sister Rosetta Tharpe/Intégrale Sister Rosetta Tharpe,* issued in four volumes by Frémeaux (FA 1301–1304), with notes in English and French. Document has released, so far, three volumes of *Sister Rosetta Tharpe: Complete Recorded Works in Chronological Order* (DOCD-5334, -5335, and -5607), covering the period between 1938 and 1947. The English label Proper Records also publishes a four-CD compilation, titled *Sister Rosetta Tharpe: The Original Soul Sister* (Properbox 51).

Listeners who want an introduction to Rosetta's music in a single CD might consult *The Gospel of the Blues* (MCA B0000533–02), which mixes her gospel work with blues pieces such as "I Want a Tall Skinny Papa." *Up Above My Head* (Indigo IGO CD 2108), which focuses more on her gospel material, is also recommended. Both offer selections from Rosetta's earliest Decca recordings, as well as samples of her duets with Marie Knight.

CD reissues of Rosetta Tharpe's LPs from the period after the mid-1950s include: *Precious Memories* (Savoy SCD 5008), *Spirituals in Rhythm* (Collector's Choice CCM-1302), and *Gospel Train* (Verve 4228411342). The latter reproduces the original 1956 LP cover and album notes.

Live recordings of Rosetta Tharpe date from the late 1950s and 1960s and vary in sound quality. In chronological order, they include: *Chris Barber's Jazz Band with Special Guest Sister Rosetta Tharpe, 1957* (Lake LACD 130), *Live in 1960* (Southland SCD-1007), and, from 1964, *Live at the Hot Club de France* (Milan ML2 35624). The last is the best representation of Rosetta live in Europe.

Katie Bell Nubin's *Soul, Soul Searching* is out of print, but "Where's Adam?" is on *Dizzy's Diamonds: The Best of the Verve Years* (Verve 314513875-2). *The Very Best of the Harmonizing Four* (Collectibles COL 6106) provides a taste of this superb quartet's music. *Rev. Kelsey and His Congregation, 1947–1951* (Document DOCD-5478) features some wonderful singing, and introduces listeners to the sounds of an important COGIC church in the 1940s. *Arizona Dranes: Complete Recorded Works in Chronological Order, 1926–1929* (DOCD-5186), collects the work of the early Sanctified pianist-singer.

Rosetta appears on many compilations, but two are particularly worthy of mention: *The Great Gospel Women* and *The Great Gospel Women, Vol. 2* (Shanachie 6004 and 6017). Produced by Anthony Heilbut, both CDs feature Rosetta in the context of the best of her contemporaries.

The soundie of "The Lonesome Road," performed with the Lucky Millinder Orchestra, is available on *Jivin' Time: Harlem Roots, Vol. 4*, Storyville Films (SV-6003), videocassette.

Scores of musicians have covered Rosetta's work—either songs she composed or songs she made famous. My personal favorite is *The Glory Road* (Numero NUM 005), which includes several of Rosetta's tunes performed by Fern Jones, an unsung white Pentecostal singer-guitarist. Finally, there is MC Records' tribute CD, *Shout, Sister, Shout!* (MC-0050), on which Marie Knight sings "Didn't It Rain." The CD also includes a video feature of Rosetta performing "Down by the Riverside" on *TV Gospel Time.*

CREDITS AND PERMISSIONS

Parts of the book draw on material previously published as "From Spirituals to Swing: Sister Rosetta Tharpe and Gospel Crossover," *American Quarterly* 55, no. 3 (September 2003), 387–416. Courtesy Johns Hopkins University Press.

Chapter 8 is based on an article that originally appeared as "Have a Little Talk: Listening to the B-side of History," *Popular Music* 24 (2005), 323–337. Copyright © Cambridge University Press.

Parts of the epilogue appeared in an earlier version as "Reviving Rosetta Tharpe: Performance and Memory in the 21st Century," *Women and Performance: A Journal of Feminist Theory* 161 (2006), 91–106. Copyright © Taylor and Francis (http://www.tandf.co.uk).

THIS TRAIN
Traditional spiritual arranged by Sister Rosetta Tharpe.
Copyright © 1938 (renewed) EMI Mills Music, Inc.
Used by Permission of Alfred Publishing Co., Inc.
All rights reserved.

PEACE IN THE VALLEY
Words and music by Thomas A. Dorsey.
Copyright © 1939 (renewed) Warner-Tamerlane Publishing Corp.
All rights reserved.

UP ABOVE MY HEAD
Traditional spiritual arranged by Sister Rosetta Tharpe.
Copyright © 1947 Webman Associates.
All rights reserved.

JUST A LITTLE TALK WITH JESUS
Words and music by Cleavant Derricks.
Copyright © 1937 Stamps-Baxter Music (BMI).
All rights reserved.

TROUBLE IN MIND
Words and music by Richard M. Jones.
Copyright © 1926, renewed by MCA Music Publishing.
All rights administered by Universal Music Corp./ASCAP.
All rights reserved.

The April 24, 1954, *Billboard* advertisement is reproduced by kind permission of Universal Music Enterprises.

NOTES

ABBREVIATIONS

AA   *Afro-American* (Washington, Baltimore, or Richmond edition)

CD   *Chicago Defender*

GS   Anthony Heilbut, *The Gospel Sound: Good News and Bad Times*, 25th Anniversary Edition (New York: Limelight Editions, 1997).

GAG Horace Clarence Boyer, with photography by Lloyd Yearwood, *The Golden Age of Gospel* (1995; reprint, Urbana and Chicago: Univ. of Illinois Press, 2000).

CHAPTER 1: COTTON PLANT

1. Brian Greer, "'A Reign of Terror': Little Rock's Last Lynching Was in 1927, But the Terrible Memories Linger," *Arkansas Times,* July 28, 2000.

2. Census of the United States, 1880, Princeton Township, Dallas County, Arkansas (Enumeration District 66); Census of the United States, 1900, Princeton Township, Dallas County, Arkansas (Enumeration District 20).

3. *The Hustler,* Special Pictorial Magazine Edition, 1, no. 19, July 14, 1905, 12.

4. Bill Sayger, *A Cotton Plant and Dark Corner Remembrancer* (Brinkley, AR: private printing, 2002), 5–7.

5. *Hustler,* 1–2.

6. Tera W. Hunter, *To 'Joy My Freedom: Southern Black Women's Lives and Labors after the Civil War* (Cambridge, MA: Harvard University Press), 175.

7. "Weird Babel of Tongues," *Los Angeles Daily Times,* April 18, 1906.

8. C. Eric Lincoln and Lawrence H. Mamiya, *The Black Church in the African American Experience* (Durham, NC: Duke University Press, 1990), 81.

9. Acts 2:4 (New International Version).

10. Anthea D. Butler, "Church Mothers and Migration in the Church of God in Christ," in *Religion in the American South: Protestants and Others in History and Culture,* ed. Beth Barton Schweiger and Donald G. Mathews (Chapel Hill, NC: University of North Carolina Press, 2004), 196, 206.

11. Butler, "Church Mothers and Migration," 201.

12. Toni Morrison, *Beloved* (New York: Random House, 1987); Lincoln and Mamiya, *The Black Church,* 354. For more on the development of COGIC and related class tensions within black communities, see Hunter, *To 'Joy My Freedom,* 177, and Leon Litwack, *Trouble in Mind: Black Southerners in the Age of Jim Crow* (New York: Alfred A. Knopf, 1998), 378–403.

13. Lincoln and Mamiya, *The Black Church,* 83.

14. Litwack, *Trouble in Mind,* 378–403. The quotation is from page 387.

15. Most dictionaries also regard "Holy Roller" as a pejorative used to describe Pentecostals of any race or ethnicity. I use the term when it is used in print or in interviews. Many of the sources I interviewed use "Holy Roller" as a term of identification thought to be understandable to non-Pentecostals—that is, as Rosetta sometimes used it, without disparaging intention.

16. Butler, "Church Mothers and Migration," 196.

CHAPTER 2: GOT ON MY TRAVELIN' SHOES

1. Mahalia Jackson with Evan McLeod Wylie, *Movin' On Up* (New York: Hawthorn Books, 1966), 62.

2. Tera W. Hunter, *To 'Joy My Freedom: Southern Black Women's Lives and Labors after the Civil War* (Cambridge, MA: Harvard University Press), 232.

3. Richard Wright, "Ethnographical Aspects of Chicago's Black Belt," December 11, 1935, The Illinois Writers' Project / "Negro in Illinois" papers, Box 53, Folder 1, Chicago Public Library, Vivian G. Harsh Research Collection of Afro-American History and Literature.

4. Hunter, *To 'Joy My Freedom,* 205.

5. "And Churches" [n.a., n.d.], The Illinois Writers' Project / "Negro in Illinois" papers, Box 45, Folder 1, Chicago Public Library, Vivian G. Harsh Research Collection of Afro-American History and Literature, 5.

6. Lawrence W. Levine, *Black Culture and Black Consciousness: Afro-American Folk Thought from Slavery to Freedom* (New York: Oxford University Press, 1977), 180.

7. François Postif, *Jazz Me Blues: Interviews et portraits de musicians de jazz et de blues* (Paris: Outre Mesure, 1999), 15–16.

8. Sister Rosetta Tharpe, "One Morning Soon," *The Gospel Truth* (Mercury SR 60080).

9. Pearl Williams-Jones, "A Brief Historical and Analytical Survey of Afro-American Gospel Music," in *We'll Understand It Better By and By: Pioneering African American Gospel Composers,* ed. Bernice Johnson Reagon (Washington, DC: Smithsonian Institution Press, 1992), 37.

10. Ellistine P. Holly, "Sister Rosetta Tharpe," in *Notable Black American Women,* ed. Jessie Carney Smith (Detroit: Gale Publishing, 1992), 1120.

11. Joyce Marie Jackson, "The Changing Nature of Gospel Music: A Southern Case Study," *African American Review* 29, no. 2 (1995): 190.

12. Jules Schwerin, *Got to Tell It: Mahalia Jackson, Queen of Gospel* (New York: Oxford University Press, 1992), 30.

13. Michael Corcoran, "Holy Roller: Arizona Dranes," *Blues & Rhythm: The Gospel Truth* 185 (2003): 14–15; Ken Romanowski, album notes, *Arizona Dranes: Complete Recorded Works in Chronological Order, 1926–1929* (DOCD-5186).

14. George D. Lewis, "Spirituals of Today" [n.d.], The Illinois Writers' Project / "Negro in Illinois" papers, Box 49, Folder 24, Chicago Public Library, Vivian G. Harsh Research Collection of Afro-American History and Literature, 1.

15. In "Negro Churches (Denominational)," another New Deal–era study, Fenton Johnson quotes Elder Lucy Smith. "We didn't buy no second-hand white church," she is reputed to have said, "but built one from the ground up," supposedly for sixty-five thousand dollars. See Johnson [n.d.], The Illinois Writers' Project / "Negro in Illinois" papers, Box 18, Folder 3, Chicago Public Library, Vivian G. Harsh Research Collection of Afro-American History and Literature.

16. Telia U. Anderson, " 'Calling on the Spirit': The Performativity of Black Women's Faith in the Baptist Church Spiritual Traditions and Its Radical Possibilities for Resistance," in African-American Performance and Theater History: A Critical Reader, ed. Harry J. Elam Jr. and David Krasner (New York: Oxford University Press, 2001), 114–131.

CHAPTER 3: FROM SPIRITUALS TO SWING

1. Nathaniel Harrington, "Benny Goodman Bids for 'Sister Tharpe': Wants Singer Out on Coast with Him," CD, July 29, 1939.

2. Harrington, "Benny Goodman Bids for 'Sister Tharpe' "; Marvel Cooke, "Holy Roller Singer Toast of Broadway: Sister Rosetta Tharpe Swings Spirituals for Sophisticated Cotton Club Clientele," New York Amsterdam Star-News, March 4, 1939.

3. Art Franklin, "Lucky Millinder and Rosetta Tharpe," Swing magazine, October 1941, 15; " 'Sister Tharpe' Thinks Her Old Role Was the Tops," CD, August 19, 1939.

4. Harrington, "Benny Goodman Bids for 'Sister Tharpe.' " For the description of Calloway's discovery of Rosetta in New York, see George D. Lewis, "Spirituals of Today" [n.d.], The Illinois Writers' Project / "Negro in Illinois" papers, Box 49, Folder 24, Chicago Public Library, Vivian G. Harsh Research Collection of Afro-American History and Literature, 14. Leighla W. Lewis, in "Sister Tharpe Swings Hymns at Cotton Club," Washington AA, January 14, 1939, reports that Calloway heard Rosetta on "one of his trips South."

5. Cooke, "Holy Roller Singer Toast of Broadway."

6. Ibid.

7. Esther 1:10–20, New Oxford Annotated Bible, 3rd edition, ed. Michael D. Coogan (New York: Oxford University Press, 2001), 710–711.

8. Cab Calloway and Bryant Rollins, Of Minnie the Moocher and Me (New York: Thomas Y. Crowell, 1976), 88.

9. Edward Kennedy Ellington, Music Is My Mistress (Garden City, NY: Doubleday & Company), 419–420.

10. Calloway and Rollins, Of Minnie the Moocher and Me, 78; Ellington, Music Is My Mistress, 77, 80.

11. Jim Haskins, The Cotton Club (New York: New American Library, 1984), 146.

12. Haskins, Cotton Club, 113–118.

13. " 'Sister Tharpe' Thinks Her Old Role Was the Tops," CD.

14. Harrington, "Benny Goodman Bids for 'Sister Tharpe.' "

15. Sherrie Tucker, Swing Shift: "All-Girl" Bands of the 1940s (Durham, NC: Duke University Press, 2000).

16. Angela Y. Davis, *Blues Legacies and Black Feminism: Gertrude "Ma" Rainey, Bessie Smith, and Billie Holiday* (New York: Pantheon, 1998), 3–41.

17. Paul Allen Anderson, *Deep River: Music and Memory in Harlem Renaissance Thought* (Durham, NC: Duke University Press, 2001), 231, 233.

18. Count Basie, as told to Albert Murray, *Good Morning Blues: The Autobiography of Count Basie* (New York: Random House, 1985), 221; "Harry 'Sweets' Edison Remembers 'From Spirituals to Swing' and Count Basie—1999," *From Spirituals to Swing,* album notes (Vanguard 169/71–2), 27; John Hammond with Irving Townsend, *John Hammond on Record: An Autobiography* (New York: Penguin Books, 1981), 203.

19. Herb, "Apollo, N.Y.," *Variety,* July 19, 1939, 38, 46.

20. "Singer Swings Same Songs in Church and Night Club," *Life,* August 28, 1939, 37.

21. Herb, "Cotton Club, N.Y.," *Variety,* May 8, 1940, 50.

22. "Sister Tharpe Gets Reprimand from Her Husband for Not Wearing Hat," *New York Sun,* September 5, 1939. Lewis, in "Sister Tharpe Swings Hymns at Cotton Club," implies that Tommy Tharpe had been in New York since January 1939.

23. " 'Sister Tharpe' Thinks Her Old Role Was the Tops," *CD.*

24. "The Church Stands for the Highest Values in Your Community," *Pittsburgh Courier,* March 11, 1939. See also Jerma A. Jackson, *Singing in My Soul: Black Gospel Music in a Secular Age* (Chapel Hill, NC: The University of North Carolina Press, 2004), 113–120, for an extended discussion of the *Pittsburgh Courier* debates.

25. Thomas A. Dorsey, "Gospel Songwriter Attacks All Hot Bands' Swinging Spirituals," *CD,* February 8, 1941.

26. Zora Neale Hurston, *The Sanctified Church: The Folklore Writings of Zora Neale Hurston* (Berkeley: Turtle Island Foundation, 1981), 103.

27. Arna Bontemps, "Rock, Church, Rock!," *Common Ground* (Autumn 1942): 80.

CHAPTER 4: SHOUT, SISTER, SHOUT

1. Whitney Balliett, "Night Clubs," *The New Yorker,* October 9, 1971, 75.

2. Josephson opened a second club, Café Society Uptown, on October 8, 1940, but Rosetta played at the downtown club. Nevertheless, the uptown and downtown performers were professionally friendly.

3. David W. Stowe, "The Politics of Café Society," *Journal of American History* 84, no. 4 (March 1998): 1388.

4. Balliett, "Night Clubs," 76–77.

5. "Accuse Sister Tharpe of Stealing Old Songs," *CD,* January 11, 1941; "Night Club Soulsaver," photograph caption, *Washington AA,* January 11, 1941.

6. David Albert "Panama" Francis, interview by Milt Hinton, Smithsonian Institution, Jazz Oral History Project, Reel 2.

7. Bill Doggett, interview by Dave Booth, December 1988. CD recording of interview courtesy of Lex Gillespie.

8. Billy Jones, "Stars," *CD,* May 17, 1941, reports that "Rosetta Tharpe, the hymn

swinger, has signed up with Lucky Millinder's band," but Roxie Moore's memory puts the date of the actual agreement several months earlier. It's possible that Rosetta, who appeared in February and March in the musical comedy *Tropicana*, signed with Millinder in February but announced the deal in May.

9. Doggett, interview by Booth.

10. Cab Calloway and Bryant Rollins, *Of Minnie the Moocher and Me* (New York: Thomas Y. Crowell Company, 1976), 71; Malcolm X, with the assistance of Alex Haley, *The Autobiography of Malcolm X* (New York: Ballantine Books, 1964), 77.

11. Elijah Wald, *Escaping the Delta: Robert Johnson and the Invention of Blues* (New York: Amistad, 2004), 93.

12. "Girls, If You Are Heavy the Apollo Will Admit You 'Free,'" *CD*, December 13, 1941.

13. "'Soundie' Using Big Name Bands," *New York Amsterdam Star-News*, November 22, 1941.

14. "A Musical Trend Comes to the Cross Roads of Public Favor," *Pittsburgh Courier*, August 2, 1941.

15. Dick Carter, "On the Air," review of Lucky Millinder at the Savoy Ballroom, New York, WNEW, Sunday, January 11, 1942, 4:00–4:30 p.m., *Billboard*, January 24, 1942, 12.

16. The recording ban went into effect on August 1, 1942, with the union demanding royalties for its members each time a recording was played on the radio or a jukebox. Although Decca settled with the AFM within a year, the dispute lasted for more than two years.

17. Francis, interview by Hinton.

18. Review of *Lucky Millinder* (Decca 18386), *New York Times*, June 28, 1942; Bill Gottlieb, "Swing Sessions," *Washington Post*, July 5, 1942. Rosetta was called "the prize of Lucky's band" in "Harlem to Broadway," *CD*, September 26, 1942.

19. "Fort Custer Victory Ball Lures Visitors," *CD*, May 3, 1942; Elizabeth Galbreath, "Typovision," *CD*, May 23, 1942.

20. Doggett, interview by Booth.

21. Tony Russell, "Clarkesdale Piccolo Blues: Jukebox Hits in Black Taverns 30 Years Ago," *Jazz & Blues* (November 1971): 30. See also Wald, *Escaping the Delta*, 98–100.

22. "Ink Spots Draw 10,600," *Baltimore AA*, May 29, 1943; "Ink Spots Draw 10,000 in St. Louis," *CD*, June 12, 1943; "Bands Up Philly Theater Take; T. Dorsey Record Still Stands; Heidt, Millinder, Osborne Next," *Billboard*, January 23, 1943, 21.

23. "Lucky Charges Sister Tharpe Pulled Sneak: Everybody Upset When Singer Quits Without Notice," *Down Beat*, September 15, 1943, 6.

24. Jack Schiffman, son of Apollo Theater owner Frank Schiffman, refers to Allen as the manager of Washington's Howard Theater, but I have been unable to confirm this. See Jack Schiffman, *Uptown: The Story of Harlem's Apollo Theatre* (New York: Cowles Book Company, 1971), 101.

25. *Rosetta Tharpe v. Thomas Tharpe*, document 372, no. 44, decree issued in District Court of Douglas County, Nebraska, May 7, 1943.

26. "Savoy Ballroom Closed: Charges of Vice Filed by Police Department and Army," *New York Times,* April 25, 1943; Malcolm X, *Autobiography,* 116.

27. Eric Hobsbawm, "The People's Swing," in *Uncommon People: Resistance, Rebellion and Jazz* (London: Weidenfeld & Nicholson, 1998), 277.

28. *I Shall Be a Witness,* Rosetta Tharpe and the Heavenly Queens Choir, RGB 3024, digital sound cassette, Recorded Sound Division, Library of Congress.

29. "Sister Tharpe with Ink Spots," *CD,* December 25, 1943; "Sister Tharpe Tops at Howard," *CD,* January 22, 1944; Ted Yates, "Around Harlemtown," *CD,* December 11, 1943.

30. "Louis Jordan, Dusty Fletcher and Sister Tharpe Take Regal," *CD,* January 8, 1944.

31. Sammy Price, *What Do They Want?: A Jazz Autobiography,* ed. Caroline Richmond (Urbana and Chicago: University of Illinois Press, 1990), 52.

32. Sammy Price, interview by Dan Morgenstern, January 21, 1980, Institute for Jazz Studies, Jazz Oral History Project, 43–45.

33. Guido van Rijn speculates that Rosetta's inspiration for "Strange Things" was a ballad by Bud Ezell with the words "strange things a-happening in this land" in the chorus. Guido van Rijn, *Roosevelt's Blues: African-American Blues and Gospel Songs on FDR* (Jackson, MS: University Press of Mississippi, 1997), 176.

34. Michael W. Harris, *The Rise of Gospel Blues: The Music of Thomas Andrew Dorsey in the Urban Church* (New York: Oxford University Press, 1992), 237–238.

35. Dewey Phillips, *Red Hot & Blue: Dewey Phillips Live Radio Broadcasts from 1952–1964,* CD, Memphis Archives (MA 7016).

36. Jerry Lee Lewis, interview by Peter Guralnick, 2005. Personal collection of Peter Guralnick.

37. Peter Guralnick, personal correspondence with the author, December 28, 2005, with material from Guralnick's notes from an interview with Johnny Cash, February 8, 1979; Johnny Cash, *Man in Black* (New York: Warner Books, 1975), 73–74; Rosanne Cash, interview by Larry King on *Larry King Live,* June 10, 2005.

38. Carl Perkins, interview by Peter Guralnick, circa February 8 or February 9, 1979.

BRIDGE: "SHE MADE THAT GUITAR TALK"

1. Pearl Bailey, *The Raw Pearl* (New York: Pocket Books, 1969), 6–7.

CHAPTER 5: LITTLE SISTER

1. "Stars to Sing May 12," display advertisement, *CD,* May 4, 1946; "Want to Hear Sister Tharpe?" *CD,* May 11, 1946.

2. Rosetta told Anthony Heilbut that Marie was three years younger. See *GS,* 193. Horace Clarence Boyer writes that Marie was born in 1918. See *GAG,* 158. Jerma A.

Jackson gives Marie's date of birth as 1923, the year I find most likely. See Jerma A. Jackson, *Singing in My Soul: Black Gospel Music in a Secular Age* (Chapel Hill: University of North Carolina Press, 2004), 121.

3. Jackson, *Singing in My Soul,* 121–122.

4. François Postif, *Jazz Me Blues: Interviews et portraits de musicians de jazz et de blues* (Paris: Editions Outre Mesure, 1999), 16.

5. "Sister Tharpe on Tour with Singers," *CD,* July 13, 1946.

6. *Say Amen, Somebody,* videocassette, directed by George T. Nierenberg (Santa Monica, CA: Xenon Entertainment Group, 1997).

7. Nat [Hentoff], "Caught in the Act," *Down Beat,* April 6, 1955, 4.

8. Sherrie Tucker, *Swing Shift: "All-Girl" Bands of the 1940s* (Durham, NC: Duke University Press, 2000), 59–62.

9. Peter Waltrous, "Back to Basics, Little Richard Is Happy at Last," *New York Times,* December 8, 1992; Charles White, *The Life and Times of Little Richard, the Quasar of Rock* (New York: Harmony Books, 1984), 17.

10. Etta James and David Ritz, *Rage to Survive: The Etta James Story* (New York: Da Capo Press, 1995), 75.

11. Willa Ward-Royster, as told to Toni Rose, *How I Got Over: Clara Ward and the World-Famous Ward Singers* (Philadelphia: Temple University Press, 1997), 68–69. Ward-Royster writes that the convention took place in 1943, but Nick Salvatore dates it as 1952. See Nick Salvatore, *Singing in a Strange Land: C. L. Franklin, the Black Church, and the Transformation of America* (New York: Little, Brown and Company, 2005), 202–203 and 359–360, note 53.

12. Ward-Royster, *How I Got Over,* 68–69.

13. David Ritz, *Divided Soul: The Life of Marvin Gaye* (1985; reprint, New York: Da Capo Press, 1991), 14; Salvatore, *Singing in a Strange Land,* 202–203; James and Ritz, *Rage to Survive,* 76.

14. Jerry Wexler, "O-o-h, Sistuh! Rosetta 'n' Her Gitar Grab Bible Belt Moola," *Billboard,* April 9, 1949, 3, 18.

15. Jay Lustig, "A Musical Tribute to a Gospel Legend." *Newark Star-Ledger,* May 8, 2005.

16. "Sister Tharpe With Rosettes; Madame Marie Knight Out," *Pittsburgh Courier,* November 26, 1949.

CHAPTER 6: AT HOME AND ON THE ROAD

1. C. A. Bustard, "Local Roots Show in Rosetta Tharpe's Music," *Richmond Times-Dispatch,* November 1, 1981. On Richmond in general, see Elsa Barkley Brown and Gregg D. Kimball, "Mapping the Terrain of Black Richmond," *Journal of Urban History* 21, no. 3 (March 1995): 296–346.

2. *GAG,* 152–153.

3. Sarah Brooks later married and became Sarah Roots; Lottie Henry became Lottie Smith. For clarity's sake, throughout this chapter, I use their maiden names.

4. The term "quartet" commonly referred to all small gospel vocal harmony groups. Sometimes "quartets" had five or even six members.

5. *GAG*, 169–170; *GS*, 356.

6. In addition to my interview with Sarah Brooks (Roots) and Lottie Henry (Smith), I am drawing on Oreen Johnson (Craddock) and Barbara Johnson (Henry), interview by Lynn Abbott, March 10, 1983. Personal collection of Lynn Abbott.

7. Sister Rosetta Tharpe, advertisement for Second Anniversary, Mosque Auditorium, Richmond, *Richmond AA,* November 18, 1950.

8. Review of Rosetta Tharpe and the Rosettes, "Silent Night" and "White Christmas" (Decca 48119), *Billboard,* November 26, 1949, 168.

9. Jody Rosen, *White Christmas: The Story of an American Song* (New York: Scribner, 2002), 137.

10. "On Television," *New York Times,* January 1, 1950.

11. "Mahalia Jackson Rejects 10G Bid," *Richmond AA,* June 10, 1950.

CHAPTER 7: "THE WORLD'S GREATEST SPIRITUAL CONCERT"

1. Tim Stinson, "A Vanishing Breed: Welcome to the Drugstore," November 2003, www.mondiale.co.uk/tpus/contributors/timnov.html.

2. Jerry Wexler, "O-o-h, Sistuh! Rosetta 'n' Her Gitar Grab Bible Belt Moola," *Billboard,* April 9, 1949, 3.

3. The quotations from Henry Whitehead and Dick Heller are from Brad Snyder, *Beyond the Shadow of the Senators: The Untold History of the Homestead Grays and the Integration of Baseball* (New York: McGraw-Hill, 2003), 11 and 305, footnote 13.

4. "28,000 See Elder Michaux Baptize 150 at Stadium" *Baltimore AA,* November 25, 1948; George D. Tyler, "Gateway to Gayway," *Baltimore AA,* November 24, 1949.

5. Smallwood Edmond Williams, *This Is My Story: A Significant Life Struggle* (Washington, DC: Wm. Willoughby Publishers, 1981), 39, 190.

6. Many sources say that Russell Morrison managed the Ink Spots, but I have not been able to verify this claim. It may be that once he became Rosetta's manager, Russell was retroactively assumed to have managed other groups. It is possible he once served as valet to Lucky Millinder. See Marv Goldberg, *More Than Words Can Say: The Ink Spots and Their Music* (Lanham, MD: The Scarecrow Press, 1998), 78.

7. Ralph Ellison, *Invisible Man* (1952; reprint, New York: Vintage International, 1995), 7.

8. "Mediation Warms as Air Conditioning Fails," *Washington Post,* July 3, 1951.

9. Rosetta Tharpe, *The Wedding Ceremony of Sister Rosetta Tharpe* (Decca DL 5382); "15,000 Attend Sister Rosetta Tharpe's Wedding," *Richmond AA,* July 14, 1951; "20,000 Watch Wedding of Sister Rosetta Tharpe," *Ebony,* October 1951, 27–30.

10. "Sister Rosetta Tharpe Weds," *Los Angeles Sentinel,* July 19, 1951.

11. "Sister Rosetta Tharpe to Wed Russell Morrison: Costly Gowns, Fireworks, Concert Added Features," *Washington AA,* June 30, 1951.

12. "Sister Rosetta Tharpe Weds," *Los Angeles Sentinel.*

13. "15,000 Attend Sister Rosetta Tharpe's Wedding," *Richmond AA.*

14. Marie and Dolly stayed close companions. Later, Dolly formed the Gates of Prayer Church in New York, where Marie was ordained a minister in 1973. For many years, they shared a Harlem apartment.

15. Alan Lomax, album notes, *Blessed Assurance: Gospel Hymns Sung by Sister Rosetta Tharpe with the Rosettes and Organ Accompaniment* (Decca DL 5354).

16. Howard Grut, "Sweet Religion, Hallilu!—At Only $2.50 a Seat," *Melody Maker*, September 6, 1952, 9; Derrick Stewart-Baxter, "Preachin' the Blues," *Jazz Journal International* 5, no. 7 (July 1952): 17; "20,000 Watch Wedding of Sister Rosetta Tharpe," *Ebony*.

CHAPTER 8: SISTER IN OPRYLAND

1. Allen Churchill, "Tin Pan Alley's Git-tar Blues," *New York Times*, July 15, 1951.

2. The quotations from Owen Bradley and Bentley Cummins are courtesy Randy Fox, from an e-mail forwarded to the author by Dawn Oberg, February 16, 2004.

3. Ray Charles and David Ritz, *Brother Ray: Ray Charles' Own Story*, 3rd paperback edition (New York: Da Capo Press, 2004), 43.

4. Ben Grevatt, "On the Beat," *Billboard*, March 9, 1959, 8.

5. Greil Marcus, *Invisible Republic: Bob Dylan's Basement Tapes* (New York: Henry Holt, 1997), 3–4.

6. Rob Bowman, "Profiles in Black and White: O. B. McClinton: Country Music, That's My Thing," *Journal of Country Music* 14, no. 2 (1992): 23.

CHAPTER 9: DON'T LEAVE ME HERE

1. Guido van Rijn, *The Truman and Eisenhower Blues: African American Blues and Gospel Songs, 1945–1960* (London: Continuum, 2004), 93–94.

2. Dick Kleiner, "Spiritual to Pops is Tough Switch," *Sheboygan Press*, January 27, 1960, 24.

3. "Clara Ward . . . Gospel Singer," *Our World*, December 1953, 38.

4. Lee Hildebrand and Opal Nations, CD notes, *Sister Wynona Carr, Dragnet for Jesus* (Specialty SPCD 7016–2).

5. Jose, review of Rosetta Tharpe and Marie Knight at the Village Vanguard, New York, *Variety* February 16, 1955, 55.

6. Nat [Hentoff], "Sister Rosetta Tharpe, Marie Knight: Village Vanguard, New York," *Down Beat*, April 6, 1955, 4.

7. "Teeners Wielding New Influence on Singles Record Market," 1956 article cited in Galen Gart, *First Pressings: The History of Rhythm & Blues*, vol. 6, *1956* (Milford, NH: Big Nickel Publications, 1991), 4.

8. Quote from "The Murder of Emmett Till," *The American Experience*, PBS online, www.pbs.org/wgbh/amex/till/peopleevents/p_till.html.

9. Alice Walker, "Nineteen Fifty-Five," in *You Can't Keep a Good Woman Down: Stories* (New York: Harcourt Brace Jovanovich, 1981).

10. "Sister Rosetta Tharpe to Star on CBS-TV," *Jet,* March 1, 1956, 66.

11. Marvel Cooke, "Holy Roller Singer Toast of Broadway," *New York Amsterdam Star-News,* March 4, 1939.

12. From a 1957 *Billboard* article cited in Galen Gart, *First Pressings: The History of Rhythm & Blues,* vol. 7, *1957* (Milford, NH: Big Nickel Publications, 1993), 146.

BRIDGE: "THE MEN WOULD STAND BACK"

1. The epigraph is from Marian McPartland, "Mary Lou: Marian McPartland Salutes One Pianist Who Remains Modern and Communicative," *Down Beat,* October 17, 1957, 12.

2. Frederic V. Grunfeld, *The Art and Times of the Guitar: An Illustrated History of Guitar and Guitarists* (London: Macmillan, 1969) 6, 11; Steve Waksman, *Instruments of Desire: The Electric Guitar and the Shaping of Musical Experience* (Cambridge, MA: Harvard University Press, 1999) 185.

3. McPartland, "Mary Lou," 12. See also Nichole T. Rustin, " 'Mary Lou Williams Plays Like a Man!' Gender, Genius, and Difference in Black Music Discourse," *South Atlantic Quarterly* 104, no. 3 (Summer 2005): 445–62.

4. Ralph Gleason, "A Gospel Singer; A Secular Guitar," *San Francisco Chronicle,* January 30, 1964.

5. Etta James, foreword to Bob Merlis and Davin Seay, *Heart & Soul: A Celebration of Black Music Style in America, 1930–1975* (New York: Billboard Books, 2002), n.p.

CHAPTER 10: REBIRTH AND REVIVAL

1. Bob Dawbarn, "Sister Rosetta Makes a Flying Start," *Melody Maker,* November 30, 1957, p. 5. The phrase "a shambles of slurring sound" is from this article, page 5.

2. Desmond Wilcox, "They Call Her 'Holy Roller': Rosetta Flies in to Rock," [London] *Daily Mirror,* November 22, 1957.

3. Burt Korall, "Rosetta . . . ," *Melody Maker,* November 23, 1957, 5.

4. Wilcox, "They Call Her 'Holy Roller.' "

5. Ibid.

6. Marybeth Hamilton, "Sexuality, Authenticity and the Making of the Blues Tradition," *Past and Present* 169 (November 2000): 138; George Melly, *Owning Up: The Trilogy* (London: Penguin, 2000), 394.

7. Chris Barber, "U.S. Jazz Scene," *Melody Maker,* May 20, 1961, 3.

8. Melly, *Owning Up,* 491.

9. Rob Bowman, DVD notes, *The American Folk Blues Festival, 1962–1966,* vol. 1 (Reelin' in the Years Productions, 2003); Val Wilmer, *Mama Said There'd Be Days Like This: My Life in the Jazz World* (London: The Women's Press, 1989), 36–37.

10. Robert Gordon, *Can't Be Satisfied: The Life and Times of Muddy Waters* (Boston: Little, Brown and Company, 2002), 163.

11. Theo Zwicky, speech presented April 19, 1964, at the New Jazz Club, Zurich. Printed in *New Jazz Club Zurich* newsletter [n.d.], 44.

12. I am creatively paraphrasing based on the following: Jacques Demêtre, "Sister Rosetta Tharpe est à Paris," *Jazz Hot* 129 (Février 1958): 16–17; Baget-Garriga, "Sister Rosetta Tharpe en Barcelona," *Publicacíon Club de Ritmo Granollers* 12, no. 142 (Febrero de 1958): 4; "Rosetta Vous Parle," *Jazz Magazine* 35 (1958): 15–17; Maurice Berman, "I've Never Been a Jazz Singer," *Melody Maker*, April 19, 1958, 7; Valerie Wilmer, "Queen of the Holy Rollers," *Jazz News,* April 8, 1960, 6; Wilcox, "They Call Her 'Holy Roller.' "

13. Chris Barber, interview by Dave Booth, June 28, 1984. Audiotape courtesy of Dave Booth.

14. Korall, "Rosetta. . . . ," 5.

15. Madeleine Gautier, "Sister Rosetta Tharpe à l'Alhambra," *Bulletin du Hot Club de France* 75 (Février 1958): 32; J. D. [Jacques Demêtre], "Sister Rosetta Tharpe à l'Alhambra," *Jazz Hot* 129 (Février 1958): 34.

16. Bowman, DVD notes, *The American Folk Blues Festival.*

17. Tyler Stovall, "The Fire This Time: Black American Expatriates and the Algerian War," *Yale French Studies* 98 (2000): 182–200.

18. Terry Cryer, *One in the Eye* (West Yorkshire: Yorkshire Art Circus, 1992), 59–60.

19. Pearl Bailey, *The Raw Pearl* (New York: Pocket Books, 1969), 112; Neil M. C. Sinclair, *The Tiger Bay Story* (Cardiff: Dragon and Tiger Enterprises, 1997), 68. Val Wilmer originally made the point to me about the importance of black American–English West Indian connections and provided the passage from Sinclair.

20. Melly, *Owning Up,* 515.

21. Bob Dawbarn, "Rosetta's Secret Is Sincerity," *Melody Maker,* April 5, 1958, 5.

22. Melly, *Owning Up,* 544.

23. *GS,* 194.

24. Wilmer, "Queen of the Holy Rollers."

CHAPTER 11: RIDING THE GOSPEL TRAIN

1. "Gospel Singer Clara Ward a Hit on Nitery Circuit," *Jet,* December 14, 1961, 6.

2. William Hamilton Jr., "Sister Rosetta Tharpe," *Jazz News,* November 1957, 6.

3. Martin Williams, album notes, *The Gospel Truth: All New Recordings of Great Gospel Hits* (Verve V/V6–8439).

4. Desmond Wilcox, "They Call Her 'Holy Roller': Rosetta Flies in to Rock," [London] *Daily Mirror,* November 22, 1957.

5. Steve Morse, "The Summers of Love," [Syracuse] *Post-Standard*, August 15, 1992.

6. Derrick Stewart-Baxter, "Blues on Record," *Jazz Journal* 12 (May 1964): 17.

7. Robert Gordon, *Can't Be Satisfied: The Life and Times of Muddy Waters* (Boston: Little, Brown and Company, 2002), 187.

8. Precise dates for *TV Gospel Time* episodes are difficult to establish. My esti-

mate of 1962 comes from Dave Hepburn, "Big Bonanza in Gospel Music," *Sepia*, March 1963, page 15, which notes that a show called *TV Gospel Time* began "only last September."

9. "TV Gospel Time Moves from New York to Memphis," *CD*, February 2, 1963; Hepburn, "Big Bonanza in Gospel Music," 15.

10. *GS*, 194.

11. Hughes Panassié, *Bulletin du Hot Club de France*, April 1968, 30.

12. *GS*, 189.

13. *GAG* gives the date as 1969, but Leiser's timeline and Roxie Moore's memory point toward 1968.

14. *GS*, 195.

15. Mark Bricklin, "Gospel Singers and Church of God Official Mourn Rosetta's Mother," *Philadelphia Tribune*, January 27, 1968.

16. Sister Rosetta Tharpe, *Singing in My Soul* (Savoy MG-14224). Heilbut makes this point about "When the Gate Swings Open" in the brief album notes.

CHAPTER 12: I LOOKED DOWN THE LINE

1. Neither Roxie Moore nor Tony Heilbut can remember the exact month when Rosetta's leg was amputated, but both say it was not long after she returned to Philadelphia.

2. Les Ledbetter, "Sunday Is Soul Day at Lincoln Center," *New York Times*, July 21, 1972.

3. Robert Sherman, "Gospel Rings Out Again at 'Soul' Fete," *New York Times*, July 27, 1972.

4. Tony Heilbut, undated letter to Rosetta Tharpe. Personal collection of Annie Morrison.

5. Courtesy of Roxie Moore. Dated October 16, 1973.

EPILOGUE: VIBRATIONS, STRONG AND MEAN

1. Dave Hepburn, "Big Bonanza in Gospel Music," *Sepia*, March 1963, 13.

2. James Greenwood, "Jazz" column, review of Jazz Expo '70: American Folk, Blues and Gospel Festival, n.d., n.p. Clipping from the personal collection of Annie Morrison.

3. Christopher Small, *Music of the Common Tongue: Survival and Celebration in Afro-American Music* (New York: Riverside Press, 1987), 387.

INDEX